# PRESS: INSIDE OUTSIDE

# PRESS: INSIDE OUTSIDE

*Rama Vajpayee*

PUBLICATIONS

KALPAZ PUBLICATIONS
DELHI - 110052

**PRESS: INSIDE OUTSIDE**
[*Journalism*]

Rs. 475

ISBN: 81-7835-076-9



Published in 2002 in India by
Kalpaz Publications
C-30, Satyawati Nagar
Ashok Vihar-III, Delhi-110052
e-mail: kalpaz@hotmail.com

*Laser Typeset at:* Alphabet, Delhi
*Printed at:* Mehra Offset Press, New Delhi

# Contents

# Preface

This work has deep bearing on several facets of press which have shown its effectiveness in moulding the views expressed at socio-political and other levels. In a democratic set-up the expression of thought of an individual through the media is highly valuable in the sense that the 'freedom of pen' is his basic and fundamental right. In this regard the State should give the maximum facility to the healthy growth of press, media and television and should not put any kind of obstacle in their growth and circulation. In fact we need up to date news everyday in order to know the new developments in our country as well as abroad. The television indeed is playing a most significant role in enlightening the people of all categories and fulfilling their demands and needs, which have become essential in their social growth.

This comprehensive survey has been well-knit in eleven chapters and has tackled each and every item with meticulous care. Whereas the freedom of press has been well highlighted, the role of news media and television did not lag behind. At the same time, it admitted about the commercialisation in press, its circulation along with several kinds of advertisements and changing role of the media along with the new trends in our society.

**Rama Vajpayee**

*One*

# Press: Inside Outside

Pressing the point which nucleous the surroundings all over and in all with powerful spike in facade of the world is — Press as such, considered as a Fourth State in Democratic set up siding the Rights of People against the exploitation, the power of pen is placed in all countries and now with Electronic Media to the latest technology of free flow to information, which is a matter of right to know towards the citizens of any free country. All sort of Government has its own flow of information with current and uptodate surroundings of the country. But the Press working under the Government authority believes to show the development like a full progressive 'dream show' to the public of country, may be tagged as a Press Inside.

But the Press as a power of a real Fourth State in democracy with all sorts of developing media technology it is still an established prior provision for sharing public purpose, is the "power of pen" in all countries which firmally disbelieve in sovereignty is the Press Outside.

But the basic difficulty is just to discover that every point and the position where Press does stand under the Government and works outside as the government and an open Media. Although this specific platform has been named as a Mass Communication. The communication with people and ruling authority. This point was first raised in 1818 under British ruling in India by Sir James Silk Bankgham through his first published paper in India where he placed the thought to people that they should free and fluent in their communication even in British Rule. The paper was Calcutta Journal, where it was expressed— "As for as Europeans only whether in or out of service the freedom or the restrictions of the press could do little good or harm and would hardly deserve any serious attention." He also told but though the danger be distant it is nevertheless there. It could corrupt and disaffect the Indian Army and work for the overthrow of the British power. It might spread among the people the principle of liberty and stimulate them to expel the strangers who rule over them and to establish a National Government. A Free Press and domination of stranger are things which are quite incompatible and can long exist-together. Thus the Press with the orientation of free opinion became an established thought for the first time in 18th century India.

The proposal for Ruling and Non Ruling sections mediating with the views of a press journal took place in 1823, by the G.O. of British Government; having licensed all sort of press publications even books or any other published material. But this move was protested by Dwarikanath Tagore and Raja Rammohun Roy. And afterthat during the tenure of Sir Charles Metcaugh this regulation was cancelled from 1823-1835. When Macaulay came to India he made Press totally free here as it was in England. But the basic and fundamental thought at that time which evoked concern was that they were working outside as there were no such sect of information media made open to the common man by the Ruling government. This was carried away from 1823 to 1857, even now as the Government of British Indian Ruling has no such flow of information of its own, so at the time of Mutiny it was thought that the Press as an open view should not be left without any ruling control. On this very need the Article XV was implemented as an indefinite censor on press.

During these periods from 1857 to 1860 so many Indian Origin Press in the form of their voices in newspaper were introduced like Amrit Bazar Patrika from Bengal and 'Akhbare Aam' from Lahore. All these kept the viewpoint of British India and not for India our own country. In 1878 the Vernacular Press Act was passed by Lord Lytton—less or more it all still is any how present in India with all its so-called set-up.

So as an open mind first free Indian Government took the charge to make the people know about the planning and development of government strategy which was formed in Democratic India for the people, by the people-turned in to the people, with the mass helpline object. As a rule, the press which tried to nucleate upon the policies of the government to a dream show line came as a press inside and the press which within unfolded wrapper tried to disbelieve in sovereignty was the press outside. Here the basic difficulty came just to discover that very point and the sole position where press does stand under the government and works outside as an open media. It has still to be disclosed and carries a matter of debate even after Prasar Bharati burst. How and who can point out at a tenable position between the subjection of press under secrecy of ruling authority and the full expression of public opinion. Because press as such had always been against the ruling power or as a matter of undercurrent of sovereignty. So this thought that what should be inclined to adopt by both side—Press as an inside story—Press as an outside play game.

The accountability of press at its hearts arises the issue and even a question of who should hold reins the government or the free press outside. The press outside called Free Press is one which has its first responsibility not to politicians but to public, whether it uses or abuses, how it takes its own and comply liberty and also the press under the government control—can be said as a press inside, instead of balancing things eventually, giving a free flow of information to the public, or pressing them at wrong points, undercurrent in between what should the main decisive point tipping toward freedom or control.

As a matter of right as the citizens of India have their own 'Rights to Know' through the government media in the form of Right to Information and it is a fundamental human right, also it is a touchstone of all freedom to which Nation has consecrated and the freedom implies the right to gather or transmit and publish news anywhere and everywhere without fetters. Here it is there one more pressing posture in connection with other big countries, press manifesto where it is considered that in developing countries they can not have a free wheeling press. It might be too deceptive and people will get too excited where the people as down to their own thinking limit have not yet developed that much of critical sense to judge stories and news without being unduly influenced or distracted.

So the question is still hanging in the air as for in or out of all services towards the Press, whether the freedom or the restrictions of the Press could do little good or harm, so they still deserve the serious attention toward free press and the press as an Information Bureau with latest information technology siding to common masses of a country as such.

# Two

# Free Press View
## (*The Power of Pen*)

This sort of burning debate was taken with critical vision in the beginning of journals by the ruling authority at the time of British India, which I have tried to glance in the beginning of this book, by which the Press Inside Outside was basically needed in India by Muno who had been sent to India for getting an informative look to open free press view at the time who ultimately came to conclusion whether the expelling liberty among people will be proper to their little educated sense or to leave them as unknown dummy in mass group without any communication of their own with the Ruling Reigns. This was even noticed by Pandit Jawaharlal Nehru—after being the first Prime Minister of free India, that the citizens of India first need to adopt the information in this free country through the Government of India in a new democratic set up to which the Indian people are originally not used to. That way it was constituted as a guarantee to the citizen's own Fundamental Right to know things done by the government in the interest of public development unlike the U.S.A. government. But the Press outside as a Print Media—printed in the form of newspapers and published by the rousing journalists or by taking it as a mission towards the public welfare News papers were and are even published by the big Business houses which has pace in between public and ruling authority. The mission was to make bridging point among Democratic white collar rulers with down to earthy public interest. But it mainly turned to Industry behind the figure of management set-up. Publishing of a newspaper underlined by onlookers a circumvent figure fitting to all sort of beneficial objects. It was no oppression, but the pressure to all over surroundings without introspection resulting what? And the motive of holding power through Press either or outside nucleated towards the multifarious object to haves and have-nots. They were expected to open the window for good and a positive healthy air, turned in to a folder of get-off from both the sections—Rulers and public.

The press outside the government but a registered work by the government constituted for useful purposes and totally committed towards the society and also the press which having been judicially determined to be a derivative of the so-called freedom, came under current a puppetry of show of incidental and accidental events, talks of politicians and there given and prepared statement by their press staff. They have to follow a subject to limitations and a separate right of angling towards inviting possibility of separate limitations, even time to time interpreted and also interrupted by judiciary already existing as a last hope for stayed backed upon the court system and its existence. So as a regard the concept of a press outside open to public siding their plus and minus and filling their section of welfare interests would have been an Angel's-God play, which appeared like that before the freedom of India eventually turned into a Devil's laugh.

From there the turning point came to Free Press a complete demand or a possibility. In the beginning of 19th century mainly the press fought for one's own feeling of expression. In human values the social opening means to get freedom to talk to communicate expressively and boldly for which the power of words and language represented, which is spoken, listen and written for expressing thoughts of all's mind and heart in variety of ways concerned with press and media. But the press is main media to tell about others feeling of express who are not educated —common and dumb people of the society.

So, seriously it becomes two faces of conceptional press with the Politics of Secrecy as a freedom of Information and people's right to know - where a citizen of India is free to receive and impart the information from ruling section without any fear. It is, as such, a duty to them to provide all sort of knowledge of their welfare interest without any obligation for which they are authorised with their position by the ruling government. But playing the game of Right and Duty and balancing with that they have had to face a kind of creeping but biting insects by which their visions come to steamy glance towards the facts. It is just because bureaucracy playing in an ironic role even in free India still looking to its people with British attitude, where the king can do no wrong. May be it customary but with the orientation of present values it is challengeable for the well spring of modern and awakened civilisation of Indian public but with proper and perfect reasonable restrictions avoiding abuses to the public life and even to important faces.

So now mass-democracy to take the latest example can be either the observation of the Press from both sides, some time prejudice by the section ruling sides of the Press who are time to time obliged by the workers of the factories. The existence of immensely powerful media of mass communication under the set-up pressing hard to the journalistic media, mass thinking, mass prejudice, mass suggestion through the common press would threaten to swamp considered as individual thinking and feeling. In all democracy the press rules which has both a classical and liberal reputation in mass democracy, who press working outside and relations to the new means of democracy which are changing with the changes of all popular government. This is a separate issue which I shall discuss in relation to the new means of communication.

When considering the function of Press outside and its essential function in a democracy is to serve the governed and not the governors it requires a sort of instant and boosting freedom for serving the common masses. But as a mission it should be addicted towards the mass interest and not a proxy to the politicians from their side.

As the news means of communication represents a major technical advancement and the oldest and still the most important is printing which has itself passed through major technical changes in particular the coming of the steam-driven machine press in 1811 and the development of ever faster cylinder and rotary presses from 1815. The major advances in transport, by road, rail, sea and air all of it themselves greatly affected printing at once in the collection of news and in the wide and quick distribution of the printed product. The development of the cable, telegraph, and telephone services even more remarkably facilitated the collection of news. Then as a new media, came sound broadcasting, the cinema and the television. But all of it came under the Press inside the government authority with the norms holding ruling authoritative policy with the. meaning to inform to educate with awareness of governmental developments done by the popular placed government.

The word 'Mass' is used regularly with both the idea of the 'masses' and a consequent idea of 'mass civilization' and 'mass democracy' to 'mass communication' and others. Here lies a central and very difficult issue which more than any other needs revision. Masses, at one time was a new word for mob, which has gradually assumed much significance. It seems probable that these social tendencies joined to confirm its meanings. First, there was a concentration of population in the industrial towns a physical massing of persons which the great increase in total population accentuated and which has continued with continuing urbanisation—which differs the crowd of village—and draw a very thin line between people and the masses. The one who works on field and with village variety industries—and another works in urban factories. The second where there was a concentration of workers into factories again a physical massing was made necessary by machine production which was welcomed well by Nehru, who told the industries, the temples of new India. Here the line of speech of press is basically changed who work outside and the press inside government is protective to them by throwing the information of labour laws.

**Development of Communication**

This social massing in the work relations made necessary by the development of large-scale collective production. This, there was a consequent development of an organised and self organizing working class - the main of today's social and political massing. The Press outside is concerned with its organising security—raising against the factories—and become the mouthpiece of their trade unions. The masses in practice have been any of these particular aggregates and because the tendencies have been interrelated it has been possible to use the term with certain unity. On the basis of each tendency, the derived ideas have arisen from urbanisation, the mass meeting from the factory in part in relation to the workers, but mainly in relation to things made by the working class considered as mass-action which was main attraction to the press working outside against the exploitation of labour classes which was named as law communication within the world of journalistic media.

Wherever the democracy exists the power of Press is over heading and an interpreting majority rule over the country. So even the placed popular government even throwing the power of authority and flowing information stated by the leaders and ministers can not overrule the power of Press outside established for siding the masses in common, which is the forceful power of democracy for establishing the government through the electoral constitutional formation. There, the press has to watch and see as an outside press and to quote and note the viewers and the newsmakers.

Here, with the viewpoint of the Press let us see and decide about the masses and the mobs. Masses have the communicative joint voices but the mob is only controllable and uncontrollable crowd raising slogans for the partial points with little interests of their own. And the Press has to watch both with all separate angles with no such mark of its own, but to view them with their identity not the opinion as masses have show down with their leaders not with the view of its own and the mob neither has the separate identity nor the opinion as they are gathering material normally uneducated or little educated or ever educated but under circumstantial force to deal with them the Press can not make a people's identity but it has to say like a public talk.

These familiar factual elements if we are to be able adequately to review the idea of "mass communication" which is the product of now kind of press with some these changes have given us more and more normally cheaper look, magazines and newspaper to read and also more bills and posters and establish authoritative broadcasting and television programmes. Various kinds of films documentaries. I think in my opinion at this stage it will be difficult to express clearly and simplify my kind of judgement but the definite judgement of value about all these very various products, yet they are all things that need to be valued with the point to discuss the press as a spreading media thought. And also I want to question here the idea of this sort of mass communication where the interaction between both sides, the Press and the public either on government media or taken by open and outside press the formula of mass communication is useful or not. I am arising this question just because two preliminary points are evident first that there is general tendency to confuse the techniques themselves with uses to which in a given society, they have been put, second that in considering these uses or the arguments are commonly selective, and even at a time to the extreme degree, which is illusive to masses and to society. Here the press with its insider vision and working towards with outside media need to be revised with all pros and cons. So the techniques of interaction between Press and person nowadays are worst at natural when it has been rewarded with power and additional facilities with perks and bunches of diffusive gifts. Here the only and one substantial objection that is made to them is that they are relatively impersonal in comparison with older techniques serving the same ends. In all kind whether a television presents a voice with photographs where the meeting presenting a man speaking or the wireless presenting voice, a cinema or theatre presented actors, raise the kind of relevant point and the suggestion with my points of view that by adding some alterations to the subjective person should be allowed an altered emphasis in the time given to particular activities. But these alterations are obviously conditioned not only by the techniques, but mainly by the whole circumstances of the common life. The point about impersonality often carries ludicrous rider. It is supposed, for instance, that it is an objection to listening to the talks and discussions that the liner can not answer the speaker back they are only about asking questions and the person specialised has to answer according to their own concerned politicised control - which from both side of Press does not feed the purpose either to its country or to the people or towards the latest happenings.

Although at very known fundamental the word 'Mass' was basically used one to a contemporary author who are very easier than to try to answer Aristotle, Burke or Mar, who took masses at their sensitive liberty to form universality among all under their section of forum. But it is other point of subject to be discussed later on.

Here, the specially stated by the Government Press Information Bureau, all state-wise information centres who deal with policies of ruling section and make them reach to common masses, even produces literature of all kind by publishing magazines and books, even purchase of books for the common readers, when the Press in free India was already established as Fourth state, a strongest pillar for the country or society and a watchdog to all sections of it. After that when the press was already working outside was it necessary for the free Indian government to place such departments for the free flow of information?

**Bureau Advent of Press II**

The question I find easy to answer in a manner the 'it was' and 'it is' a duty of ruling sections to make people know that under agenda in provincial and country-wise development, the 'work' of the government is looking behind the welfare of all sections of the society or the minorities for section of financially weaks and the people the citizens of India — who form the government. At one end they from responsive help to the Press working outside by filling their newspapers with the advertisements of all their popular government programmes.

Here I can have a little peep in constitution of India's base and look, which opens the front that the preamble which begins with the "we the people of India having solemnly resolved to constitute India into a sovereign socialist secular democratic Republic. And to secure to all its citizens that they should have justice social economic and political liberty of thought, expression, belief faith and worship. Equality of status and of all opportunity and to promote among them all fraternity assuring the dignity of individual and the unity and the integrity of the Nation." This is the supreme thought constituted in a democratic set-up and the press and media under and inside the government has to keep the wave alive in popular government by expressing the policies made for this constitution and the citizens of India. Their work is mainly in the states and in all the state governments, the press defends and protects the interest of all and for all four figures described. The press inside has to adopt, enact and give all information of the work done and develop the citizens of India and should be protective to their own fundamental rights. The people of India have to get a constant and free flow of information as a rule of people's right to information. They are responsible to give the information the right of all sect are preserved served with vivid affluence and with usual acceptable manner to both the people and society.

Now informally it could be discussed that what kind of parliamentary privileges has been given and also immunities of either house of Parliament and of its committees and members have been laid down in Article 105 of the Constitution, where the freedom to speech in Parliament and the immunity of members from any proceeding in any court in respect of anything said or any vote given by them in Parliament or any committee thereof until defined by Parliament by law, continue in actual practice to be governed by the precedents of the British House of Commons as they existed on the day our constitution came into force. Clause (3) of Article 105 as amended by the Constitution (which was 44th Amendment) Act 1978, provides that the power, privileges and immunities of each house of Parliament and of the members and the committees of each house shall be such as may from time to time be defined by Parliament by law and until so defined shall be that those of the house and of its members and committee immediately before the coming into force of this amending Act (on 19th June 1997).

With very small descriptions the constituted Parliament put the right as a matter of right the freedom of speech to all, either person in public or person in common and the press has to watch both the section of people here the press and all government media who authoritatively place the guarantee of man in common to protect his voice and propagate the agenda of government introducing their all welfare project. This thought was already there at the time Lord Spin in 1880—that the British Government will provide all sort of facility to people as a right to know. But at the time of Dodwell, who was quite aware of this fact that the

Indian Press would never like the British policy, so give them full freedom to open and say accordingly would not be wise for the government. Because at that time day by day Indian public in British ruling was boiling with revolutionary thoughts and their press outside were bubbling with hot and fire brand writings in newspapers. So to check them first the British Government started some journals of their own who were the propaganda of their policies who tried to show what sort of developments in all field of life have been done by the Britishers. Secondly they passed the "Indian Press Act. In 1910 and dictated the owners and publishers, editors of the Press had to pay the sum of Rs. 500 to 2000, as a bond to the magistrate. At that very time it was most criticised and was debated by all the intellectuals in the country mostly in Bengal.

At this very point the press inside the government and the press outside the government were basically divided and separated with views and stands of writing which took a full course afterwards in defining the criteria of journalism that started the British attitude towards India and Indian people. As the rulers of Britain used to summarise their liberal viewpoint only the utility of India to Britain, which they found that military power which India could not contribute even they thought governing India was not of much benefit to Britain, by which Indians felt hurt and disgusted. Defending that the timely ruling government opened their mouth by publishing their own journal and even pamphlets.

So the very decisive point where press started working in side of the ruling policy which believed in sovereignty and the press working outside might be under less or more control by Britishers worked and that way the imperialists and the missionaries thinking in country went their separate ways. Imperialism of Britishers who convicted India a monumentous for their empire where the 'Men' would be restored to be use of their reason and with this viewpoint they increasingly enjoyed the comforts of life upon their shoulders and attained the security and happiness of a well-ordered society of their own. Further an Indian itself would become attached to this empire through Christianity who were proud to say that undoubtedly the most important communication which according to the Hindus could receive through the medium of their language which is English and the knowledge of their religion.

All these opinions were floating in the air by means of Press outside which awakened the educated masses that how planting their language their knowledge of technologies their opinions, in religion spreading throughout the Asiatic territories. The Britishers put up a great work beyond the reach of contingencies, probably they wedded the inhabitants of these territories. A very little of imperial attitudes of this viewpoint spreading Christianity in India and use of Indian men for their own comfort.

But keeping in mind the sense of responsibility towards ruling India or the problems of preserving empire the imperial statesmen offered only minimal reforms in India stated big in their own published press journals through their imperialistic spokesmanship in dealing with political organisation, the economic activity, and the social and religious order in India he control his attention on the maintenance of British power in India. Such an imperial outlook no matter how generally held in those groups and interests which were most concerned with Indian affairs and first dominated Indian policy, was basically unsatisfactory in British society which in the long run most imperial leaders stayed aloof from this concept and they turned into love with India as a good sign to progress for Indian man in common. But as a fact by the British section of press which again I would like to call press inside as such which always used word 'Hindu' in their publishing with the matter of religion. First time before that, there was no such conception for to spring the word 'Hindoo' or religion by the section of press as it was meant for giving news of happenings in the country. First published in a paper Elphistone's opinion of the Hindoo religion to be one great cause of the people of this country being so far behind Europeans in laws and morals and that man even commented that "I am likewise persuaded that the Natives must gradually become enlightened and that their religion must fall unless an injudicious spirit of opposition to it should be inspired with new life." It is a visionary thought felt by a British spokesman. In British newspaper argued that for the development of Christianity if Britain interferes in Indian religion, so such kind of interference in Indian religion, so such kind of interference would present western enlightenment from growing. First time in the section of press insiding ruling resign stated this kind of statement of Britisher and after that Munro who swiftly officials guilty of ill-treating Indians, likewise suspended and removed the officials who used their official prestige as a way of spreading Christian Doctrines to the people. This first attack by the press through the Britishers to say about freedom of religion, which was constituted after Independence in free India in Parliamentary constitution which followed the same ruling but amended time to time as of its need.

**Technique of Information**

The Cultural and Educational right they feed helping to their mental digestion with programmes and cultural shows, through which they educate public. But again question as I think to be the 'big' ban matter of debate, arises, that is, it all being fulfilled and really needful to public. Do they really know about all such facilities by them. Do they really look and think even these dreamy-landed banners and posters and food in a farm entertainment programme served to them by their sister departments. The press inside also promotes by permitting the publishing for small and medium kind of newspapers who are meant totally to look after exteriors of Indian and their internal problems. All such kind of newspapers always look towards the insiders of the government press and acceptability thrown by them and the advertisement which feed the financial need of the papers. So how and where that point could be discovered, which hankers in my mind that the press inside and the press outside actually come to any decisive corner or undercurrent they are bound to see each other face to face the people of the country.

Now where a well-managed information technology has marked the boundary by walls, doors and enforced by laws, guards and even by well-trained dogs mustered under government press, they are formally defining or constantly continuing to define situation by including and excluding and making participation of their own choice. Today such boundaries of government press and media functioning to define social situations only to the extent that information can still be restricted by restricting physical access.

As a known factuality the massages who provide the press inside, in all early media, stone, clay, papyrus, parchment and paper had physical value and weight like Ashok Shilalekh Tamrapatra etc being heavy and people had to go to a specific place to experience them. Even when they are portable however they still had to be physically transported from one place to another and they move with people who pass. Telling this story of past my concept is to define putting thoughts of political popular reign at the time exhibiting then ideas in minds of people hammering people, that they must see with a magic eye, catching them in a though wild prison from which they may look the popular show of any popular government is the idea behind.

May it be called a factual democracy and who is free from whom to destroy each other freedom or to communicate and solve the problems of the society. So the problem is that what sort of relationship the Press from both sections is going to be formed between people and then for what purpose to experience each other.

*Three*

# Freedom of Press

## During British Rule

So the freedom of speech, freedom of religion keeping with one's self identity came out to public by insider form of Press. Freedom of education had been a questionnaire to British India and it was said with open flow of information. But even in bringing progress to India the British had expected gratitude and support from the Indians, as by them it was offered a fresh look towards the British ruling by Indian, but can openly condemn the fact that it was the backwardness of Indian people and that was the reason for the disturbance. And for Indians within the Muslims Native the First Afghan War was not a barbarism. The British rulers said the people they believed barbarous and backward could challenge or injure civilized people as they thought of themselves. So they censored the Indian Press, and seized the machineries used for publishing and cancelled the licenses of newspaper owners out of their own fear. As a result, *The Times* from London spoke for this public in demanding a swift and decisive punishment of all who mutinied English people and revolt. This was the revolt against their freedom of choices to religion first tried by all sort of small and even big newspapers who disbelieved in sovereignty. But as both the sections of people are equally sensitive in their faith to their respective religions it was the last for Hindu mind also who are basically considered liberal and believe in welcoming all good thoughts to them the revolt was the last stand for them against the western civilization. *The Times* thought and the newspaper proposed that the proper course was to sweep away every political establishment and every social usage which prevented British power and western progress from being 'universal and complete'.

So at this point and moment the feeling of being closely in

their opening mouth to public, *'The Times'* was stated deliberately and also aligned with joining the section of people belonging to AH Humes Congress, which was the first politically well-placed party in British India, The classification and a snobby certification to the press working outside, with untold attachment with politically and apprehend stood party, get its placement eventually. The English language a part of the western education which the Indian gradually received in the exercise free Press in the encouragement of political organisations in India and in the British conviction that a liberal constitutional government was the highest political achievement of a civilised society, where Indians absorbed the principles which were to justify and help inspire their movement for Independence. From there, War would be fought by pen in place of sword through the Free Press as an outside press in India —the first flame to fight for their freedom with thoughts, views, opinions not merely confined within the limits of verbal aggression.

Apart from some imperial statesmen who had always insisted on preserving the real supremacy of Britain in India, the bulk of British opinion about Free Press anticipated the eventual separation of the two countries. After 1858, the British had not done very much to preserve Indian for self-government. Indeed, the British often seemed to give false roar in India to the liberties and constitutioned system which they cherished at home that is the thought that they never exercised against Free Press with the thinking that their love to imperial greatness could not be revised as people produced by them as an intelligent knowing their mannerism with glossy codes. But above all, they had to think that India's Independence was must and unavoidable. And part of main press done outside turned into a pointed hard weapon in the form of press outside not believing in ruling thoughts which gradually evaporated in anti-established thought and then converted in to yell journalism. A side by side food for so-called pressmen.

As a western learning into Indian education, partially started using westernising mean in the field of all other journalistic media like literature, art-cultural settings. The effect of British attitudes towards the society and culture of India was equally important and decidedly more beneficial. Such attitudes of course ranged from a desire to preserve Indian society and culture in fact to a wish to anglicise Hindus completely. Of course neither viewpoint was wholly maintained. Both westernisation of Indian society and preservation of Indian culture which comes under the field of expression in the section of open and outside press with orientation to bring out this part of expression with open vision and this sort of development in the society among the intellectuals came as a good significance. The press with their open and vigour columns brought a wave in print media with lovely and lively illustrations. Here the press outside was more clear in the beginning there was no ragging or the renowned personalities as what is observed now-a-days.

The major impule in press section in the beginning on the highest level, was the conservative desire to preserve the literature and learning of India, as a very prominent purpose. For that, even Sir William Jones intended to encourage not only European interest in Indian culture but to inspire Hindus and Muslims both reinvigorate their intellectual activity. With his own countrymen Jones achieved significant results. As any part of the expressive writing come under the press formation, who build up people's mind and educate them to authencity is the working outside media with the flow of informative knowledge. So it was resulted into happy emulgation of art-culture and literature now-a-days the pages of open print media with newspapers and magazines. Here a group of Indian and British scholars and historians revealed the greatness of India's past and the basic concept of Indo-European language.

Whatever their political purposes regardless of their prejudices, historians such as William Robertson, James Mill, Mount Stuart and Elephynstone, all showed not only Britons but Indians this historical greatness. They began the discovery of India culminated in the biggest Indian National Movement.

The introduction of western ideas, however had the major effect on Indian society and culture, so the reader of a newspaper or journals, magazines and all press material was aware and awakened with zealous view, with eager eyes to see to read the matter of its own kind with the change of the society. As early as

1800, the British were inducing Indian artists to paint pictures according to British nations about what was romantic. As a matter of rule I shall say that painting a picture is a most visual and established powerful media of press in start, so provoked them to try pictures of Indian romance and to follow Renaissance artistic criteria in their techniques. Needing a recognition and British patronage many Indian artists, therefore, started to westernise themselves and though their work was frequently inferior compared to the indigenous Indian art the way was open for first rate, western artistic standards and techniques to gain ground in India. So it failed. But the placement of Indian painting done by original artists played a role of mass-to-mass visualisation of art in a form of the greatness of ancient Indian to the viewers as a medium.

The press outside mainly synchronized with the freedom of struggle with its birth and growth till 1947. But most of the time the role of politicians and the political activists before Independence and even that of journalists like Lokmanya, Mahatma Gandhi or Aurobindo were the outstanding examples of those combining in themselves with two kind of role. They were the setter of an open press outside. So before Independence they had to meet setbacks and occasions to expand also. At that time the total number of daily newspaers were about 17,168 with a total circulation of 216.6 millions copies. At a glance about 10 per cent readers followed newspaper reading with of being such a low percentage of newspapers restricting factor was the percentage of very low point of mass literacy which made the demand less. There was one more very big factor the difficulty of money. Because at the time of freedom movement it was supported by so many rich and poor sort of well wisher for country's freedom fighting. But now in free India an open press was not a missionary fighter but now the object of the press was basically to give news with 'tidings new or interesting information and fresh events reporting'. As sometime Ben Bardlee told about that the news is the first rough draft of history, a days with day-to-day challenges any outside press has face, which contains a pool of money which had made the press outside a perfect industry and its primary premise is that success in almost every field is now reliant on the application of new type of communication technologies. But the vision of the new communication revolution is somewhat bleak and also not perfectly useful for printing section of the press. The computers can do for them, but all sort of technology is not used in innovatory and creative manner, but is simply reinforcing old structures with existing power relations and established ideologies in new ways. As an alarm of changes in society so drastically is sensed by people they want to read and know about it. When it is going to be with effect of latest technology then people get together and try to explore the idea that there is going to be some sort of revolution as such. The information technology is mostly followed the press inside the government to make people's right to know. But suddenly success is just about any field has become impossible without the latest information technology, either in farming, manufacturing, education, policing, medicine, entertainment, banking or whatever I. T. is apparently set to change everything that human beings do in advanced society. It is all dealt by the press outside working for the society to go with its proper circulation of the paper it appears that this the only way forward. Initiations in the process of handling, transmission, storage and retrieved is the key to future prosperity and to qualitatively different ways of life and failure to proceed this direction carries dire consequences. So not surprisingly this "one way forward" is greeted by others with sense of forebiding so it should be properly adopted by outside press and also the press inside for giving the free flow of information to all to whom they are meant for concern and deputed by the ruling popular government, which will be the wealth of information for department attached and to whom it is concerned.

As Indian mind remained rooted essentially in traditional religious belief of the civilisation. In their attitude towards the intellectual and spiritual changes only the Britishers fortunately maintained belief that the change must be voluntary. As already John Stuart Mill wrote that the British could not force another nation to become civilised according to foreign standard. And in the end Indians preserved what was useful in their own traditions and adapted what was necessary front. To say all that, has only the meaning, that first time in these period Indian were found expressive by their own thought for their traditional values which was dumped after Hindu reign and Buddhist era which only came into possibility just getting the expressive media like press which gave them a voice to speak and say their esthetic feeling by means of art which was at that times visual expression.

The political effect of British attitude was probably the most striking of all and such effects were continually felt both in the period and afterwards in press media. Although in the beginning Bruke's conservative philosophy checked the worst effect of early imperialism and helped stabilise political conditions in India for nearly a generation. Provided with this conservative outlook officials and their successors began with some success to establish good government in various parts of India. But there was a force at work in British attitudes which disrupted conservative stability and continued imperial expansion meant the end of princely states and the traditional mode by which Indian had governed themselves. The sort of change introduced in the society of that time in such a manner, the Press from both sides holding British attitude and siding countrymen was responsible, liberal reforms provided new ideas as to how such a nation as India should be governed. But the Indians reform protested being not governed through their pen with medium of press. The reason why together imperial expansion and liberal political ideas kept in India in a statement. As going by the record, the great revolt of 1857-58 was the climax of this development, a last effort of Indians to rule themselves in their traditional way. By this time no such spokesman like press was alive against the government, so the messages were being spread by 'Rotis' hand to man a specific way of expressing thought of revolution, this also would be counted as a communicative media pressing their thoughts in masses or the men in India. And by the time the more important political contribution of ruling authority British attitudes had now made through the pattern of education had now made its entrance, so India had received its seeds of self-government which eventually resulted in its emergence as an independent state. As a result, the western education which Indians gradually received in the exercise of a free press, in the encouragement of political organisation and in the British conviction that a liberal constitutional government was the highest political achievement of civilised society. Indians absorbed the principles which were to justify and help inspire their movement for Independence through the medium of press.

Aside from some imperial statesman some notable Englishmen eventually tried to conceive the concept of Free Press with free Indian voice as a flow of their knowledge to their own identity. That is the why the greatness of imperialism could be reserved. By which it was known to all at that time that India's Independence was unavoidable. As all of us know that the base of Indian Press or journalism begins with the freedom movement, which established later on an important source of knowledge and awareness.

This section of press brave out from its crippling image to roaring wave with the freedom of movement to the freedom of press. A very little history at a glance can be taken here to continue the main living to that very decisive point where press divide and also I would like to talk about its all fields and limitation both with a short discussion of what to say and how to say.

In between rulers and the commoners who is getting what and what is their right. How much welfare is being done by the government concerned to the public, what is wrong and right for whom is being questioned and valuated by the press as such. The tussle begins when the truth is tried to ban by the government for mustering their own policy. As in the time of British this division was clear called as National and British when the ruler at the time concepted as an open outsiders. So the press like "Anglo Indian" and Nation who provoked the movement for freedom and people's own rights.

After II World War for its own interest British government gave some liberty to the national agenda after the result of 'Gandhi-Irwin Pact', as a result, the Congress shined sudden with influence and Indian Government Rule 1933 took a stand for the time. But it was all vanished after the II World War as the British could not continue with their own promises, so the leader and people of India irritated with revolved door-to-door and a group of patriotic revolutionaries turned the Indian freedom movement in to bloody revolution which was followed by Indian National Press and so many big and small sort of newspapers, pamphlets pressing the freedom movement as "Quit India" a roaring message to the British Government.

**After Independence**

From that time till 1947 all sort of progress towards this point was one and only fought by the Free Press which was succeeded to communicate between government and the people in common. Here the fields of press like paper, books, literature plays a big role of expression as media of press to communicate a country's feeling and thoughts. As a result, they all had to suffer all kind of torture. Ban upon literature and newspapers made the section divide whether the government is correct in its version or the truth said by Press puts the facts with modesty and sincerity. Knowing about what and what not made the people aware who raised an issue of Free Press without any suppress that should get the correct news from given by the newspaper. The question float as a sea wave against this exploration named as freedom of press. But at that moment the press doing outside government was completely a missionary work.

So, getting the same prestige the press as such stood as a 'Forth' State and the main pillar of parliament constituted India as a free country after a very long and fire-brand blood shedding struggle. But as a real surprise that even holding such big importance of being of the press for them keeping alive with free thoughts no such kind of ruling was established by the free Indian government in democratic India. It was commonly considered under rule by common freedom of speech and freedom of equality as a matter of right to all. But the Press was not even being given the fundamental right of smelling the undercurrent fear of Press worked in freedom movement, and fearing that it may not turn into anti-established media against the free Indian government and also after objecting a complete from for freedom movement press had no such issue to right as a pen warrior.

The current flowed with new and developing movements of industries. Here the Press in small section covered the benefit of peasants and the big urban press followed the good and bad of workers dislocated from villages and working in urban factories. The second kind of conceived thought followed the conceptional uninformity to reform and revolt but not even clear for whom? Taking the side of masses, all sat under the banner of Marx's who was with communistic pattern of society. The section of art literature and theatre in free India unlike the time of Britishers as the educated and neo-civilized Indians followed the mixture of thoughts in their own writing or any kind of creation but were not up to the mark according to people's traditionality neither among the original western creators, so they could not get a sort of popularity not appraised by English originals.

But this section of writers and creators followed by the same thought could get a big hand by a specific section of press for their express and also awarded by the government with 1936's progressive movement of India. Coating the names like Premchand, a novelist and storywriter who wrote for very common men and specially upon the peasant's life and Sazzad Jashir. Just in the freedom movement Hindu and Muslim and all small and big communities fought together for the country. So at this platform all stood together with their mind of liberal thoughts may it differ to the traditionality of Indian values.

This very point I would like to say that till now all sort of expressive media under consideration with siding common man came under press outside as such which they all follow with giving variety and shapes with proper and current illustration to thoughts. So fields and expansion of press as an open media took its own flying wings and gradually centered in the hands of big industrialists of India. And the press inside was taken as a free flow to information given and propagated the policies of the government and the fulfilled or trying to fulfill the right to know and right to information. Government of free democratic India took the responsibility to feed the public interest with its own wings and figures. I would even like to say that all sister concern feeding the interest of informative wing settled by the government of India, under their own secrecy were placed to show the dreams of goodness of free India who was established by the people, for the people and to the people. But in a factual side they were supposed to purchase the intelligential and that architectural society who may become the 'Yes person' to the section of the government liking under wrong and not uttered governing power.

But why it was needed at this time. Why it was meant for where in any type of Democratic country there should be complete transparency between common person and governing power or the ruling power. Secrecy for what? Siding for whom? This question in connection with Press stood even in British period when the concept of free press originally came into the light. And why so very bulk of priorities to the press which entered in the world of man as a mission to do or die. It was considered a risky and most adventurous job. To find and figure out right or wrong to have its own right to calculate things with open eye and clear vision, this right was given to them stating as a Forth state by free Indian government.

Here about the press inside the government, as it was never such visioned out in the time of British Indian Government. Firstly, the first Prime Minister Pandit Jawaharlal Nehru smelled the danger that press in India should be a synergy between both the press and the government, as he found that the people of India is not so well educated that it could adopt the openness of events and thoughts as it is concerning the problems related to their own welfare even. The press may also misguide and misinterpret them against the government policy if they are left out more free and frequent. This a very thin line to draw and pace in reference to press inside and the press outside. Nehru could better sense it at the momentary figure and tried to give a ground to it by the under ground thoughts stating and standing the frame from the siding or from the side of the government under so many departments working for the welfare of the society and attached them with section of all informative government media.

**Education of Press**

A press working beyond and outside the government for the countrymen with their good or bad human stories, their prospects and to their problems as it any newspaper hold the events and news first to state it on their banner headlines and columns. The subject of their vision was the first happenings all around, may be political, social, criminal, eventual, all sort of current affairs with their spreading feed captured and gathered by camera and by their correspondents to which the editors wing had to decide to give the quality and importance for that very events or even the stated view by any important political leaders who could cause the lead. With this there is no connection with that kind of press who is under the government media, but they attained the check post liking working through the government section without showing any open hinderance. But under current the press outside without the utterance of the facts belong to press inside.

Here let me talk about the field considered under the press which with the expression massaging or educating to people. First to discuss the news and the literature spread over by government communicative media after press with establishment of Indian Broadcasting media with very little references as I have not to define or write the history of Journalism but the subject on top priority is to see all pressing communication side under the government and beyond the government. It starts with Ashok Stambh, then first Indian press publication like Bengal Gazzette to all sort of provincial literature, poetry, plays all communicative arts like pupperty and films everything comes under this media but as a free and open on its own wings. But I can say that the debate on press itself is a history of press as it is noted even the history of modern newspapers in India in more than 200 years ago started from January 29, 1780 with Bengal Gazzette brought by an Englishman James August Hicky which were swiftly followed with the growth of literacy and development in regions more in India written and read in regional languages, even now as the electronic media has picked up the same line like newspaper more than four decades. They were more and more nearer to public with their widespread impact. This impact was thought as early as Maurya rulers 250 B.C. and Ashok was first to recognize the importance of media so finding new as a new every time was difficult to the newspaper owners.

The press outside now depended totally upon news as called itself with the name like "News-Paper" that means to fill it with events and also with "News is anything that makes a reader say which turned a so-called saying by Charles Damo that "when a dog bites a man that is not news, but when a man bites a dog that is news. It also be like a quest but not traverse—so the 'wrong doing of a person is always a news and good deeds come as a normal duties expected by the so-called society which wants to rule on personalities not on persons or upon common hands for which even Hicky paid a price for denouncing the then Governor. Warren Hastings by going to jail and forfeiting his postal facilities since there the fearless editors have been persecuted and even now the categorised bold press outside is always under fire all the time.

This kind of laws are mostly unwritten and untold. So the press outside has to face numerous curbs in the form of legislations restricting the publications of news and views. But these still remain faithfulness for clear and sincere reporting of events and speeches. It should be remembered of justice Krishna Iyer who suggested in a seminar in 1980 organized by Delhi Union of Journalists about the rule relating to contempt of court and privileges of Parliament Statutory Protection for not disclosing source of information should be codified so that the press could discharge its duty more freely and fearlessly.

As a rule the headline of a newspaper as press outside has all the resounding impact of a damp squib, it turns the story into every thing news is not if is in a dullest managed which may have something to say but not the news. Because for a story in press outside needs to have impact and it has to be relevant. The press outside totally exists upon news so for the news to be relevant and it has to be proximity to a reader, listener or an audience. At time somebody once described news as an arranging for North, East, West and South. But I think the news is narrower than that as the tremors in south would be unlike to trouble the sect of as the problem is too far away.

So first I shall try to find out the main roots of the Information Society ideas which surround the press in an open era. There are many investigating facets of the new information age which are now-a-days in such a communicative flow. As a rule he chose a permanent material of nature stone as a source of medium to inform about his policies connecting the views he wanted to spread in public and also all kind of implementation in ruling which was time to time needed. And thus throughout the length and breadth of his empire he on cardinal points got his inscriptions engraved an stone pillars and rocks in the language and script of the people of their advantage as well as that of the illiterate masses and inspired them to follow the lead given by their ruler. His inscriptions thus became at one and same time, a blueprint of state policy, the white paper of what was being done and also with was kind of success, a government of India official's handout as well as annual journal of socio-economic change. This was the first evidential experience of communicative press inside the government which is still followed by the government of India today at the very point functioning the government and also enlarging the scope of communication by throughing open its columns to air the problems of people. Even now the government press working is still followed by the same manner, I would like to call it the press inside.

**Primary Right**

The constitution 'Right to Know' is one of the fundamental propositions in the functioning of the press. I can very strictly say that the media or the press at its outside working has not been properly and already defined in a democratic political structure of this country. Although it is excepted that the press in performing its role of disseminating information to the reading public must be must have access to information there is a large and larger grey area on what kind of information it may have access to even there is massive wall of Official Secrets Acts, which in its present form may be invoked to deny the press uninterreputed information on a wide range of subjects and when prosecute a newspaper should the act be violated.

The wide range of clear reach of the Act has been one reason why it has been applied so rarely so far in the country. Now this has been an issue to the current debate on whether the Act needs to be amended. It is said on one hand the act, as it is argued by all that it has passed no problem in the functioning of the press, therefore, it should be left alone, but there is another view also that some of the provision of the Act should be reviewed and there being no guarantee that they will not be used in the future to impose severe restrictions on the press inside in a very perfect legal manner.

The second Press Commission has observed like the way with this one of the main obstacles to the free flow of legitimate information to the people in India is the existence of certain provisions in the official secret Act of 1923, which was basically modelled on the way of British Act of 1920. And this Act was amended by the Amending Act 24 of 1967. The usual felt necessity for amending Section 5 of the Act had been considered by several committees and also by several commissions. The whole of the matter was examined by the Press Law Enquiry Committee in 1948 when the first Press Commission, and first Press Commission in 1954 then the Law Commission in 1971 and by a study group comprising of officials from the Cabinet Secretariat and Ministers of Home Affairs, Finance and even Defence in 1977. When the Law Commission recommended some usual changes with regard to punishment under the Act, the press Law Enquiry Committee and the Press Commission did not suggest any change in this Act as they thought that the Act as a whole was being administered in most eminent and reasonable manner, but here the first press commission was the view that nearly because a document was mark secret or confidential it should not attract the provisions of the Act if in the interest of public it should be well published.

Now the question arises or even not whether there were only a very few prosecutions under Section 5 but the possibility of its being used to curb the freedom for free and flowing expressions. The Section undoubtably had chilling effect on the freedom of the press as a whole inside and outside both. And the main prohibition form communication under Section 5 is that any secret official code or password or any sketch, plan, model article note, document or information which relates to or is used in a prohibited place or relates to anything in such a place or which is likely to assist directly or indirectly an enemy or which is likely to affect the sovereignty and integrity of India, the security of the state or friendly relations with foreign states or which has been made or obtained in a contravention of this Act.

Where the prohibition is mainly addressed to :-

"Any person having in his possession or control the thing prohibited."

"It has been entrusted in confidence to him by any person holding office government of which he has mainly obtained or to which he has had access owing to his position as a person who holds or has held a contract made on behalf of the government or as a person who holds or has held such an office or contract."

This is to note here that what is punishable under section is—

"Willful communication of the prohibited thing to any person other than a person to whom it is authorised to be communicated."

Using information contained in it for the benefit of any foreign power or in any other manner prejudicial to the safety of the state.

'Retaining the prohibited thing in one's possession or control when one has no right to retain it or when it is contrary to one's duty to retain it or willfull failure to comply with directions issued by lawful authority with regards to the return or disposal thereof: and

'Failure to take reasonable care of the prohibited thing or so conducting one self as to endanger the safety of the prohibited thing.'

The express like "prohibited place" has been very widely defined. Any pace belonging to or used for the purpose of government which is the time being declared by the government by notification in the official gazette to be so becomes "prohibited place".

So the coverage of this Section widely is a matter of research and also very wide. The chief vice in the Section is this that its catch all characters covering all kind of secret official information whatever be the effect of disclosure. The official information covered by the Section is extensively broad. It includes any official code, password, sketch, plan model, article, note, document or as said before information provided it is 'secret' and the Section itself does not define any definition in the Act, it is secret or what is an official secret. In the absence of any definition in the Act, it is for the government to decide what it should treat as secret and what it should not. The Section gives a blanket permission to the executive to prosecute any person disclosing official information or any person voluntarily receiving such information knowing or having reasonable grounds to believe that such information is being given to him in contravention of the Act. The only redeeming feature perhaps is that "mens era" is a necessary ingredient of the offence under the Act.

So I confirm that there is no doubt that this Section as it stands can prevent any kind of information about any affair of government being disclosed to the public and there is widespread public opinion in the country that the Section has to be modified or repealed and also substituted by a more liberal one.

It is known as earlier the Franks Committee in England said that the scope of Section 2 of the British Act which corresponds to Section 5 of our Act is enormously wide 'any law which impinges on the freedom of information in a democracy should be more tightly drawn.' An English Judge has said that the time had come to pension off Section 2 of the British Act.

Now let me talk about it freely in connection with the press inside which has its own responsibility to give a free flow of information. At that point the consideration of this question of amending the Section but we think that it would make the Section more cumbersome and difficult to understand, as keep the opinion that it would be more appropriate to repeal the Section and substitute it by other provisions suited to meet the state as well as the right of the people to know the affairs of the state affecting them. It is very essential in my own viewpoint that to restrict the operation of Section 5 by prescribing the types of information which need a restrict protection from disclosure. These types or categories will necessarily be broad; but primarily it will be the task of the executive to determine whether a document falls under any of the specified categories. This will definitely create an atmosphere in the bureaucracy that anything and everything which they consider to be secret would not gain the protection of the Act. In this respect we think that the provisions of Part II of the British Freedom of Information Bill can serve as a model in framing the new provisions. Broadly these provisions entitle the Minister to classify the documents which are to be treated as secret and the main categories of the documents include those relating to defence, security and intelligence as their discloser would certainly cause serious injuries to the interests of the nation or even endanger life or safety of the citizen. Under these provisions any document which would furnish such kind of information could also be perfectly classified as a "secrecy" even may be its only contents if anyhow disclosed on their own would not have any such effect, so the cause 24 of the Bill specified the descriptions of documents and information to which Part II applies mainly. They are :- 'documents relating to defence, security or intelligence classified as provided under clause 26, information relating to defence, security intelligence where it is certified to the court by the Secretary of State that the document ought to have been classified information likely to be helpful in the commission of offences or in facilitating escape from legal custody or the disclosure of which would be likely to impede prevention or detection of crime or apprehension of offenders and information relating to any identifiable individual. It is not necessary that our draftsmen should restrict themselves to these subjects mentioned above. It will be open to them to include other appropriate subjects also which are necessary in the interest of maintaining the safety and security of the state without going further into the details the scheme envisaged in Part II to take the place of the Section proposed to be revealed appears to us to be reasonable and all the provisions of this Part may be adopted with appropriate modifications and the usual changes. The other all provision in the Official Secret Act may be carefully examined by an expert body to see which of them deserve modification and thereafter those provisions could also be incorporated in the new legislation proposed.

On such kind of information the Press may have access to as a matter of right and the procedure to be followed, the Commission suggests. The broad scheme of these legislative measures in other countries is to give the citizen access to official documents on the basis of an application. If the request is not granted and order must be passed stating the reason and communicated to the person making the application. In all these legislation certain categories of documents like those relating the defence, foreign affairs, material protected by other statutes, trade secrets and other confidential business information, internal and inner communication, which are deliberative or containing advice, recommendations and proposals and the like are executed. In information all about individuals, investing investigatory records and records even relating to examinations of banks and other financial institutions, by the agencies that supervise them etc. are also exempted and the citizens have no right of access to them. Each and every country has its own scheme of exemptions.

So if I want to review it there is difference in legal and constitutional practice in the various countries. Basic and a very clear vision is that there is great difference in legal and constitutional practice in all other countries. As a clear and open division is between both the constitutional and the legal it is systematically and closely has been modelled on Westminster on the one hand and on the other governments with parliamentary democracy but also with a more or less highly developed system of administrative law. The involvement of third parties whether it may be court or may it be quasi-judicial bodies in assessing the merits of ministerial decisions on its disclosure is help to present a complete weakening of their accountability to Parliament, with the complementary danger of politicising the courts or all other quasi-judicial bodies, it is also feared that the courts are in no way competent to decide on the merits of a question whether a particular sort of document will tend to endanger the defence or the foreign policy of the country as that is primarily a task of the executive.

This all comes under these Section of pressing pointed which is accepted that not to be disclosed by the government or by the any government press working inside it. In respect of the right of any access to public documents also we think that the provisions in Part I of the British Information Bill can be studied, again with profit and our legislation modelled on that part with all and appropriate changes. The suggestions in this Bill is complaints about rejection of and application for official accesses will lie only to Parliamentary Commissioner. I think so that it is only proper that we should adopt this method instead of entrusting the task to the courts which are already overburdened with so much of other work. At that point the draftsman will have to think a perfect and functionary correspondence or corresponding to the Parliamentary Commissioners in U.K. for entrusting the work of review for the review upon to day's state and the conditions.

**Liberty to Press**

Freedom of speech is a great idea and glitters, but of those who bleat loudest about it have rather more liberty than the rest of us. So let me discuss its pros and cons to all side of it even beyond the vision but to talk about any ruling and running government is always questionable that the freedom for what as they are set and purely bound to cover the secrecy of the government, mostly in the occasion like when negotiations are going on with foreign governments, but the press outside need a glance in the full gaze of publicity, where government is determined to require a certain degree of secrecy. So this sincerely is not very unusual that during war and all external aggression as things are going on to day's clamour about Indian government apt to come on India's own decisive visions punching the minds of all other nations who does see India in a different gaze, the government may be interested in keeping certain matters hidden from its own citizens at least for some-time so that the enemy does not get any fortuitous advantage. Besides the morale of the people in general and of the forces is not to be jeopardised. At this point the secrecy of the government to the press should not be opened as it is an important factor even in personal matters also for the example regarding health records, financial status or banking operations of individuals. Even universities can not dispense with secrecy all in the conduct of examinations and tests. Another factor that research organisations and research consultants have to have certain modicum of secrecy keeping in view their purpose. Even business and industrial organisations who often press for more openness in governmental policies and procedures.

Although in the time of British India and even in Britain as on the other hand it was stick to its 1911 Act, over the years public opinion has been veering round to the view of Section 2 the 1911 Act is an anachronism. And several committees, the Fluton Committee and the Frank Committee to mention two have properly underlined the need for reform, the basic thought of freedom of information the government itself has brought out a white paper and a green paper to lend support to more openness. At the time of Thatcher Government in Britain which it the time unfocused a bill in the House of Commons conceding the scope for the enlargement of openness but, in view apparently of the spying scandal which explored in that country at that the new Bill had been withdrawn out of countries security. As a known fact Canada and Australia follow British outlook and its tradition in practice but has moved forward with measures pending before their legislature to extend freedom of information to areas which remained inaccessible to the public. As regards India, the Official Secret Acts are modelled on the British Statute and its Clause 5 is a "catch-all" provision, according to many commentature and jurists.

But there is a big gap between secrecy to the government and about personal right to privacy. "Secrecy" and "Privacy" are two different aspects, upon which one contains the governmental confidence another to keep personal faces alive with own identity and figures, both should not to be disturbed by the press outside. But to produce sensations for public, correspondents seek such kind of news may it not be news but they make it news by their vision. Which is moreover alleged. There has been mushroom growth of magazines and journals which are indulging in good deal of what is called "yellow journalism". The political high ups and particularly those in ministerial ranks in the states appear to have been greatly perturbed about the stories which are published in these magazines mainly in all the regional languages in which these are intrusion into privacy, a complete character assassination and even an attempt at political or other blackmailing like every things else it will not be wise to generalise or to tar a section of press with one brush. There may be blacksheep and their existence and its presence must be acknowledged in all walks of life. But the proper course would be to locate such incorrigible ones by bringing to the notice of press council such kind of violation and contraventions of journalistic ethics as are committed by them so that a competent body which is wholly and totally independent and impartial can adjudicate.

But it is all for self regulation which will be discussed later on but in short I would like to make others know the model for several countries is obviously Sweden where freedom of information has not only the longest tradition but it recognised as a constitutional right and in outside Europe, the United States has gone Swedish way but apparently not without a prolonged public struggle for recognition of the right to freedom of information and in the face of recorded hesitation on the part of the President's time.

Till today the Official Secret Acts of both Britain and India are not directly concerned with openness in government. So they no doubt primarily deal with information that needs to be protected from most of the unauthorised disclosure. I can say instead of right to know it can be defined as a need to know among top civil servants as a reasonable way in common to prevent the leakage of sensitive information of all kind of sensitive information is deviously by a classification of documents and by strictly enforcing the above rule with the added provision of a regular procedure of classification of documents periodically, when they cease to be sensitive any more. Another safeguard can be to decisive factor or a system which really works regarding the correctness of the classification of information by entrusting this kind of responsibility to a group of ministers who can exercise the necessary political judgement.

In the parliamentary form of the government there is one more added problem of ministerial responsibility to Parliament and the ministers collectively being accountable to the people through Parliament. This is quite often cited as a reason for official unwillingness to disclose information but according to some, a direct correlation between ministerial responsibility and official secrecy may not be established. In any case the general consensus in Britain seems to be liberalise and range of official information, the disclosure of which should no longer be a criminal offence.

I see vis-a-vis that the freedom of the press and official information another area where there is considerable scope for a fresh look. Those who for a free access to information argue that they are not trying to assent any special privilege, but only want to protect, what they consider to be, the press's own social function of informing the public. They further say that to the extent that access to information is denied to press, there is a likelihood of a credibility gap between the government and the press and consequently the public. On the contrary, if information is denied, the media will come to rely on leaks and these such 'leaks' may happen to be inspired or prejudiced both ways where it effects credibility. So the denial of official information, specially to the press often leads to court cases in many of countries and their judicial interpretations have a vital bearing on complete openness.

As this debate is constantly going on and so much of thinking where law and its practices differ from country to country, no general formulation is possible as to the limits and nature of secrecy in any administration.

I would like to quote Robson and certainly conclude by drawing attention that 'knowledge by the people about their own government is indispensable if the democracy is to succeed. The government can not operate successfully if its activities veiled in ignorance, misunderstanding and mystery. Public authorities must come in to the market place and tell people simply and clearly what they are trying to do and why. They should explain and justify their method, they should be frank about difficulties and shortcoming only by a deliberate effort of this kind can prejudice and ignorant or malevolent criticism be basically avoided and a discriminating body of public opinion built up.

Once a that time Home Secretary of the Government of India expressed in his addressing in Indian Institute of Public administration which was found under the presidentship of Late Shri Jawaharlal Nehru in March 1954 that "without such a body of informed opinion the government is unlikely to be judged fairly. So it will not be praised for its successes or should be blamed for its failures. And if the public cannot judge the quality of its government with some discrimination that quality is unlikely to be high. Instead of sound and high schemes of constructive public administration we are likely to have demagogy bread, and circuses as at a time in Argentina under Person or sabrerattling as Italy under Fascism. Hence part of the task of government is to enlighten the people about its purposes and for programmes."

Let me take a little upon like going from press to media section.

# Four

# Role of Television in Printing Press

## Media's Effect on Press

It may be questioned out of difference between media and press. This is a very clear picture before us that media and press cover at a point before like press opens information to all sometimes educates people who came under literacy but at the divided point with the broadcasting came to early in India with a powerful medium. The main criteria of broadcast journalism was thought to deliver the solution in its viewpoint except pushing up the news, which was mainly as it is, which was followed by its illustrated clippings as an audiovisual media. Radio mainly is the premier medium for the new writings. But it would be discussed later on one thing at a priority that audio and video media both has its placing as a friend to people. A sharing a communication and an intimate friend with interactions when these other people are not present with the media communicate with all persons alone at a time of relaxtation, once a telephone, radio or a television is in house spatial isolation and isolation and guarding of entrances have no effect on information flow. I can guess that electronic messages seep through walls and leap across great distance and read to the viewer with this feeling efforts, whether the effect of such media on our society are good bad or natural the reprocessing of our physical and social environment may be or it is evolutionary.

As print media tend to create new totally observing definition, and reading is best done alone in a quiet place designed for reading. These places are designed for reading. These places are basically designed to separate people, often into single person's cubes. A reader of course is connected with other people by reading what they have written or what has been written about them but the reader tend to be removed from those physically present.

Indeed when someone hands you a greeting card, you must ignore them for a second in order to read it. In this sense, reading is anti-social, it isolates the reader from live interactions. Reading is liner and absorbing. It is difficult to walk, talk eat exercise, make love or drive a car on self while a person is reading. Yet most of these activities are possible while watching television, and all are possible while listening to Radio, so in these ways electronic media invades places, yet do not occupy these places in the ways that other media such as books do when television not only changes the definition of the situation in placed, but it does so in an unstable and inconsistent manner.

So that kind of media under a section of Press outside like electronic media destroy the splashiness of place and time. Television and radio and I consider even telephone as a communicative media turn into private places into more public once by making them more accessible to outside world. Even I find that a car stereos, wristwatches, televisions, and personal sound systems such as the Sony walkman make public places private and comment people direct to media in my consideration a press as an entertainer out side as a metabolically recreation of mind and heart both, but such media what is happening almost any where can be happening whenever people are, yet when we are everywhere we are also no place in particular.

The press as inside working for public service it is defended for them that press section working for the public services as if they existed only for the poor when in fact their rationale is to create common conditions of life for all classes. But I take here the subjection of broadcasting media for public services, which has been tagged as an openly entertaining media but its main section is the news broadcasted for people and grades its own and intensive credibility with current and prompt flow of news conducted with accuracy of time binding. So in their differing ways reading news in newspaper is an exercise of mind to feel it even and also you are opt to think and discuss it but to listen news from radio, you tend to pass it on at one state of hearing. But I have to come to this pointing out figure that the broadcasting stands under inside press and a government media with its names and formation.

I find in many other modern states and even in Britain Public

Service forms of broadcasting have entailed the organisation of radio and television services primarily as public utilities resources rather than as profitable commodities. This emphasis has encompassed their organisation and control as national cultural institutions owned, regulated and run in the public interest and dedicated to the public provision of information and entertainment both. In these terms, broadcasters have been obliged to serve the public in various ways rather than simply to follow the dictates of commercial markets. The history of the development of broadcasting in many nations and states is almost from 1920s onwards has been profoundly influenced by the values and discourses of public services either in the form of publicity owned state monopolies as for example the B.B.C. of pre-1955, or more recently as significant public element within mixed systems which allow for competition between commercial and public variants of radio and television. Thus the ethos of public service broadcasting and the practices associated with it have changed considerably since earlier decades of the century. Scannell's historical assessment and what follows is again only a complete extract from the whole essay needs to be set in the context of two particular issues. First the accelerating demise of the public service ideal which has occurred particularly as a result of the policies of deregulation in British Broadcast sector from last few years and the expansion of new commercial and technological form of media to challenge the previous dominance of public service media.

**Influence of Electronic Media**

The use of electronic media has led to redefinition of the nature of imprisonment as one has to sit and watch to a *de-facto* revision of the prison classification system, here the radio makes people free to face and fallow information and feeling heard by ears, which does not harm physically.

At another side electronic media bring information and experience to every place from every place, may be any kind of happenings under new values and also with event, hostages guests to space flights drams which can be played on stage of anyone's living-room. And the characters in these sort of dramas are almost experienced almost as if they were sitting on the living-room sofa.

But to watch all that one has to watch it on sitting on a sofa for the face to face interaction than is the information conveyed by books or letters and relationship with others through the electronic media are accessible to virtually everyone without regard to physical location and with social position.

I can say then that electronic media however have changed the relative significance of live and meditated encounters. Through this electronic media of communication, social kind of performers now go where would not or could not ravel and audiences are now 'Present' distant events. But you had to be there to experience this kind of informal and intimate interaction. So it can be categorised type of communication, so a sort of relationship is formed between people who experience each other only through this media. Where you are not with society but you are in society through media. I read in a magazine that in western media Donald Hortan and R. Richard Wohl in one of his perspective article on media written in 1950 with suggestion that even when the communication is most unidirectional such as in radio and television a special kind of relationship develops that did not and could not develop or exist in print media. What is unusual and improper about the new mass-media, they suggest, is that they after illusion of a face-to-face interaction with performers and political figures. The conditions of response to the performer are analogous to those in primary group. The most remote and illustriously men are met as if they were in the circle of one's peers.

As a result of electronically, mediated interaction, the definition of situations and of behaviour is no longer determined by physical location. To be physically alone with someone is no longer necessary to be socially alone with them when there are other people there on the telephone or radio or then television, intimate encounters are changed. I would also like to say that the full social meaning of a "prison" for example has been changed as a result of electronic media of communication. Prisons once more than the places of physical interaction, they were places of informational isolation as well. A prisoner was not only limited in movement but also an experimented "excommunicated" from society. The placement of prisoners in secure, isolated location once led to both physical and informational separation from society. Today, however, many prisoners share with the larger society the privileges of radio, television and telephones even. This was separated within line to press and media specially the norms of broadcast media gives or produces the solution or give a remedial treatment to its listener, and they are awarded it with gift like moving and listening both while doing work or even at walking sleeping and at awaking stage, is the most important part of the Broadcast media, whether it is good or bad but is difficult to say, but certainly it is quite different without any doubt.

But in my views the new media lead to a new type of relationship which they call 'para-social interaction. They argue that although the relationship is mediated, it psychologically resembles face-to-face interaction, viewers came to feel they know the people they meet on television in the same way they know their friends and associates. In fact many viewers begin to believe that they know and understand a performer better than all other viewers do. So paradoxically the para social performer is able to establish intimacy with millions. The content of their performance is mostly small talk and running gages. Yet they are likeable and interesting in same way that a close friend is a liable and interesting. The viewers can rely on them on to be "Themselves." Within this framework, it makes sense that stories about any character threats to resign from any show, and his arrest for suspicion of drunk driving and his divorce settlement have been reported on the network news and in front page headlines. It is not an essential point for news in broadcast media or for television network news, it can only take in print media. So I find as a result of close personal observation, many athletes, musicians, journalists and politicians are now judged not only on the basis of their personalities which is basically a base line to electronic media only on the basis of their talent personalities which is perfectly defined face-to-face on electronic media, is certainly not any way possible in the section of press in print media. There noted headlines are eventual base, but personalities are covered in a with talk which does not exceed to that which both audio and audio visual media which shows action and reaction on faces, known to public it is print media shown in photographs covered by the photo journalists.

Here different aspects of life are covered by all section of press outside, someone's considered as a personalities, their happiness, grief, and mourning of same bodies death, it all is covered when by press working outside in print media, it is defined words of encouragement hilarious comedial tips with this a magic is created by press and electronic media. It can be defined as expressed like this, that unlike the loss of a real friend or relative the death of a media friend does not provide traditional rituals, or clear ways to comfort the bereaved as a viewer and media friendly who is attached to see, read and listen media by assessing it fully enjoying it, but indeed the mourning of a para-social friend or I can say a personality is filled with paradox and helplessness. Attempts to comfort the dead person's family with words or flowers are intrusion by strangers, and intensely felt personal grief is simultaneously strengthened and weakened by the extend to which it is shared with the mass. In order to banish the demons of grief and helplessness, therefore, thousands of people take to the stress or hold vigils near the para-social friend's home or at place of death. This is the one difference opted by the press and media outside with which government media is not that way concerned to share good or bad of the persons or personalities.

The media, provides the most ritualised channels of mourning which press outside in print media could not and press under Section of government working is never and anymore concerned with this sort of events continuation with presentations and expressions Radio television present special and retrospective and many people use the telephone to contact real friends who shared the intimacy with the para-social friend this is a kind of provision press outside wings which gives highlights upon those kind of para-social friends which press inside never do. But the final irony is that in some ways the para-social performer does not die. It is only told and projected by the press in outside media not the press inside government. For the only means through which people came to know him or her records films, videotape of those are used in the focussing process. The relationship is frozen rather than destroyed in part, it is the potential and hope for increased intimacy that dies, and the never to be face-to-face consummation of the relationship is mourned.

So the para-social relationship with the press outside has also led to a new form of murder also and new murder motive, here the electronic media shows a new type of murder mystery where police generally distinguish between two types of murder those committed by a person who knows the victim and those one committed by a stranger, and there is now a third category, the para-social murder, while the media and police noted that someone's murder was a complete 'stranger' meaning that two had never physically met they overlooked the powerful para-social ties between them. This cannot be picturised in open press and print media.

This analysis suggests as well as that any where there's telephone is no longer the same home, those entering many places no longer find them informationally special. As places visited for the first time now look familiar if they have already been seen on television. And places that were once very different are now more and more similar because nearly almost in every country in at a same point in India because nearly every place has radio and television set and telephone. I see that with electronic media most places from a child's room to the priests's home and even to the prisoner's cell, now equally have a very strong common denominator. Those aspects of group identify, socialisation and hierarchy that were once dependent on particular physical locations and special kind of experiences available in them have been already altered by electronic media.

In Indian set up it is a public service media under the government towards the public, pressing the challenge to hold a responsive outlook with constructive vision to inform, to educate and make them listen to current affairs with attitude towards finding solutions. So the broadcasting is defensible as a public service which can only be a service to public. 'Public' means in the context of broadcasting remains remarkably under examined in debates about the social role of radio and television now and in future. The broadcasters are confused so too are politicians and academics. Formerly it has always been treated radio and television in terms of their immediate interests. So the whole history of the relationship between broadcasting and the world politics is one of manipulation and pressures overtly and covertly both exerted to broadcast news and discussion by politicians, parties and governments. As for academics in this country has been that the media are manipulative, audiences are beguiled against their better interests and the benevolent, disinterested role of education is mainly to teach critical awareness of how these manipulations take place "behind men's backs".

Many developing and totalitarian nations see the issue of media control in a different light. Their government often seek to use the media as a complete instrument of social control, education and national development. But it only effects and commented upon open press or open media telling something to the people living in the country and sensing the air around.

Press outside is totally connected with peoples viewpoint, but it is being given only a thin layer in newspaper for reader's view. In radio leaving the section of news it is covered by its features and section of writing which peeps in the eyes of others to see the world of people's day-to-day feeling and views. I see press release broadcasting in connection with politician if it is too much to go ahead one automatically go and get a ministry and then somebody from opposition. The similar sort of warning applies to using pressure groups for reaction and comment which beware of vested interests. The big pressure groups include trade unions and employer's organisations. Smaller groups such as so many observance society which wants to keep a day free from commercialism. So many charities also act as a pressure group upon press outside media. Beware of most unrepresentative groups of only handful members. Bonafide pressure groups have an important contribution to make to public debate.

The protest against press working outside is the pressure group trying to give its voice as wide a public hearing as possible. Methodically, a three-lane highway is to be constructed across greenfields to run alongside a housing estate. Resident, environmentalists and opposition politicians from an action group to stage a march on some big hall. This all could be explained in print media as public hearing and in radio and television through recording and camera which make the event as visual as possible. But here the press in only floating the message of the politicians without any news or views as in front of the politician people pretesting are dressed in different costumes with banners in hand. To ensure radio coverage they chant and sing specially. Here is a monotonous and usual work of press and media only to hold responsive vision at sight, no need of opening mouth of its own. No fancy brand news or accuracy of the opinion. But more than a formal and with no interest of people or any person concerned without his or her own interest involved.

Here a little gaze where press does set with motive of being for which the freedom is required where first we find freedom of information as ever told that a fundamental human right and is touchstone of all the freedoms to which even the United Nations is consecrated and that freedom implies the right to gather, transmit and publish news anywhere and everywhere without fetters.

One more point had been assured by the open press that in developing countries we can not have a free wheeling press. People have not yet developed the critical sense of judging stories without being unduly influenced or distracted. It is even a question mark after Prasar Bharati. If I see for the Independence there can be no higher law in journalism than to tell the truth and shame the devil and remain detached from great. This is one of the viewpoint for press outside as an open and free press for any country. A perfect and clear law of journalism. But here the reporters are puppets, they are to simply respond to the pull of the most powerful strings.

On the front of the press outside several major questions lie at the heart of the censorship issue for checking by the governmental authority to the press outside working, like first, by censoring what we see or hear is the government exercising commendable responsibility in sparing less well educated viewers from 'harmful' opinions. They may not have the mental capacity to judge for themselves or is the government displaying a paternalistic arrogance that underestimates and patronises its citizens? It is wise and responsible government to ensure that a tool as powerful as the media is used as a positive force for social control, national development and the common good? Or in political censorship simply a cynical way for the government to preserve its power by silencing the more outspoken voices of opposition? All these questions come down to the right or otherwise of a government to decide for us what we can do. But the censorship in all section of press outside and government interference is no more rife in many countries. As Britain 'half free' press as it has been called, has a good deal more freedom than its counterparts under some regimes where freedom of speech is something it would be wiser not to discuss.

In areas of political instability governments will attempt to exercise control over the media which would otherwise become powerful rallying point for the opposition. Failed to do so, it is argued, could lead to destabilisation in a country which may already be suffering from unrest, famine, political or religious strife, but the media working inside as broadcast media for broadcasters in nation governed by a single party system with no concept of a loyal opposition, the task of providing an unbiased and factual account of events can be frought with danger. As a result, so many journalists are killed all over the country who are committed to the press outside with norm of perfect journalism. As beyond India as increased censorship was mainly reported to countries like Zimbabwe, South Africa and areas of South America while censorship was relaxed in some degree in Nigeria and South Korea.

With the myth of objectivity we see that the B.B.C. has no editorial opinions of its own. It has an obligation not to take sides, but a duty to reflect all main views on a given issue, where the very selection of the news involves bias, there is some bias in every programme about public policy. The selection of the policy to be discussed and those to discuss it means bias. But the outside need a touch of complete unbiased opinion as such.

So complete impartiality is like perfection, and ideal for which many will strive but none will wholly attain. Even the most respected and regarded journalist can only be the sum of his/her beliefs, experienced and attitudes and product of his/her society, culture and upbringing. No one can be free from bias, however hard he/she may try to be or to compensate by applying professional standards of objectivity, for objectivity itself, subjectivity appraised must by nature be an unreliable yardstick.

So working for the press outside the journalists' duty is to recognise the individuality of bias without ever surrendering to it. In matter of press dealing outside with the problem of personal bias through a combination of professional integrity and an exhaustive system of checks and balances, like, people do have their politics, quite definitely but they are very good at keeping them out news, as they never get through any way because there are too many checks and balances, too many people asking questions. There is a dual personality which tells that as an observer this is not for them talking politics just me talking about things from both sides with which he is not directly involved merely telling that what is what.

Under the press outside the process of eradicating bias begins by recognising that every argument has at least two sides and that the truth probably lies somewhere between them. The journalist must stand back and view the argument from all sides before scrupulously drawing out the key points to produce as full, balanced impartial a picture as possible in the time available. When I base upon the chosen subject or created with my own wings as press inside outside that does claim the norms and ethics of journalism which are basics for open press media. So the first law of journalism is to confirm existing prejudice rather than to contradict it. And here is another journalistic dilemma : that there is never enough airtime to point the masterpiece he/she would wish. Even the fullest report of an issue can be at best a sketch and at worst a caricature of events.

But sometime the seasoned journalists who tread the margins between factual information and reasoned opinion, the path was established by an American journalist who did much to haul America out of the destructive introspection of an era with its fanatical witch-hunts against public figures with real or imaginated links with communism. But the British news tradition tends to shy away from the projection of personality, preferring to aim for the factual approach that permits viewers and listeners to make up their own minds on an issue.

When times change and there are signs that the pendulum may be swinging towards a more personal style of telling rather than announcing the news, this can be seen most clearly where factual reporting crosses over into interpretation and analysis which is often presented in a personal way by the reporter.

In the press outside bears a reporter traditionally not only to refrain from comments but also to speak in natural tones, never giving any intimation of his feelings. Any flicker or emotion would signal both an intellectual loss of self control and violation of the sacred code of objectivity, so a campaigning or committed journalism, must by necessity be biased journalism, yet it has its place. In 1983 I read a report of B.B.C. on the famine in Ethiopia was credited with opening the eyes of the world to the crises and leading to an unprecedented for the relief of flood stricken region. This report was described by the Media Weak magazine described as—'unashamedly emotive' with no ground of humanitarian feeling as such, and it was quoted from the press officer of the UNICEF (U.K.) it seems as though he no longer merely reporting, but actually experiencing something and again it was quoted by ITN'S chief editor. In scenes of the great tragedy and conflict a reporter has to be touched by what he is seeing. He said I don't think the report would be as valuable if we didn't get a feeling of involvement and concern on behalf of the reporter.

As it is a question on open press media that could the press working outside is able to cope up with the so-called impartiality under fire. Here the strongest test of media impartiality comes at times of internal division or external conflict. But nothing nails colours to the most more quickly than a good old fashioned war.

Thus the independence of the press working outside has been challenged at critical times. And at times as a principle it has survived. Once a B.B.C.'s external senior duty editor expressed, that the most pressure I have ever been under was certainly during the Falklands War. Communication was controlled by the Ministry of Defence and this meant they effectively had us by the 'bias' "because they could cut the line of communications with our correspondents unless we told the line and agreed to delay stories. On some we delayed for as long as 24 hours. I don't thing it is anything would ever agree again with hindsight". Here comes the actual tussle of press working against the sovereignty finding out the facts for openings to the people from inside the government press section for which the press person on duty has been appointed in all sect of governmental machinaries for giving the information to newspaper or a media open to public a press outside lined from government. But the reporting here is disordered when the reporter doesn't get the news in time, one side the demand of the public then the responsibility of the press. It is possible for the very presence of reporters and camera crews to create news by making a tense situation worst.

The main problem from the side of an open press does stand that it is mainly not welcomed by the press inside under pressure of government. For the press outside feel at that point difficult to distinguish where the coverage of an incident becomes incitement. But when peeping inside the governmental set-up the reporter finds only calculated statements given by the person concerned in this hide of some time under official secrecy and sometime Parliamentarial procedure. So many reporters must have been tempted to ginger up a coverage or a reporting of these 'insiders' is always a critical and biased danger upon them who is prior and work for outside press and committed to his/her countrymen.

**Photography**

As in the press outside the camera for both print and visual media is used as evidential and strong weapon and seen visualised and picture published in any newspaper might be useful in evidence. This spiral of distrust tightens if camera crews are forced to retreat to the safety of police lines to film disorder as happened increasingly during years in all democratic countries. In behind the police security given to public the police sometime fail before mob or under pressure of some V.V.I.P.'s wing where the police is available to face the facts, the officials and the policemen before are not able to face the press outside or camera forcing upon to shelter behind that 'person' or 'Dioter' concerned inevitably produces a distorted and one sided views of the action which will see the other side as the aggressors resulting in accusation of bias.

Although a camera bias can be present even in run of the mill industrial relations. If the striking workers are filmed as an unruly mass blocking the roadway and the management are interviewed by newspaper and T.V. both in the calm sanctuary of their offices, the impression will be that management represents the virtues of order and reason, while workers are seen as the forces of disorder.

And in a visual media of an outside press have another danger in the presence of the cameras is that they may be seen to be legitimising or endorsing what is happening and encouraging that to continue and a very camera person will know who has ever had a good shot laid to waste by cavorting and yelling like the mum, the mere presence of lens can bring out the performer is sometime most of us mean those press persons working for outside media. This is why that the media is not always welcomed where there is any kind of disorder especially when it is coupled with violence and crime. The camera or recorder or print media on the streets may be seen as a threat by those who fear for their identification specially if the press or the open visual media is turned over the authorities.

Once during a wave of riots in Britain a reporter was killed, another was slashed across the face with a knife, and T.V. crews were stoned and charged by irate mobs and many reporters were attacked, at that time rioters, who are even now in India in all its sensitive places they are fenatic and see the press outside as an open arm of police, because the newspapers are giving away pictures taken at the riots to police. I see here under the police and countries own Criminal Evidence Acts in which the police have the right to requisition the published pictures which might be useful in evidence.

Here the camera may also distort the news by highlighting the point of action : a three hour demonstration by 100, 000 passes peacefully until a group of twenty trouble makers through stones and bottles at the police, it is a reverse side of press performance and if such skirmish lasts eight minutes before police drag the culprits off into waiting vans. Here the camera of a news-paper and the camera of a visual media of an outside press works different. A film captured in camera by a pressman can only click a side of the part-not the whole fight as a forty second film report on the evening bulletin include twenty seconds on disturbance which can not be captured in a still photograph. The impression is of a largely violent demonstration. The only way to comensate for the contextual distortion is to stress the relatively small scale of the incident.

Distortion of news in the press outside can only be controlled by self regulation as prevailing news values sometime be a distorting mirror on the world. So the decisions about what to cover are made with one eye on the clock and the other on audience appeal. They may be made by news editors away from the scene or live-action cameramen in the heat of the moment. That is why they are always made under pressure. So the four main dert causes of distortion were isolated in a working paper on the media such like emphasis on action, conflict and personalities selection of particular events and themes for coverage especially disorder and upheaval. Labelling or stereo typing in the reporting of section of the community such as minority groups and women. The snowball effect where the media covers a story because the media is covering a story.

Sensalisation is also one point for the press outside attached with commercial section of newspaper for its selling and circulations. So the newspaper wants a hungry reporters for it to eat sensitive news and feed it to the newspaper. But when the reporters hunger is for a good story with upbeat actuality can lead down the road to sensationalism especially on a thin news day when the editor is scouting for a strain lead. The easiest solution is the unethical one which is to 'hype' a story and blow it up out of proportion. Thus a suggestion that overtime might be cut at a local steelworks unless more orders can be found becomes, jobs threat as steel works grinds to a halt and so on. Unless the facts are permitted to speak for themselves without embellishment, fact gives way to fiction as the story is inflated until it can stand up as headline. Making something out of not very much can easily give way to making something out of nothing these are such thing which are the goods and bads of press outside committed to the people as such.

There is one more aspect to be seen that the press outside has an open responsibility create a good taste of their reader when the press under government has only responsibility to entertain people through the connecting department and to give information to public of policies of government and of popular government concerned. In other word I can say this press never concern with problem such a rioting. Police encounter, accident occurred in places, it is very much perfect but even the press outside. Though committed to people but never have a direct fight with government or with private sectors as depending upon advertisement, or D.A.V.P. support for running a newspaper as an industry but not formally declared.

# *Five*

# Activity of the Media in Democracy

**Performance**

Here let me put same vision upon sovereignty it, democracy from there the press divided. The very first point to be entered that imperialism from years was challenged by an idiomatic word Democracy and followed by the democratic theory and practice like to day. From this way to that way the press as an informative media turned up into pressing media. As we all know that the key traditions of democratic thinking above all those which stem from republicanism, liberalism and even Marxism appear to be severely strained in the face of major 20th century developments. Among these developments are to be counted the dynamics of a world economy which produce instabilities and difficulties within states and between states which outreach the control of any single polity. The rapid growth of transnational link and which have stimulated new forms of collective decision-making, involving states inter governmental organization and international pressure groups, the expansion and intensification of transnational communication systems the proliferation of military technologies and arms as a stable feature of the contemporary political world and the development of pressing translation problems, involving for instance environmental challenges like acid rain damage to the ozone layer and the "green" house effect which do not acknowledge national boundaries and frontiers. Explaining this section which seem beyond the press talk I only mean to open that unknown fronts which is being faced by the press outside as a neutral and with rapid growth of complex interconnections and interrelations between states and societies, often referred to as the process of 'globalisation, along with the intersection of national and international forces and processes pose questions that remain largely unexplored. These centre on the challenges to democracy deriving on the one hand from the world political economy and the web of relations and networks which stretch across national borders and on the other from the divergence that sometimes exists between the totality of those effected by the political decision and those who participated in making it within a democratic state.

When the press under the government mainly deals with non-aligned news-pool or it can be said they mainly put the point to inform people of their well-being and if any news goes beyond the welfare of the society, they never highlight it. And if it is a must give in their broadcasting media or on television network they have taken the permission of the District Magistrate, for instance I quote the news of riots, as all the newspapers and television channels show and print it big banner either show it to people stonning a person to another amount the mob, but the reason of provocation if not known properly, but guessed by the press outside working which opens this front sometimes oriented to its own bent upon opinions either to one of the group concern with any religion or sects and sometimes cast and creeds. But it is captured by the camera of press it is almost mob created violence but the person who begin with not known. So cause of it is behind the scene. So what a press camera see in its picture it is never clear in concept. We normally see that this kind of happening are provocated by but when a riot takes place in football match and in a cricket match between India and Pakistan. The riotorial reason is quite different. The riot in an auditorium of football match is only a feeling of individuality deal with the state of mind of a person sitting there may for his siders defeat or may be for good or bad play. But the riot placed in India on the ground of India Pakistan test cricket match is the result of a bias religions feeling judged by people of both sides in their state of mind of thought which they with the oriented view-point.

Thus the total upon all as "what is going an" around is the duty of press as and outside media and the Forth State of democracy with the nature to cope-up and bridge the people in between, keeping the knowledge of all section including the pursuit of political knowledge on old disciplinary grounds which not an adequate for today's policies. But to be followed by the press as it is.

The pursuit of following question is central to this enterprise is the idea of democratic politics progressively comprised by the intersection of national international forces and pressures, which are main talk of the subject handling by the pressures? Is the notion of national self-determination becoming an anachronism in a world of interconnected political authorities and power citizenship rights? Is the principle of territorial representation the single most appropriate principle for the determination of the basis of political representation? Are there duties beyond borders? If so what are the political and legal implications of these duties? It is a question that how should press agencies should deal it with to control democratic level with aspect of local, legal and regional and global.

Democratic political theory has to be rethought and along with it a study of underlying principles and practices of the democratic politics are necessary for carrying an open outlook upon parliamentary setup and constitutional proceeding and feeling newspapers for political reasons with statements given by politician. As press outside is the only canvas to picture a scene of society and sites of power in the democracy, with its principle problems developments all over and around, but to remark a fiery brand comment upon bad happening in the field of all governmental surrounding to clinch and pinch the public mind and heart both.

When define a good history of past about the country in present, the sovereignty as a popular reign of the time can also be showed down when to point out for a bad democracy of the eventual time, with discussion of civil association and the states. The press has to file a complete figure with events happening around of democratic good in democracy of popular government. Which press inside can not so the press section of government gives authority to press outside to deal with it.

From here I come to the main object of writing this book. The motion of writing is only to draw a every thin line that how the both section of press work inwardly and outwardly and the broadcast media under control, and known as a government media including television network with its inner motive towards people, handling this very point I would first try to define the field and limitation of the press of both sides. Means of expression and all communicative folder of thoughts which interacts with masses in common leading to the points one by one I would first prefer to say that media and glamour both are connected figures but why. And equal roar for freedom of press but in my mind as I find people half awaken, so the freedom for whom and also why. It has a mental psychological base of the question, but detained upon the relations towards media flow and whispered by the people. In between I can draw a face of democratical form of neorich society keeping arms on both side, introducing newspapers every day.

I have to peep into the heart of democracy, challenging sovereignty through the press, fighting with people. It is the history of almost every country but not to see free but to retain identical values of country's culture. This side of protection has been mainly taken up by that section of press which is mainly under government which maintains untold sovereignty of popular ruling government, as the 'organ of social thought' as a next name to democracy viewed in a manner and as an agency with a specific task to do, one to regulate and another to coordinate uses people which was possible by the means of pressing media as a new thought of revolution. I even call in other terms the juridico-discursive' concept of power which can not cope with the major modern role of the state, at this point to divide the role of communication relation and a social distance with authoritative power of command, the power of pen under the outside press is the only and one thought to keep the earned democracy alive. Democracy is necessity because in a complex public-service state, governmental practices must be effectual and therefore based impractically sound information about their reception by society and this kind of issues as debate are raised by the press outside.

So the press has to keep a watch upon the language used in thought and action. It is much more important to the section of the government media. Where a word used for announcement or to public has its official meaning and terms of secrecy under governmental secrecy, because it is an statement open to public on their responsibility. Under their policy they prefer to use word No or and in telling Not in some important matter a word to risk skipping over it without any contractions. Normally they put it in

CAPITAL. For it a simple reason is that people have to come up for a breadth every now and again.

Sometime sentence used in the press language look fine in print, but it sounds unfinished when it is read loud in radio and television. Secondly the language used in media speaking stray from conventional rhythms of speech. Usually where English is spoken sentence will rise and fall and end with the voice turned down, unless that sentence is a question, when the voice will rise at the end.

While print journalists concentrate on cutting words out, broadcaster will sometimes extend sentences to make them sound more and more normal and natural in spoken form.

Here the government media like radio, television carry it with peaceful appeal to mass and announces to maintain law and order, and as a news credit they give it to last listening not the front line not like other magazines and newspapers. There political orientation blow it up to another exciting follow up with no norms, and even in the same newspaper you find a big column advertisement placing an appeal given by the Chief Minister or by the Prime Minister with the announcement to 'set-piece'. Maintaining the newspaper like an industry which kind of line in the field of journalism the paper is going to maintain or the magazines, I shall discuss it in minute observation later but instances are quite vice-versa in the credibility ground.

Most of the section of press mainly ruled by the pressure groups not only the government. And these pressure groups have and important role in carrying out to make to public debate which make a press to get fall into some categories where the main voice is not of the newspaper itself but of punching line under the journalistic table. The television does take it as a leas story when something big has been happened in a big riot and people died in mob, which normally reported by the reporters and captured by video camera and photographers, but as a rule name of victims identity should not be disclosed to keep the morale high of people, that they shouldn't be afraid of other section. Gradually adopted professional skill is the main criteria to pick up the situation polity and policy both.

Some news releases carry embargoes, which means they are

not to be used before a certain release date. This is a parallel section of the news opening. This collected news is a trial brand of coming occasion. In these types of projection mainly interviews and statements and but in these cases the contractions are better to deal the situation, when statements given by concerned not certain for future print or broadcast. In the matter most obvious differences between written and spoken languages is the use of contractions words like can't, couldn't, wouldn't, shouldn't, we'll, she'll, they'll, didn't and even shouldn't, and can't might look peculiar on paper, but are the substance are spoken English. But it is not for writing. In one's next conversation, should try to avoid contractions and see how difficult you find it and how stilted it sounds. Broadcasting is about conversation so contractions are a must. That is why a little contractions can be a dangerous thing. Shortened form of a word in print media and even in radio talk confuse the year and to reader can be misleading to the listener "He couldn't agree to the proposal" sounds like could agree. These type shortened words are use in the reporting of a murder or upon any sensational news.

Another main division between print media and broadcast media and in television is that the trial resumes at one's unfinished while the trail is due to resume at one's clock is louge but more rhythmic and more definite shape and conclusion.

**Language of the Media**

One more problem about the media language which can often show-up only when the copy is read out loud is that of the unintentional rhythm. But in India Hindi as a spoken language goes down, so the norm in spoken media like radio, television are strict in speaking the words as follows. A little alteration may casually and sometime occasionally be acceptable, but sometimes several similar sounds in spoken aloud sound stupid, while a superfluity of hissing's 'S' and 'C' sound sibilant. Say this sentence yourself and see the effect. These are the warning for speaking media it is not a question for print media as such.

For the filed work for a press journalist in Press outside will be at good to take two daily newspapers one popular and another serious and read some of the stories at loud. Which newspaper style sounds more like conversational language the popular style or serious style? What makes the difference? He should take the hardest story to read and go through its using in easy listening formula. Now read out loud and see how it sounds. Is it any better or can it still be improved. Then should find a better way to write this story and to bring the point home and try to do it again. This will improve the language of press in the media.

Now specially if I talk about radio a popular broadcast media and powerful form of medium and its role is becoming increasingly important in developmental communication. After free press the radio and television become a popular weapon introduced by the government of India against the voice, the press. But it took its place as a very popular media and could overcome all section's pressure by giving programmes in a constructive manner, this happen one good to this point and All India Radio kept the news section in terms separate identity and popularized it to interiors even in the villages. According to survey in India, All India Radio ranks second after the print media, in terms of absolute reach and penetration, either the side we are still not be able to keep away with the thought that our bureaucracy and diplomat thinking is even based upon British attitude and filtered towards now a day democracy there the channels to be listen to the British Broadcasting world service it still based on open credibility to be listened and to be believed by Indian people. I myself find it one of the giants of broadcasting and enjoys an unparalleled reputation. For the purpose of this book it provides a global point of contact with British radio. It is some years now since the sun finally set on British Empire. And yet, in one respect this country still does rule the waves—the air waves. The B.B.C.'s External Services with more than 100 million listeners around the world, has achieved a reputation for political independence the reliability gives it a stature no other national radio can match.

I still see now and listen about past that the sun may indeed have set on British Empire but that is easily forgotten from within the magisterial headquarters of the world services as the stirring strains of Imperial Echoes herald the start of another Radio Newsreel. I say as you lean back, half stut your eyes, and let the newsreader, is well modulated and oh-so British intonations wash over you, the world is much as it was between two world wars and the Empire Services is still in its hey day. Passing from those days to even now in Indian Democracy we are still bearing the legend 'To the friendship of English speaking people' and step slung the pale, travertine-clad corridors and up the wide and winding staircase, the effect is reminiscent of an art deco hotel or once elegant gentleman's club. There only when you enter the doors of the newsroom on the forth floor does elegance good to utility. Where the brown carpeting, battered wooden desks and achro columns give a worm but comfortable air, like a faded easy chair or battered pair of slippers.

**News by Wireless**

Now come to being with All India Radio, actuality of which commenced as shown not in 1927 with inauguration of the Indian Broadcasting Company but four year earlier. So according to a contemporary newspaper report FE Rosher, Managing Director of the Indian states and Eastern Agency Limited approached Government of India in 1922 with a few establishments of broadcasting services in India. And a few months later as result of a Broadcasting conference held in Delhi sanction was accorded for the transmission of programmes. Operating in conjunction with the Radio Club of Bengal, the Calcutta Station Broadcast its first programme in November 1923 while a similar service was inaugurated in June 1924 on behalf of the Bombay Radio Club, both these on small transmitters loaned by the Marcony Company. Smaller Station were also set-up in Madras, Karachi and Rangoon.

More than half a century old, the Indian broadcasting system remains government controlled. The constitution of India which come in to force of January 26, 1950 placed broadcasting placed broadcasting in the Union list, where the entry 31 in the list I of the seventh schedule reads : "Post and Telegraph, Telephones, Wireless, Broadcasting and other like forms of communications.

With the proclamation of the internal Emergency on June 1974 Akashwani was brought under censorship and the AIR code was discarded as 'absolute' and not restored until and after the general election in March 1977.

Recommendation to make it autonomous in a bid to increase, its credibility and accessibility to the listeners were made as early as 1966 by the Chanda Committee, and later by the Verghese Committee in 1978. The government has not yet taken any steps to implement the recommendations. The debate on the merits or demerits of autonomy are still counting.

I am talking about its freedom or the control but I guess that it was inadequately tapped. But whatever might be the future structure of the broadcasting system, it will remain an important communication medium. I still see it, unfortunate that inspite of potentialities, it still remain an inadequative tapped resource. Against the minimum desirable diffusion rate suggested by UNESCO of 50 radio sets per 1000 people long time before. When in India there was 21 radio licenses per 1000. Community radio sets and particularly the ubiquitious transistor have played an important role in reaching farflung villages. But it is feared that they are more recognized as a source of entertainment than that of a medium for serious news or the development instructions. It is about time that one asked whether the entire purpose of the radio as a tool for transforming society in a developing country is not being frustrated. So it commenting an All India Radio serious programmes, one observer notes : 'They have lented to become AIR's Achille's Heel. If it is an education, inadequacy of the number of receiving sets becomes a crucial negative factor. If it is a matter of 'straight' talks radio adopts a 'tongue-in-the-check' style that sometime or often mentally alive listener is agitate where missing the sound carving style of news. May be it is a criteria of governmental policy in the broadcasting media but there are, however, ills that are in the nature of the set-up. this was the opinion of an observer. But in my view-point if I see the sense and sensitivity of news both flowing to the listeners. By the norms of broadcast journalism, the news should be in a farm and constructive, but the interest of listener here differ, as he wants the sensation of the news, which better provided by the newspapers of outside press even it is sometimes inflammatory.

The one very point that suppose a nine minute bulletin of world news is broadcasting at intervals, interspread with shorter news summaries. There a foreign correspondent's reports are featured in the four fifteen minutes newsreels. This kind of limitation in time is also an actualized binding for the news, which followed with hard bindings of time restrictions, which can only cover the hardest facts of news concerned. Here the listener is benefited only to hear when it is not in a stay mood, radio provides you the news 'read' by and 'listen' to process with a style, solid with factual and even earlier done and checked and double checked for its accuracy. One more plus point is there that the news read in radio thumps-up in mind in currents, but the news given in print media, pours a thought in mind, both are concerned to news values given to public.

Why to give it, is it a duty to inform or people wants something to know. If I analyse with my conceptional thinking I feel so the difference between man and animal is the missing enviety. As our Unished has already claimed right to in the form of 'Athato Brahma Jigyansa". A neurotic action in man is the main thought about inquisity to know and when it is quietened eventually posed by an intelligensia that the posed figure of 'Aham', on 'self' where on his own terms he thinks of himself as a wisest man, and at that point the eagerness is dead man's polity is dead to know each other there is no news containary kind of news values. So the news is for a common man and conception towards life in society with human values.

Here the news broadcast by radio clicks the mind for a second, but the grip of its news is followed by the press as such begin with print media, which really presses the point where it should clinch the mind but not in a provocative manner. I can draw a very thin line in between the news and the sensitive news given by the pressing print media and media like radio and television with it own norms and condition. One of the editor of Radio says that, keeping up the information is a major task, but trying to keep it on a top of the news is like climbing up a mountain that's terribly slippery. You never get to the top even when you are very close to it, you just keep slipping back again. If you can manage to stand in the same place then you are almost ahead of the game. Normally in new room of a radio station is unlike most other the newsroom is without reporters. Mostly the journalists are in the field are the stringer and foreign correspondents. But the difference that radio does not have a desk of specialized subjects as it is in the newspaper line. So the radio news does not consists with the follow-ups. It is at a place where the agencies work most importantly than a man as live figure who brings news or sends it to the newsroom from their allotted sights.

New as follows by radio gives an opening to the events, either the proceeding going on in Parliament or the happenings in the fields of different sections like—economic, political, defence all other world affairs, all in occupied place in newsroom, but in newspapers the newsroom is basically almost inclusively the enclave of sub-editors.

Here same time radio news effects you but find when it affects you it is a noted excitement of the whole thing, the excitement of the being at the centre and that one of the first things that strikes you here. You are at the centre of the world events, you know everything that's going on. You become the part of that.

I quote here, for instance as seventy five voice dispatches are filed daily by the B.B.C.'s world wide network of correspondents from every international trouble spot and scene of upheaval. Bulletins go out on the 24 hours a day. From some fifty studies programmes criss-cross the globe with broadcasts in thirty seven languages, a total of 734 hours a week of news and general programming. In addition the news is re-broadcast by station in fifty countries-1300 G.M.T. Bulletin alone in twenty countries including Canada, Australia, the West Indies and Hong Kong and the B.B.C.'s domestic service has correspondents in the worlds major capitals. Its external services broadcast their reports and plug the gaps in coverage with their own correspondents. I mean to tell about B.B.C. that the backbone of the operation is mainly the news bulletin in every aspects and language even in Indian Broadcast but the methodical manner in missing as in other countries and even the straightness of the news which is time to time has been questioned by the front foot willing of Prasar Bharati. For running things in order as decided in the newsroom each story from the teleprinters should be passed to the central copytaster who basically hands potential news items to the senior duty editor, this way radio can assure to speak with more or less the same voice.

Like India B.B.C. has no pressures, no advice, no guidance at all from other or the own country office, the last thing that Foreign office wants is to be involved with B.B.C. and the last thing they want is to be involved with them. This fundamental out-look of news interaction with country sources by means of getting the news.

**Funding of Fourth-estate**

All India Radio as not only funded by the government but a Government Institution under Ministry of Information and Broadcast totally under Government, when B.B.C. itself has all the same facility by the Government but not dancing on its tune so the credibility and truth containing to the news is such as people would listen in carefully smelling the facts of talk and they would never stop to listen, which is never a possibility of All India Radio as it can not peep inside the whole. Where losses the wings of news but to be listened by people in hurry and at first opening basis.

I may say that impartiality means that is only conflict or dispute media always try report the views of both the sides. So they do this who-ever may be involved in either Britain or America or any other country and if it is a domestic dispute, whether government is involved or any other side they open it with courage, when radio gives weightage to it at least, or have a policy to speak in a twisting language or talk goodie goodie form. So it is not entirely acceptable to people. Here the regions are quite content, indeed relived there the editorial decisions making process is focused in the news department, because then they are sure that radio speaks with one editorial voice and has one stamp of journalism.

Let me come again to the debate on autonomy in view of these problems, it could worthwhile to resuscitate the debate sparked off some time back by the Chanda Committee's observation : if radio organization were to be made autonomous and its programmes based on the concept of social responsibility, its value and effectiveness would be considerably enhanced. It would create public confidence and lead to the acceptance of its programmes and objective and unbiased and consequently their impact would be far greater.

One could even go further and discuss the possibilities of

decentralization of the broadcasting medium. The working committee of International Broadcast Institute at its annual meeting Nicosia in 1973 suggested : 'Government and society should be encouraged to consider ways of increasing participation of groups and individuals within particular committees. This would develop a new approach to communication's issues, providing assistance into continuous struggle of man for the right to communicate : Regional programmes with particulation of village people could go a long way enabling rural groups to communicate with others at their own level, horizontally so that the experience gained by one group could be available to another.

The need of press begins as the imperialism has already set-up a wing to send information of its own authority where the people should listen about the policies created for the welfare of them. It is a for their own welfare as the revenues of land and taxes from trading class and other working section so there was no voice of public beyond it except the court and courtier section who used to listen the public for their complains of victimization and other complain but the decision was based on their outlook of judgement sometime good sometime bad.

So I can say this was the problem of people not the problems of imperialism. Two critical approaches to the liberal theory of sovereignty as it was sensed in 1945 near about when a dramatic reduction in both the variety of intellectual positions and the agenda of issues in western and Indian political theory and jurisprudence. I see that the political argument has been virtually reduced to a contest between positions within contest of liberal democratic theory. But theory of it was based on economic revolution rather than upon. So in western country it have been all with popular democratic radicalism of the 1968 student movement but eclipsed in public political argument. So it mainly entered through Literature and Arts, paintings and so many others as a non-traditional wings of art and culture.

The language of democratic socialism starts here with this who are relatively radical and seek to challenge the economic *status quo* now believe in representative democracy and liberal/ constitutional government as their unquestioned point of departure. From now the started containing human stories in their papers and electronic media took it producing them with their own voices. But the press inside the government media covered it up with their welfare programmes giving for poor, backward and so many other ways consisting good of the society. But there are some genuine benefit of this democratic socialism which follow from this dramatic restrictions of the terms of political argument, coming as Fascist, Nazi and Stalinist political ideas because now utterly marginal. It is also case the restriction may be more apparent than the real. Here the press has taken side of masses and printed the literature which is concerned with the revolutions for man's hunger, its fight against the society. The process outside here sided with common man and its down to earth reality. A different political argument in different political argument in liberal democratic terms does after relatively broad spectrum of positions and opinions. From here a context of political theorizing which includes both side of press, addicted to the masses is a broad one. But the hegemony of liberal democratic political argument tends to obscure the fact that we are thinking in terms which were already obsolete in the 19th century.

Till now the independence was nearer to gain, and there was no forum for fighting anymore but to see the conflicts of masses. The newspaper took the side and liability both for uttering its agenda, and so many of small medium and big type of journals magazines assured the responsibility of fighting with spirit of man's fight towards life and down to earth problem containing bread-butter and water problems. The other also government press started popularizing there responsibility to the mass-advertising its own policy. When the press in Print Media used to have its own column for human stories given with evident factuality.

Here representative democracy, parliamentary government and liberal constitutionalism are the doctrines re-used and re-cycled much as they were passed on the patter of constant and Mill and Dicy. In Britain the modern big government has used these doctrines as a means of legitimation and has suffered precious little restraint in its action thereby. The 'sovereign power' of peoples representatives gathered in the legislature has been placed at a service of the executive through enabling legislation. The division of conservative and liberal starts with this now, this dividine line of work and action in the press section divided the viewpoint of independence occurred in India. It simply became questionable and its battle stood at the point of economy. They tried to seek and to make the world fit for individualist liberalism rather than to recognize the obsolescence of the political doctrine. Radical liberal democrats, on the other hand do not really perceive the problem, in that they seek to extend the scope of government action without devising new means of control of co-ordination of governmental agencies.

But in other countries the shock of Nazism and Stalinism scared the vast mass of western politicians and there electorates into a rigid adherence to liberal democratic doctrines The agenda in some of the newspaper rigidified to a excessive degree and even now it remains rigid. From the place the rise of New Right has served to enforce the terms of argument by pitting classical liberalism against democracy which begins in India with movement of trade union workers and with so many other unionistic mass revolution. The majority of the theorists of the new right do not challenge either sovereignty of the state or the basis of this sovereignty in representative. As they seek to restrict the function of the state whilst at the same time conceiving of it as a sovereign public power able to assure public peace. Even a state restricted in its functions to war, police and justice if such were possible under modern economic and social conditions raises the problems involved in liberal democratic conceptions of sovereignty in its acute form. Where the conservative theories of liberal theories of rule of law and social democratic theories of an interventionist social welfare state alike ancient evade the central questions of how to ensure public accountability and control when faced with modern multiform big government. The former imagine it possible to reduce the problem to nothing by taking the state back to the mid-nineteenth century and the latter, if they really see the problem due in with adhoc palliatives like Freedom of Information Act.

The terms of debate have not always being so enclosed and so in the first three decades of this century, liberal democratic political theory and the national of popular sovereignty through representative government were widely challenged. This challenge came from supporters of classical Marxism, from labour and administrative syndicalists from 'pluralists' and guild socialists and from proto-fascists and fascists. Much of this challenge was mere demagogic rhetoric and was made on behalf of doctrines of social organization which were little better than absurd. Anti liberal criticism of rural as Maurras or Mussolini may be telling on occasion, but their alternatives to liberal democracy are poisonous and one can only heave a sigh of relief that they have no place in modern political argument in India specially.

In particular we need to be especially careful about the last two hundred years the period when Marx and Marxism faced their contemporaries and near contemporaries as political competitors and where ruthless in there usage of them as such. It is in that period of liberal political theory elaborated its doctrines and stated the social political and legal conditions for the irreducible minimum of freedom of citizens by with the press concerns. In particular it is necessary to revalate attempts to refine and defend liberalism in the conjuncture of the death of the Marx.

The tussle of Fashionable Conservative remedies which drastically reduce the scope of state action in order to enhance the public choice are in no sense and enhancement of democratic control. There are two main reasons for this :

Reducing what is done in the name of the state matters not one which if the tasks are taken on by large scale private corporate bureaucracies, organizations which dwarf many 19th and 20th century state. In that case we merely substitute even less accountable big private government for big public government.

The loss of public provision in health, education and welfare makes a significant proportion of the people less and not more able to influence public affairs. A healthy well informed and secure population is more likely to pay attention to the doings of government than an ill educated or living in fear of the doctors bill or sack.

It is how radicals and liberals who hank after a Bill of right concerning human and its values as human right. As in one department of the government such as Human Resource and Development Ministry is its standby in India. They see it as a means of checking government power. Proposing formally to endow citizens with rights by law, to prevent the infringement of the private sphere by the state is try to remain in 19th century. It relies on an external check upon government rather of transformation of governmental practices. It is a remedy after abuse of power against the power.

**Liberal Views**

Liberal pluralism makes the freedom of the citizens and associations freely chosen by citizens its primary value and main theoretical concern. But the very notion of a legal order implies a 'pluralism' of another sort, it is difficult to concessive of a legal order in a society without institutional differentiation and yet with a single blinding code of conduct 'Law' is a point here but not a legal order. A legal order is not primarily a code of sanctioned norms applied to the conduct of individual. The decalogue is law in the sense of a set or rules governing conduct applied by authorities whose powers have become customary, bit it does not as such give right to legal orders. So I can simply that between "law" and "positive morality" has 'value' even if it is unsustainable in his own theoritical terms. But the basic word which I have used in the beginning for the press outside which disbelieves in sovereignty. So a complete form of discussion is compulsory to discuss about this kind of a sovereignty in other country's versions. Mainly in early years a tribal chieftain is a 'sovereign' with the concept of sovereignty, if his status is that of an uncommanded commander. But the chief is not a separate public power to twist one terms his terms he is merely and expression and executor of customary positive morality. A separate public power, regulating through a legal order, exists when its talks of regulation is open, ended and its role is independent of given customs or the opinion of a singular body of subordinates. The separate power and independent legal order exists because they regulate a public sphere of institutional complexity, individuals who occupy multiple and distinct roles, institutions and associations with a distinct function and corporate life. Then given this complex "civil society", determinateness and primary belong of necessity to the public power. It begins to resemble a 'sovereign' in one sense.

Gradually as newspaper the newspapers are setting themselves towards society the society must be composed of associations and differentiated roles to require a 'sovereign'. So I can say that law in the developed sense of a legal order implies three major elements.

A society with a legal order necessarily exhibits the conflict of interests : such systemic conflict and its regulation are simply different aspects of the same phenomenon. Therefore even in a society with a supreme and all powerful ruler like the Roman Emperor there will be conflict and its intellectual reflection. A legal order has always implied alternatives within itself, different conceptions of the political form and function of that order "law is about public issues in a legal order not merely a set of closed rules for governing individual conduct". In this sense since the very beginnings of jurisprudence there have been options and arguments as to the form and content of law. Legal reasoning has existed to debate the public issues that arise from the conflicting interests.

The first is a realm of diffentiated agencies of decision, a complex of independent decision making agencies interacting in some definite area of activity and where conduct is not given or exhaustively prescribed. Such a realm require regulation static custom will not suffice, but regulation does not, as such presuppose a single separate public power. Trade associations or castles are examples of such regulation.

As we have seen the existence of just one realm of differentiated agencies of decision does not imply a legal order merely some regulatory arrangements. It is a interaction of number of distinct realms of such agencies that changes the picture. Such an interaction require one overall instance of regulation separate from and not reducible to any one area of activity or agent. The complex interactions district realms and agent prohibit regulation by ad-hoc negosiation between the representatives of different realms. Therefore such as instance of regulation must be both separate and compelling, a single public power. But it can not be ad-hoc rule of "sovereign". It power to rules may or may not be unlimited in content but can not be inform. So the commands to determinate their source have an indeterminacy of form, that threatens regulation and coordination. Command is acceptable if law a superior addition but not a task is to facilitate interactions numerous and complexly related sphere of activity agents within them. It follows that public power must itself take a rule governed and relatively predictable form, the question is not merely identifying the "sovereign" by rules of recognition but ensuring that the "sovereign's" legislation is of some utility. That is because regulating action of the public power is itself codified then its inactments are not merely knowable as such as "laws" but are sufficiently non capricious that they do indeed serve to regulate the affairs of complex society.

It is said that the Roman Empire is first fully recognizable order. Its later rulers claimed a "sovereignty" sufficient to please most hardened ruler. Its legislation was dominated by the principle that "the ruler's will has the force of law". Through the fiction of Lex Regia the Emperor claimed an absolutism sufficient for the most seperest hobbist. But what is regulated by such laws is a complex multinational, assembles of citizens, cities and corporations and associations. The Emperor's will is the source of law but if the Emperor's word is law, it is only so in meaningful sense, possessing social utility, if that word takes the form of law and not whims or merely particular commands. The elaboration and codification of Roman Law represent a continued effort to meet this standard, despite considerable instability and periods of arbitrary rule.

This very ling talk about sovereignty does only mean that where the Emperor's words were the rules itself, to protest against that very point press had to stand against it and uttered words of its own which disbelieved in sovereignty. From I would like to touch the points of all branches of governmental information as such under the Ministry of Information and Broadcast where the truths are normally buried under part of official secrecy I have already define in a long term about Official secrecy its rules regulations. But I have predict that in Official Secrecy one has to be introwordly protect the secrets of the government and open such facts which fascinate people or the masses. As I have already referred things earlier about official secrecy. But relating to the official secret act, the loopwholes of the secrecy like some time a matter is important under the Official Secrecy Act but in public or country interest one has to utter the words in open light. Here the officer concern will prefer to go to jail under the judicial proceeding either he would utter the facts. It depends upon the mentality and tolerance of an officer and the feeling towards the common man or the binding of laws to the government. All person in this section the bureaucrat and those who touch the line in joining figures specially in State Government all had this opinions if such time comes before, it will a problem to decide them but formally all answers were the same, that they can sacrifice themselves not the dignity of law but my questionnaire is toward the procedure of law, under the judicial proceeding would they prefer to go to jail or utter the facts. This clinching point was not acceptable to anyone of the State Authority of Government namely as Press working inside comes under like Press Information Bureau. Field publicity section and other sister heads of that line mainly under Ministry of Information and Broadcasting. All keep the same goal to feed goodi goodi items to public for the direction of their mind towards the view that Government keep the public interest first in mind. By informing the policies of the government and open the frontage of their development with entertaining their minds keeping traditionality and origination of there cultural rituals, through the campaign in Melas and projecting Mahotsava with joining hands with all kind of association is the job of the Department of Information.

Is it proper and enough to feel the truth inside. As big and small newspapers are headed by departmental stamping and added with the advertisements under the D.A.V.P. rule. Here is not a question to feel fight but the main reason is to say about all kind of norms followed by the section of the press cope up with policy of the government and about Human Rights. Here I feel in this matter most of all countries play in the matter double standard game. I can only talk in the matter to who I send a letter or wherever I found quest for getting something but the reply was in a manner of polite refusal, or sometime and somewhere well warmed welcome, another side I had follow a breakthrough to get something out of horses mouth, which was very difficult and risky game, nobody wanted to interact or talk directly as with the matter, I had concern but with steady goal whatever I could get in process. I intend to right here.

Lets have a look on other countries press who guarantees the freedom of the country's press, but seeing that side it is a talk of open press, where every person has the right of free expression of opinion in speech in writing, print or the visual media within the limits of legal regulations. The press should not be subjected to censorship nor restricted by the rule of as indicated in article 13 of the constitution. This is the report of Australia. In Germany it was viewed that more than 90 per cent of Germans inform or entertain themselves through the mass media, and around 40 millions Germans in as in India, they are prior and subsequent of utterances in written or spoken words or in images. We see that the West Germany can be said to be a 'Media' paradise where maximum copies of newspapers are sold everyday.

Relationship between government media in as it have been largely influenced by the fact that the printing press is organized in accordance with private law, while broadcasting is governed by the public law affording in protection against free competition.

At a glance in China's largest city Shanghai and the most interior part of the country the newspaper reaches there and the people tries to understand the meaning of news. In China only children of small age groups read newspaper daily. Here in the country the newspaper takes up the biggest share of the growing crop of the print media. China mainly leads third world in the number of there publication but even in comparison to India it has a long way to go.

The impact of Russia has been a deep influence in India in Russia right to information is wide and guaranteed by the country's constitution in Article 49-50. Why every citizen has the right to express his or her opinion on any state or public matter. Under the constitution no one can be punished or prosecuted for voicing constitutive criticism against either the government or its policies and actions. The people can and do freely criticise the drawbacks in the activity of the State Machinery and public bodies.

Small wonder that criticism makes up approximately one fifth of the matter is printed in Soviet periodicals.

One may also emphasise that mass media in the U.S.S.R. does not enjoy "absolute freedom". Freedom of the press in the Soviet Union has reasonable limits. War propaganda the propagation of racial or national hostility, morality or violence, propaganda aimed at undermining Government out, as well as the spreading of standerous fractions about the Soviet social and state system are banner are published by law. Here the newspapers are published in 56 languages of the nations and nationalities inhabiting the Soviet Union besides in 10 foreign languages.

Radio and T.V. also pay and important role in the Soviet peoples life. In fact all mass media and print media function at single integrated system in the U.S.S.R. and as with press, radio, television in the U.S.S.R. are run by the State. There are many of mass-circulated Soviet Dailies and periodicals holds annual conferences of readers. At the end of each year they publish an evolution of the work of the paper, present plants from improving their work and appeal to readers to send in their replies are summarised and later published as a social bulletin, containing guidelines for the coming years.

Radio and television pay no small role in the integrated system of the mass media. Soviet Television service virtually turned millions of people into participant in important political, cultural and other events. Broadcast and Telecast talks on various social and political subjects, on philosophy, history and economics are very popular.

This brief set of press doing in other country.

The Indian press working outside the government started and fought for freedom with Indian freedom movement. It has been an open truth that freedom of open press begins against that rule of constitution where it was thought the country has got a conditional freedom, it has to go long way fighting against poverty, provincial problems, illiteracy varieties of social revolution, problem of capitalists, and still hanging 'sovereignty' upon the head of the country, and the people of India who recently achieved this freedom after years of revolutionary sacrifices. And this kind of freedom I feel was give to India as a defeatest policy gift to Indian people by the British Government when it had no option.

So it was a problem to think that is our country is mentally free and alive to adopt and enjoy the stage of full freedom. Probably Nehru had told that "with broken administration and with communal hot environment how the full freedom to press should be given in hands of those are aggressive in their writing with present condition of the country having the pain of partition. The provision of rule and ruling stands in Democratic country and in any country's democracy. In a partial manner it was correct and it is not correct to day I feel so. But with the very point a sided holding of press like issuing licence for opening and publishing of a newspaper, giving aids of the press and by the entertainment feeding to people and thus defusing their minds towards other side is a complexity of the government. So the open press is doing under governmental policy in a hiding and conservative manner.

But the turning point stands by the thought when the newspaper publishing came as an industry. It was not duly a media of expression of thought and views containing the part of news. Now the news wings of the press are the first head of the industry. So in condition of this it was divided informative media like and the News headlines were the criteria of the newspaper, secondly with the views of writing given by experts it occurred the freedom of expression as such. And the constitution of India has given a provision to right of freedom and the right to information, and the strongest right to speech. Mainly the press open was given freed but little and considered as a pillar of the democracy as a Forth State in Constitution of India. But as told earlier little freedom, little control was obtained by press under the article 19, as right to freedom, with the view of right to expression either the freedom of speech, freedom of opinion, had been given by the constitution, but the freedom was in parts and no full freedom to anything not being referred in any law of constitution.

The press law was constituted quite a later to India. And all control upon it was under government. And at another side Information Bureau, Press Information Bureau and District Information Centres at every provincial districts all comes under the liability of press inside working of government for giving a free flow of Information to people press working under governmental side has an authority educate and treat people for their goods. Thus the informations by the government and non-government floating towards people was taken as a responsibility by the government. In these conditions a free press had to have a double standard for running the newspaper. Here I would like to see a little but history of this side of press, working in free India. Although there is no reliable data on the number and circulation of newspapers at the time of partition of the country or for any earlier period, the first comprehensive effort on this was made by the first press commission in 1952. It revealed that at the end of 1952 there were about 330 dailies, 1189 weeklies, 1733 journals of other periodicities. While the commission could not secure data on the circulation of periodicals and dailies had a total circulation of a little over 28 lakhs. This is a data of 1950 but this number of circulation of newspapers was low for population of India's size, at that time there was a little potentiality for a large readership and mostly in rural areas than in Urban Areas. According to the communication the reason preventing growth in circulation were primarily the cost and lack of distribution facilities. It will be interesting to note that out of 330 dailies in India. The noted and even a shameful piece of country is that no paper was published in Sanskrit as it is an oldest language of the country and the base of so many languages, and also to be noted that no paper in Kashmiri was also published. The number and circulation of dailies in different languages was like this. The number of English newspaper was 41 as a daily newspaper with the circulation 7 lakhs per day. In Hindi there were 78 papers in Assami 7 in Bengali 23 in Gujarati 25 in Kannada 21 in Malayalam 26 in Marathi 3 in Oriya 9 in Punjabi 7 in Sindhi 12 in Tamil in Telugu 6 papers 70 papers in Urdu 2 in Manipuri, Chinese.

Out of all, some 90 newspapers were published from the four Metropolitan Centres, Delhi, Bombay, Madras and Calcutta, remaining dailies were published from state capitals. The largest number of dailies were published from Bombay around 69 and 49 from Uttar Pradesh 26 in West Bengal 25 in Madras and Mysore 21 in Punjabi 19 each in Delhi Cochin and Travancore 17 from Hyderabad 11 from Madhya Pradesh 9 each from Madhya Bharat and Bihar 6 each in Rajasthan and Ajmer 4 in Orissa 3 each in Saurashtra Kuch and Bhopal 2 each from Assam and Manipur. The Dailies Hindi, Urdu and English were published from practically all the States.

**Long-March of Newspapers**

The circulation of English Newspapers was higher in Urban area then the circulation of other languages daily. Only the newspapers in Bengali which commanded a higher circulation in the eastern cities of the country than the English papers. Actually the circulation of all English paper was concentrated in larger cities and towns. The corresponding proportion of Indian language newspapers was two-fifths. The expansion of these papers in metro cities may be the reason of spending power in cities. The papers who circulated in rural areas suffer the scarcity of advertisements. So the regularity of those papers was also in trouble.

Some most Important paper who commenced publication before independence I can count for further discussion of their credibility. As the first Part on the pattern of British Times of India which was begin in 1838 and the circulation of that paper from that year to 1952 at about 51, 481 to 94, 237 and second leading paper Mail started in 1867 with circulation of 17,730 till 1952 it was 34, 115 and The Statesman in 1875 was in number of circulation about 51, 433 and increased till 1952, 65,032 and The Hindustan Times in 1924 was 12,361 and till 1952 it reached in count about 48,141 and the papers in other Indian languages Swadesh Mitran. Kerala Kaumudi, Andhra Patrika, Samaj, Tej, Mathrubhoomi, Sholapur Samachar Sakal and Hindustan, in Hindi was that times most credible newspaper. The main newspapers like Times of India, Statesman, mail all were owned by the Britishers. Later it was owned by Indian Businessman and from highly trade person. As I have already referred that the first English newspaper was from Calcutta an English weekly known as 'Hicky's Gazette' which came into being on 29th January 178. And I see the oldest and even existing paper newspaper today is Bombay Samachar a Gujarat daily from Bombay established in 1822.

In the same flow of picking and categorizing the newspaper published in India which are more than 100 years old are mainly listed alike Bombay Samachar a Gujarati daily from Bombay which started in 1822 second was also a Gujarati daily Jam-e-Jamashed Gujarati daily Bombay started in 1832. Then the first English Newspaper Times of India it was also from Bombay in 1838 again a Gujarati newspaper Gujarat Mitra and Gujarat Darpan a Gujarati daily from Surat started in 1863. The first English daily from Uttar Pradesh in Pioneer from Lucknow which started in 1865. The 'Mail' an English daily from Madras started in 1867. From Calcutta with its naming identification Amrit Bazar Patrika, and English daily started in 1868 one other English daily also from Calcutta Statesman, once a Britisher owned paper started in 1875, "Hindu" as English daily paper began in 1879 from Madras.

Surprisingly the four paper which came in to the notice in Press Commission were the very first Times of India. Mail, Statesman and Hindu and besides that there were 15 centerarian periodicals.

All these newspapers came closer to the First Press Commission with the major reasons like inadequate appreciation of the dynamism of these newspaper industry facing lack of adequate finances and inefficient management. Few more reasons were there for the closer by which they came into notice of Press Commission like political changes, at the time they stood up to alien Government before partition and supported popular causes, were also forced to close down and the main reason was the partition in India and a large scale migration of population, this also effected the readers and matter of writing at that very moment.

The later position of newspaper in between 1952 till 1980 years the Indian newspapers have recorded a phenomenal rise both in number and circulation. As anticipated the Indian language newspapers have had a much faster rate of growth than English newspapers. It is also seen that in 1952 the circulation of about daily English newspaper and about 80 Hindi dailies have taken a rise and growth in all fields of newspapers. A report given by the register of the newspaper for the years earlier, the Indian regional languages daily have made a greater gain.

And parallel with the regional languages the newspapers in Hindi mounted high at 25 per cent of the total circulation of dailies, which came over 135 lacks of circulation of dailies from 25 lacks.

Todays circulation Hindi newspapers are at the top with numbers of more than one thousand in which about 400 daily papers are only from U.P. and in Hindi and Urdu both, and about

100 daily newspapers in India are very important. They are published from all provinces in India.

Now as an early the newspaper of the languages as Hindi, English, Malayalam, Marathi, Gujarati, Bengali, Tamil, Telugu, Urdu, Kannada, Punjabi, Assamese, Sindhi, Sanskrit and more other languages about 1173 papers were published till 1979 and it has now come to more than 3000 around in all over India.

Now the big daily newspaper should be visioned out like Anand Bazar Patrika in Bengali, from Calcutta till now have the circulation of 11011, then Jugantar another Bengali daily, from Calcutta has the circulation of 90, 878. An important daily in English from Madras The Hindu also bounce till 95, 868 and The Times of India in English from Bombay had number old in 1952 around 72, 002 and 3 times more from all other places even from Lucknow. Another one more important paper in Telugu from Madras Andhra Prabha, also has the circulation of todays meaning about 84, 831. Gradually the number of such dailies increasing not at a closure point as day by day big daily papers management turned into an industry or related to industry. The combined circulation of big dailies increased about 17 times over the 1952 figure. Similarly the circulation of medium dailies increased by 25 per cent and of small dailies. In Indian languages the highest circulative number of a daily is still stands that is Anand Bazar Patrika from Calcutta with its largest circulated single edition. Again from 1979 there were a circulation of more than 1, 00, 000 copies of daily in which ten were in English 5 in Hindi 3 in Malayalam and Gujarati and Marathi, two in Bengali and one each in Kannada and Tamil.

But otherside small and medium newspapers have its slow growth which is obviously because of financial difficulties and secondly a very poor revenue of sale and very low pulling power of their advertising. The fact was carried out by the Press Communication, which was no better.

But during this time after independence a number of periodicals in owned by Anand Bazar Patrika group like Sunday and so many others with large circulations have emerged in present years. While the combined circulation of big periodicals increased by more than five times in the last 20 years, when small and medium kind of newspapers could hardly manage to double to their circulation.

The press at this section had their own composing arrangements. The first Press Commission report newspaper have three makes of mechanical machinery in the country, amount these two machines were for line composing and third for mono. The Commission simply observed that line composing was little popular than the mono one. Today new technology has been developed like computer-offset offset coloured. But this is not the subject for this book to be discussed. So leaving this I would like to give some very important issues and about papers numeral, identity and credibility known around.

One more very important question is that a newspaper is playing an important role in all kinds of industries. It is also questioned that when the main work of governmental policy and to inform with free flow towards the public as there own right know turned a duty of government press and all sort of information was given by them to public was simply under their right to information. Then the left upon subject containing news in main with news values remained for the section of press outside. Mainly Hindi press were more observing in masses. And besides Bengali and English the first Persian paper, the first Urdu newspaper and the first Hindi newspaper was published in Bengal. The first Hindi paper the Udant Martand started in 1826 from Calcutta. It was a weekly owned and edited by Jugal Kishore Sukul but it was closed in 1927. The same person started one more newspapers Samdand Martand which started in 1850 but stopped after in 1929 Raja Rammohun Roy launched a paper named Bangdoot in four language including in Hindi. One more language paper was the Martand. In 1852 Shyam Sunder Sen introduced a paper in Hindi daily named Samachar Sudha Varsha. This paper was based on the news of market and shipping reports.

In 1884 Banaras Akhbar was published in Deva Nagari Script. It was edited by Govind Raghunath Thatter under the patronage of Raja Shive Prasad Hind. Sudhakar was launched Tara Mohan Mitra from Banaras. Few other daily in Hindi like Budh 'Prakash' and Lokmitra published from Agra. During 1857 most of Hindi paper closed down because of the imposed restrictions on the press after the rebellion. One paper in 1883 from London was started in Hindi and English both by Raja Ram Pal Singh of Kala Kamker named 'Hindustan'. But after the return to India it was converted into Hindi Daily, the important factor of this newspaper was that Bal Mukund Gupta, Pandit Madan Mohan Malviya and Pratap Narayan Mishra worked as an editorial staff. One more weekly was published in 1890 the name - Bangwasi from Calcutta, Ambika Prasad Vajpayee served as an editor in Bangwasi. The talent journalists of these days were Bal Mukund Gupta, Baby Vishu Rao Paradkar, Laxman Narayan Garde. In these period Bharat Jeevan from Banaras and Rajasthan Patrika from Ajmer opened in 1889 were the important weekly. A next welcome addition to a periodical general was 'Saraswati' which was launched in 1900 and was an important Hindi Journal. In 1907 Madan Mohan Malviya started Abhudaya from Allahabad and Purushotam Das Jondan worked as an editor in that with Ambika Prasad Vajpayee, Bharat Mitra a weekly was converted into daily in 1911, which set a norm in journalism in Hindi Daily. Baburao Vishnu Paradkar, another stalwart joined Ambika Prasad Vajpayee as a joint editor. Basically without having a big circulation Bharat Mitra carried a message of the freedom movement to Hindi readers all over the country and abroad also. But in 1919 Vajpayee revised and launched a company called Indian National Publishers Limited which gave birth to daily in 1920 the newspapers named Swatantra Bharat. And in 1920 even on the same when Swatantra Bharat was launched in Lucknow 'Aj' was launched in Banaras. This was in consultancy with Dr. Bhavan Das and founder of Kashi Vidya Peeth Raja Shiva Prasad Gupta was financier of this paper and other things. Sri Prakash was the first editor of 'Aj'. Both the papers were the foremost campaigners of the freedom struggle, due to constant repressive moves of British regime Swatantra closed down in 1930. But 'Aj' continued the publication and also it was and it is now from Lucknow also, published other centre also. As Vajpayee and Paradkar were the singular contributors of journalism so they were known as Saupadaka charga.

There were so many counterparts of Hindi in English dailies, such as increasing importance of Hindi dailies in 1928 from Allahabad the first daily Leader launched its counterpart Bharat.

As the Hindustan Times followed with Hindustan in Hindi in 1936 and the Indian Nation with Aryavarta from Patna in 1942. In 1947 Lucknow. The National Herald and Pioneer both came out with Nava Jeevan. The first editor of Nava Jeevan was Pandit Laxman Narayan Garde whose acknowledged as third senior most after Vajpayee and Paradkar. This time Mr. Ashokji served Swatantra Bharat.

The popularity of Hindi was increasing day by day and the Hindi Dailies spread out over a vast area from Calcutta till Nagpur, up to now some of them had arranged a telegraphic news supply but event to day and times before so many others depended upon English Dailies and openly lifted materials from these papers. The very first 'Aj' a Hindi Daily equipped itself with teleprinter news service. The cause of being Hindi daily was a second world war, who evoked people and accelerated the growth of Hindi press. So the number of papers from so many different countries came out to meet the fast growing demand of papers mainly in Hindi. The important figures and features was that it served as a news Press also. As every body knows that before independence Hindi press played most important role. And a number of magazines monthly like Vishal Bharat Saraswati and the main importance to it that they produced a number of good writers. In these period the monthly like, Maya, Manorama also published from Allahabad in 1929 and in 1924. From Lucknow Madhuri and Sudha came out as noted part of Hindi driving. One of the most popular and based on religious ethics having philosophy and it was devoted to Indian mythology, the monthly Kalyan came out in 1926 under the editorship of Hanuman Prasad Poddar. The only monthly circulated till 1979 1,58,760 copies.

The main importance of Hindi was that it was not surround to Hindi belt only but it covered all states which are known as non Hindi areas and union territories. In the period of 70 to 80 the Hindi Press outstopped the English press which were its nearest rival both in number and in circulation.

Uttar Pradesh itself had more than 2000 daily in Hindi now, and equally Hindi press established itself in Rajasthan, Madhya Pradesh, Bihar, Haryana, Himachal, Delhi, Maharashtra, Bengal and Punjab as such a substantial Hindi Press.

As of 1980 there 335 Hindi dailies with combined circulation of 37,18000 of this notable 6 metropolitan dailies as Nava Bharat Times of Bombay from Delhi Hindustan. Two more dailies have opened a professional enterprises, as Punjab Kesary and Nai Dunia, one from Punjab and another from Indore. Hindi periodicals occupied the place with problems of society and they are as much as in any other language but the subject range is almost as wide as in English. But while touching the area of sports, science, engineering and economics they are over shadowed by their English counterparts. Number of Journals have prospered in Hindi. So too the literary cultural category sometimes purveying crime and sex through fiction as in Manorama now.

Let the mirror go to side of other regional languages like Tamil, Telugu and Malayalam and other most of them where these are more others. But let me come to one by one with feeling of the regional soil. As Tamil's first monthly is Tamil Pathirikai which was placed in 1855 edited by Rev. P. Percival. Being introduced by a missionary person it was mainly a type of propaganda organ by the Christian missionaries. But against that a significant publication of 1880 of Tamil was Swadesh Mitran. It carries news and literacy articles, in 1898 it became a daily newspaper. The noted part of this that the biggest poet Subrahmaniyam Bharti who brought the paper 'India' pleading for national freedom. But due to the official harassment it could not survive more than 3 years.

Today's Indian Express has been replaced by Tamil's Dinmani established by Sadanand in 1934. Another Tamil paper was launched in 1917 by V. Kalyan Sundaram, a pioneer of modern Tamil style in writing. Anti casteism first started from Tamil Nadu with the divisive expansion of Christian Missionaries who float the literature on mission towards the conversion of lower and defeated and untouched identify like interior tribals, schedule castes and those who are less identified by the high caste people of the society. They were kept back from all kinds of development. As I would like to say that Tamil is the oldest language of India and established much before Pali at the time of Vikramaditya to King Siddharth late as 'Budha period' when the main concept to acknowledgement towards the common man took a proper part in the time of Ashoka and we all consider it a time of press giving information through stone writing which came out as an expressive media.

As we know due to the development of these missionaries the Christianity spreaded in Indians at the time of living Britishers in India, was a left over as a crucial base to rule India even after. At this point some upcoming leader tried to join these backstaged persons at a platform through political angle. So one of them a founder member of Dravinian Party C.N. Annaduri started a daily paper called 'Viduthalai'. But this paper caused a deterioration in its sales being its of an anti-Brahmin writings. The daily started in 1942 from Madurai 'Dinathanthi' by S.B. Adityan a pioneer in mass circulation. It is still published from about eight centres in Tamil Nadu and has a combined circulation of over 350000 copies but more than that. As in families with increasing literacy many of home journal including the periodicals like Ananda Niketan, Kalki, Kumudam were popularity of the time. The Anand Vikatan was converted into a weekly by S.S. Vasan. Its circulation vastly improved with the help of such talented writers as Kalki Krishnamoorthy who started his own journal in 1941 and titled in Kalki. The competition between Ananda Vikatan and Kalki was much commercialised magazines. Kumudam was also founded one of the political figure S.A.P. Annamalai which is now the largest circulated weekly in the country.

As I told that the Tamil is the oldest language of India and it was, and Tamil society was dominated by the Brahmins till cruelty by the legendary concept of Karmakand in daily life. The lower cast took the shelter in the neo-educative progressive society. There we find that the style of the language of the Tamil papers falls into two styles, one with plenty of Sankritised, another with English and the other with uses Tamil. The former finds easier acceptably. Even the effort to reform the Tamil Script has been successfully registered by newspapers. So one side opened with Brahmin Tamil another with the purist Tamil. But till no kind of investigative journalism was there. But paper were filled with political attacks.

Now the Malayalam journalism which is with the history of more than 128 years, the south Belt was more influenced with the initial crowd of Christian missionaries. So in Kerala journalism of regional language was pioneered by the Christians missionaries.

As a result of this influence the first journal in Malayalam was published from Tillichery in 1847 by Dr. Herman Gundat of the Basel Mission named Rajya Samacharam and was mainly devoted to Christian missionaries instead of the public. There are three marked stages of the development of Malayalam journalism. The first period which started with the publication of Rajya Samacharam continued till the end of the last century. So many of journals came into existence during this period but gradually faded after sometime. And few amount these like Deepika and Malyalam Manorama have survived to become leading dailies. The early journals were mostly missionary oriented. The period of between 1900 to 1947 may be described as the second stage in development of Malayalam journalism. This period is marked for the struggle of freedom and for independence which was adequately reflected in the columns of newspapers like Mathribhoomi, Malayalam Rajyam Deenbandhu and others.

The period since independence till the present could be characterised as the modern phase in Malyalam journalism. The second and oldest newspaper in Malayalam the Deepika was launched from Kottayam in 1887. The Malayala Manorama began publication as a weekly in 1890. One of founding fathers of Malayalam journalism Kanathi Verghese Mappildi who earlier edited Kerala Mitram was also the first editor of Malayala Manorama, which was converted into daily in 1928. The weekly edition of these newspaper was started in 1937.

While older newspapers like Malayala Manorama and Kerala Kaumudi and Deepika fought for political rights. Several newspapers were established during the twenties and the thirties to champion the cause of the nationalist movement. The most prominent among these were the Mathribhoomi 1923 and Malayala Rajyam in 1929.

So many communities and sects in Kerala have their own newspapers and few of them attained a very high circulation. As Kerala Kaumudi was started for championing the cause of the Ezhava community. While Malayala Manorama voiced the interests of the Christianity and their community, Deepika projected the interests of the Catholics, Chandrika in 1934 from Calicut was the official organ of Indian Union Muslim League. There are 36

Malayalam dailies with a combined circulation of more 3,00,000 and about 628, periodicals with a circulation of 28, 37, 000.

As in politics the party papers educate the leaders of the respective parties interest by interpreting news and conveying new ideas for teaching their own followers. Party workers often quote the party papers even in personal talks. So these newspapers are mainly very weak in bringing out the malfunctioning of the government machinery. Some papers are at a given time pro-government and anti-government. Due to lack of effort to critically study the working of Government Department, people are septical of what a newspaper says. And what is much worse always a guilty government escapes the public censure. Here in this the newspapers are so saturated with politics that development topics and rural news get short shift.

The major papers set apart the day of the week to cover art, films and culture etc. Except in these case there is little dependability about columns or special articles. Agriculture opportunities and employment, women column and international short stories and sports coverage are innovations of the 1970's and there is paucity of trained writers and photographers of quality.

Now I came to great Maratha's empire the Maharashtra or Bombay the Goanian's name the growth of regional language paper was not only slower but quite late as the start of a paper in Marathi is noted here in 1955. It was only because the lower literacy in Maharashtra in relation to Kerala. The diffusion rates of newspaper 21.5 copies per 1000 population in Maharashtra as again so copies in Kerala and 29.5 copies in Gujarat. This inspite of Marathi dailies being published from nearly every district unlike, in say Bengali and despite the fact of that the number of dailies in Marathi (131) is next only to that in Hindi. So the progress of Marathi press is impressive but relatively and spectacular.

Marathi press have evolved from being views papers only before 1947. The important paper Sakal was started in 1932 by Dr. N.B. Parulakar is properly and scientifically produced has a developed social conscience and expresses itself in the language of common man. It has steadily expanded its circulation, partly by tapping the hitherto unexplored interest of the working class population. It is today one of the three biggest Marathi dailies. It has combined journalistic idealism with business sense.

One more important paper by R.N. Goenka's Express group launched a paper in 1947 named Loksatta, which had the initial backing of a going concern, good coverage, quality production, business organization and efficient distribution. It could reach remote places and literally throttle its competition like 'Prabhat'. It is a good example of the supremacy of the profit motive over journalistic purpose. Today this paper leads in circulation.

The same pattern of Times by Times of India Group again by a capitalist venture the Maharashtra Times was launched in 1982. Naturally it was benefitted with all the advantages of such parentage. It has built up circulation, quality and prestige. Its news coverage is balanced and editorial comments outspoken.

While the big papers came up in Bombay and Pune, a number of papers were started in the districts in all the regions, some of them to fight for particular political causes e.g. Marathwara for the liberation of Hyderabad and Maratha for the unlingual state of Marathi speaking people. Both these bore the stamp of their editors Anant Rao Bhakle Rao and P.K. Attre respectively. Personalities and were successful in their mission though Maratha had to wind up in 1976 seven years after Attres death as a private enterprise like any other.

Curiously, the issue of the linguistic state caused the closure of Lokmanya, a Marathi Daily owned by the Saurashtra. Trust controlled by Gujarati. The effort of the staff and workers of Lokmanya to continue it were effectually thwarted. The vision of Samyukta Maharashtra gave birth in 1958 to the cooperative daily Lokmitra to the cooperative daily Lokmitra under S.M. Joshi's leadership. As most prospective advertisers were unsympathetic to separate Marathi speaking state, but unfortunately the paper was starved of advertisements, until it died despite a heroic gesture by its staff to work in subsistence wages.

Till 1950 the Periodicals Press, so weeklies dominated the Marathi Press. There are now 916 and above periodicals with a circulation are few. The district periodicals with a circulation of 16, 68, 000 between them. But those with a sizeable are very few. The district periodicals are mainly in no shape, due to the unhealthy mushrooming of unwanted journals with little circulation and with no impact.

Now the most important and the first opener in my basic concept of press outside which is a contentment against 'Sovereignty' or so called imperialism. As Calcutta had considered at a time a very luxurious city. During the time of William Bentinck, a notable newspaper 'Sambad Prabhakar' was published under the editorship of Ishwarchand Gupta, a famous poet and scribe of the early 19th century Bengal. At first it was tri-weekly. From 1839 it became full-fledged daily. It was the first Bengali daily The Prabhakar become a household work in readers in Bengal. India's Patriotism and Nationalism were spared through its pages. Eminent writers of the period like Bankim Chandra Chatterjee and Din Bandhu Mitra contributed to this newspaper. The Amrit Bazar Patrika now the oldest in English daily in Calcutta was originally published in English. It was to circumvent the vernacular Press Act of 1878. The Amrit Bazar Patrika switched over to English. Patrika's founder editor Sisir Ghosh is remembered for his forthright writings and his underlating fight against the British indigo planters whose high headedness and zoolam ruined the already impoverished peasantry of Bengal.

And infact a large member of journals in Bengal was published during the later half of the 19th century, but the notable mention should be made of Som Prakash a weekly which earned quite a name. It was published in 1858 under the editorship of Pandit Dwarkanath Vidyabhushan and continued upto 1874 leaving a glorious tradition of effective journalism.

The Bengal Press has two aspects of its growth and influence: One is in the literacy field while the other is in socio-political field. All literary men of stature and distinction in Bengal including Bankim Chandra Chatterjee and Rabindra Nath Tagore had sometimes or other been engaged in publishing and editing periodicals. Bankim Chandra Chatterjee started a monthly journal Banga Darshan which carried his invaluable contribution to Bengal literature along with his commentaries on such burning issues of the day. The conditions of peasantry in Bengal and the trend of social reform movement started by stalwarts like Ram Mohan Roy and Ishwar Chandra Vidyasagar.

One of the three major dailies mentioned in the First Press Commission report schedule, the oldest one viz. Dainik Basumati, enjoying the patronage of 10 per cent of the total Bengali newspapers sometime ago the victim of the management crisis. This forced on it a prolonged closure in mid-seventies culminating in its take over by the state government and reappearance, minus of course a good deal of its halo, circulation and prestige. It is a full-fledged state managed unit today.

In 1937 and in 1922 there were two sister dailies two Jugantar and the Anand Bazar Patrika both added greatly in circulation and both are at present in great from Anand Bazar Patrika at the peak with circulation of nearly 500,000 flash-point hardly reach by anyone else in the country, while Jugantar the sister daily its vigorous about a lakh less. A new Bengali daily 'Aj Kal' came in to existence in 1981 with more emphasis in its columns on new features.

As we all know that Urdu and Hindi press was in equal working conditions. But to say sorry that after independence minus government run papers not a single Urdu periodical in India that can boast a centenary. The heritage had suffered a discontinuity due to partition and the consequent migration. Yet there are some 33 newspapers and periodicals in Urdu in India with a standing of 50 10 100 years though not many have much life left in them. In this age group, Urdu papers are the only of numerous quality with the 1956 state's reorganization on linguistic lines, regional languages got recognition as official language and patronage from the governments. The sole exception was Urdu which found no land for its root to develop. Even in Kashmir its encouragement was negligible. Thus the potential Urdu leadership spread across the country, got reflected to other languages including English.

Over 1955-1976 8 in Hindi 9 in English and 16 other periodicals cross the one lakh circulation mark. By 1976 only two out of 976 Urdu periodicals could take their circulation beyond 50 thousand.

Circulation may be less or more but the Urdu newspapers are counted largest in number after English, Hindi and Marathi but also in Tamil, Malayalam, Bengali and Gujarati; Urdu does not have any official status in any state, neither it has used in higher education.

Urdu periodicals fall in to four categories broadly; news and current affairs, cultural and literary, religions and educational. A large number of so-called news and current affairs periodicals do not publish regularly.

In the newspaper a world sensationalism is the road on which normally most of the newspaper lean. One more over emphasis on the problem of the Muslim minorities lead to a neglect of important national and international events. Even the minority problems are discussed with or by playing up emotions. From Urdu press which first started playing emotions and thoughts of a section thus it was divide in to yellow section of journalism, discussed with the beginning of the press. This tactic can be succeed as Blitz Urdu and Nasheman could prove. The former dramatises then later mixes with new and views to appeal to the ill-informed and poor Muslim leaders. Most of the others are small one man shows with plagiarized contents. And the persons who are the contributors of these papers or periodical are paid nothing and are poor.

Very few among the literary and cultural category of about ISO have high quality. The comparable ones in Pakistan are more prosperous but of lower standard. Sharma, Biswin Sadi, Ruby, Pakeezah, Shabritan, Huma, Bano, a women's daily Khilona and Payame-Talim for children have any how established themselves. Among those that kept alive high standards are Shair, Ahang and Sabaras, Marrif, Burhan, Jamia, Shali-hoon, all monthly and Shaoor, Jawaz, and Tanazur quarterlies Shugoofa is devoted to literary humour. There are some good Government Publication like 'Ajkal', Naya Daur. The literary magazines are secular unlike the run of news-magazines.

There are some 85 religious periodicals : Aasthama, Hude, Dean Dunia and Tajalli among the better known. These do not generally mix up religion and current affairs and have a positive and healthy influence. Surprisingly in Urdu educational periodicals are almost non-existent. As to be found that main problems facing Urdu newspapers are— They are financially unstables — readers have little buying capacity. The well to do are small in number.

The few have money show but little interest in Urdu literature. One more point that Urdu literature is also scattered that distribution is also a problem in terms of time distance and cost. Public libraries do not take Urdu periodicals seriously. There are legal restrictions in circulating these neighbouring countries.

Urdu dailies and periodicals in Andhra Pradesh Karnataka and Tamil Nadu count for one-fifth of the Urdu papers, in the country and one-forth of the National Circulation. Andhra leads with 250 papers including 10 dailies with a circulation of 150, 000 and Tamil Nadu has six papers including with a circulation 22,000. The total Muslim population in the three states would be around 8 million.

Mainly the Muslim living in South India use the main language of the state. Only the community encourages Urdu papers. May not be high in circulation but in groups they are increasing because of the due facility in for study in the language Urdu. This facility toward economic condition of Muslims in the region for there adequative development. The pace of poliferation is faster in Andhra but circulation wise Kandtaka papers are better in Urdu. In fact the growth of the individual paper appear to be in inverse proportion to be increased in the number of papers, a case of two many papers chasing a defined segment of the literate population and a limited quantum of advertisements. In Tamil Nadu the growth of number of circulation has been subdued. On the whole, the environment in the region has not been adverse to the growth of the Urdu press. To the extent complaints exists about discrimination by the governments they are not a major consequence. In Andhra and Karnataka most papers are owned by individuals while in Tamil Nadu the pattern is partnership. The majority of editors are above thirty years and probable without much formal education. For about half the number journalism was not a full apart from a couple of dailies each in Hyderabad and Bangalore and one daily in Madras. The average circulation is well below 6000. And the largest had round 25, 000. The weekly Nasheman of Bangalore is an exception with a circulation of 96,000 but it points to growth possibilities. Nearly all the papers work with Skeleton staff limited news gathering facilities. Most of the papers do not have their own press. One press in Hyderabad only caters to 81 Urdu papers.

One more difficulty that not every daily have a newsprint quota and the most periodicals do not get it and the Nepa quality has a negative effect on the image of Urdu papers which one mainly suffering otherwise in their production values. There are also complaints about the fixing of the quota being unconcerned with its growth potential. Few other complaints are lack of the facility for press telegrams, absence of accredition to periodicals.

The pressure on the Urdu press are said to be from advertisement patronage, political groups and members of the ruling party and about business interests.

These calligraphers are not enough in number of these affects working conditions. Mainly there is an agreement amount sub-editors and reporters on the need for formal training but especially in Urdu papers not all editors think so. Among then few or sometime most of the editors latter feel so that professional standards are relatively good.

In southern India, Urdu press are better in their shapes and forms then its counterparts in U.P. In U.P. Hindi-Urdu language dividive 'Lafad' is more sensational instead of growing the section of Urdu press to stand equally sound and positive for Urdu literature. One more problem comes up for Urdu press that they have no main matter for it like all other daily papers unlike Hindi, and one of it is a problem the literature in Urdu found in its legendary form is mainly Afsanagoi or Shro-Shairi, not with sound problems of the society and neither they carry a road for burning issues and stimulative wings of media expression like all other dailies in Hindi or in English.

The Urdu papers and periodicals are second after English and better than Hindi put with standard or stands of its own credibility. They are mainly run through the government support. The second of not being popular to it, that is the writing language. Urdu is popular in its Juban much more and variably produced by Hindi films after partition.

So it may be taken as large number of Urdu medium schools with good enrolments figures and the comparatively good economic conditions of Urdu speaking population, mostly in Business and generally a helpful attitude of the State Government due in turn perhaps to better emotional equation between the various communal segments of population.

And on the way to help the Urdu press to restore its self respect may be to encourage newspapers to be brought out by working journalists on a cooperative basis. Another world be for government to adopt a literal attitude towards the Urdu press as a matter of compensatory justice, without expecting reciprocal support. But to fight with it the Muslims must have a feeling that Urdu as a Hindustani court language not the language of their own community than can increase not even its potential.

As it is told that the first regional paper started in a Gujarati from Bombay. It is also noted that among all other regional languages Gujarati dailies were fast growing. Three of the paper have crossed the circulation rate up to 2 lakhs named Sandesh, Gujarat Samachar and Bombay Samachar, and three papers together have grown nearly 22 per cent in its circulation for a total Gujarati speaking population of 26 million. The phulchhab of Rajkot about 85, 000 circulation more than doubled its circulation over this period. Gujarat has 782 newspapers in Gujarati amount them 46 dailies and 688 periodicals with a circulation of 1, 090, 000 and 1, 648, 000 respectively.

In most of these papers a balance between news and features is missing. The Ahmedabad papers overdo features while the Saurashtra papers say they have no space for them. Only some like Janmabhoomi, Gujarat Mitra and Jana Shakti show a little bit sense of proportion. A number of dailies are printing senseless features, fabricates stories and tailored forecasts and they try to sell and just to compete each other, which in my opinion useless task with no norms ethics as such.

*Six*

# Growth and Circulation

### Circulation of Newspaper

This the neglect by the press of the main occupation of the majority of Indians which is slowly changing. Forming figures regularity in a few papers are occasionally in others. But the press is yet to establish a healthy link between farming and social awareness Jansatta is breaking new ground in this respect.

Even small papers subscribe to news agency too is able to survive. Translation of Articles in English is very common, but the translator are poorly paid. So two are contributors of most papers. The printing equipment of bigger dailies are reasonably modern. And the mono composing and stereo rotary is the known usual pattern. Jai Hind has photo type setting and web-offset printing.

Now let me come to define about one more regional language paper in Telugu. The Telugu journal has most English journals amount 180 are only in Andhra Pradesh with the circulation of 2.36 lakhs. The Telugu language press continues its steady growth over the years. In 1999, there were as many as 503 publications. Among them were 31 dailies, 135 weeklies and 337 other periodicals. The annual increase in Telugu newspapers was 4.1 per cent. While an is published from Andhra Pradesh, these are still 45 dailies coming out from Tamil Nadu and in particular Madras city, where Telugu journalism took its birth when the city was the capital of Telugus and Tamils and the centre for higher education.

The History of the Telugu Press started to the first half of the 19th century. The Satyadoota a monthly periodical was circulated by Christian Missionaries in 1835 from Madras city. The Virthani referred to by C.P. Brown in his records and edited by Mandigula Venkatrama Sastri made its appearance in 1838 and Varthamana

Tharangani edited by Puovada Venkat Rao started publication from Madras city in 1842. The real beginning of Telugu journalism could be said to have begun Kandukuri Veeresalingum Pantulu. He started Vivek Vardhani in 1874 and Hasya Sanjeevani a little later. Veerasalingum Pantulu continued a vigorous campaign against corruption in the government and against superstition and obscurantism in the society as Telugudesham is known for this. Started towards the close of the last century was another a notable paper Andhra Bakasika edited by A.P. Parthsarathy Naidu. The early years of current century heralded the birth of Krishna Patrika by Konda Vankatappaiah Pantulu, Dasa Narayana Rao and others. It was edited for nearly for four decades by Manturi Krishna Rao Pantulu.

But the History of daily journalism in Telugu owes its beginning to Bombay city from where the weekly Andhra Patrika was started in 1908 by K. Nageshwar Rao. Its venue was shifted to Madras when it was converted into a daily. Another addition was started from Vijayawada in 1965. The monthly Bharthi was brought out in 1924 and the Andhra Patrika illustrated weekly in 1930. The Andhra Patrika had a monopoly of Telugu dailies till 1938 when Andhra Prabha was started by Ramnath Goenka. The Prabha also started a new daily. Andhra Jyoti in 1960 from Vijayawada. The Andhra Bhoomi was also started in 1960 from Hyderabad city by the Deacon chronical group.

Then came on the scene the Enadu in 1974 blazing a new trial in Telugu popular journalism. This journal was started by Ramoji Rao first from Vishakhapattanam. Enadu has four editions now from Hyderabad, Vijayawada and Tirupati in a short span of seven years. It has reached the highest and enviable circulation of about 4.60 lakhs.

Among the defunct papers, the notables were the Jama-Vani edited by Thapi Dharma Rao and Golkonda Patrika founded by Saravavarapu Pratap Reddy. The oldest editing periodical in Telugu is the monthly Udhawani established in 1887 in Madras city. The "Chandamama" monthly for children that comes out also from Madras is the largest circulated periodical now published in several languages including English and Hindi.

This has been taken according to the Report of the Registrar of newspapers the circulation of Telugu papers in 1979 was 17.88 lakhs with an annual growth rate of 9.8 per cent and now the number may be more.

Unlike Urdu Hindi for the placement of National Language was promoted in other provinces. But the speaking language of three provinces were not Hindi. The Main Hindi Belt is still considered the only Uttar Pradesh than Madhya Pradesh and Bihar. The very old newspaper, Vishwamitra from Calcutta, Dainik Ajit from Jalandhar, Teesra Pahar from Jodhpur, Seeanchal from Nainital, Seema Sandesh from Ganga Nagar, Prayagraj Times from Allahabad, Desh Ki Dharti from Kota, Shera Haryana from Faridabad, Dainik Madhya Pradesh from Kan, Hindi Dainik from Saharanpur, Gujarat Vaibava from Ahmedabad, Young Leader from Ahmedabad, Nava Swadesh from Satana, Jug Prakash from Mirzapur, Pratah Kamal from Mujaffarpur, Naveen Dunia from Jabalpur, Sabera Sanket from Madhya Pradesh, Vishwa Manava from Saharanpur, Samvet Shikhar from Raipur, Yog-Dharma, Dainik Asom from Gauhati, Dainik Samachar secretary Bhopal, Gandeevea from Varanasi, Samavet Shikhar from Raipur, Savera Sanket from Madhya Pradesh, Pratahkal Udaipur, Surya Rekha Seekar, Jamanat Dhanbad, Dainik Hindustan New Delhi, Rashtradoot from Jaipur, Nava Jyoti Ajmer, Nava Bharat Times New Delhi, Punjab Kesari from Jalandhar, Dainik Tribune from Chandigarh, Current News from Delhi, Dainik Arun Desh from Bhilwara, Dainik Uttarkal from Gauhati, Lok Tej from Surat, Bijnaur Times from Bijnaur, Sainik from Agra, Badri Vishal from Haridwar, Sandhya Jyoti, Amar Ujala Nainital, Madhya Kshetra from Guna, Begu Sarai Times, Begu Sarai, Nawa Amar Bharat, Moradabad, Dainik Vishwa Pariwar from Jhansi, Nyayadhish from Allahabad, Dainik Jagat Kranti, Pratidin from Amarawati, Dainik Maharashtra from Meerut, Hind from Ghaziabad, Desh Pran from Ranchi, Tarun Mitra from Jaunpur, Sanmarg from Calcutta, Doon Darpan from Dehradoon, Dainik Gram Swaraj from Gorakhpur, Kashi Warta from Varanasi, Swadesh from Gwalior, Mussorie Times from Mussorie.

In Uttar Pradesh about 391 newspapers of small and medium kinds are published and licensed from Press Information Bureau from Uttar Pradesh. These papers are mainly survived due to

D.A.V.P.'s advertisement and they carry very much of those reading materials which contains local sensationals, and if it is not a question mark on it, may be so, but one definite thing is that these dailies mainly in Uttar Pradesh have been mushrooming a licensed warranty to open a bridging towards the press inside and outside both.

The owners of the newspapers sometimes carry the policy of the being popular government, but for getting a kind of favour hidden in arms from that concerned government. One very point touch the corner in the section of press is contented with little or more power in hands of the owner to get exchanged by whom it concerned. Any registered press is a registered power of base politics in hands of a press owner to denote the facts in an actual manner. So to open a window outside is a criteria towards the press, and the window should be open for people and for those who does not have any voice of its own.

It does impact of this imposing question as to whether there any limitations on a journalists right to obtain information in respect of matters of public interest as have already discussed it earlier here I have see what kind of literature is basically press of the government is producing and under Bureaucracy how much it exposed to common masses. As suppose take the matter of publications done by Press Information Bureau. The publications are mainly in Hindi. Even in Annual Book published nearly in Hindi and English both carry the contents from history to down to the latest information of provincial base and qualities of the place, as in Uttar Pradesh Annual I see it gives facts from geographical area and about the population about tourism and so other parts of that places, dances and sort of information is needed under the free flow of information. It is being given to public as a form of duty of the government press itself. It is almost a directory built by government to place the right to know as firm right to people and give a genealogical history to place the glitter of the past. All is in a positive manner and followed by information of all sorts in itself. The magazines in Uttar Pradesh from the sector started with views which can carry no argument and view differ to the government policy with matter of popularity.

**Role of Periodicals**

Papers and periodicals registered in Hindi have better circulation than Urdu, and they are something doing well and committed also but a very few of them not all. Most of these papers which come under small newspaper have gaps in their printing, but some have better circulation. In all these 391 newspapers properly licenced from Information Bureau are all small newspapers and may be talked about few papers circulation. First paper from Allahabad is Urdu Apna Dost with circulation 52, 976, Amar Ujala also Agra 95,973. From Lucknow Pioneer in English and Swatantra Bharat in Hindi, both does have the circulation of 55, 866 and 55,596. In Hindi Jagaran contains the circulation of 78, 669 and Times of India in English has in Lucknow has 46,032 circulations. Nava Bharat Times in 1993 had 33,100 in numbers parallel to Nava Jeevan had a circulation of 37 named Pratidin. This paper broke the burst news at the time of late Smt. Indira Gandhi's death. The paper employ found a boy floating some pamphlet in pink which spreaded the news 8 hours before the death as declared. The paper 'Aj' started from Varanasi has circulation in Lucknow 36,495. In Lucknow paper launched in hitting the ground manner to communicate with common man which put a climax to the readers by giving human story is Rashtriya Sahara with the circulation of 1,14,310 counted almost before, when Hindustan Times in English and Hindi, but within that both the papers even carry the same kind of countdown in its readers gain. But one thing is most alarming and even predictable to the viewers that it carry the literature which is much more concern with the masses, of little literacy. High intellegensia is not very much concern with. The paper's circulation here gives a stroke of increasement just it treats to the man and the problems related with their own plusminus having food to grant it. At time in Varanasi Sanmarg, and Gandeeva were filled with fire brand Hinduism talks and took its proper place in society. But after time could not follow the number of circulation but is printed still today. From Varanasi 'Aj' is still heading Hindi paper even after the start of Swatantra Bharat.

As in Magazine in Hindi, Manorama at time a complete women magazine and new it turned towards sex and crime magazine with no ideology of life as such, carrying the live stories elaborate and critic language, in a flow discussion about those newspaper also which covers mainly surrounding not the things as a whole and are bound to side a sect a community and the feeling at one kind of people. It can be Hindu. The Telegraph, varies a Awadh, India Today a magazine which tried to writer in a modern form Samkalin Janmat, a pure Marxist magazine.

The periodical running in U.P. as printed talk matters have the count about more than thousands and less than lacks. I decide it in provincial serial. I see about 22 periodicals weekly and fortnightly are being published in District Agra and all are carrying the policy of the government much more and the local matters in provocative manner. That it might feed them from both side. Inside the press they are benefitted by D.A.V.P.'s advertisement and outside the bridge of blackmailing point cool them down with other manner. Near about seven periodicals are from Allahabad, 15 from Azamgarh, 5 periodicals from District Almora, 19 weekly and fortnightly is coming out from District Aligarh, more than other places in sum of 32 periodicals are from Badaun, 8 in total weekly only are published from Balia. At the rate of 10 weeklies are published from Banda. 16 weeklies are from Barabanki, which delegates Deva Mela every year and black-up to Urdu and addiction of Urduatism in people here around. The count of Urdu papers is bigger than Hindi.

Equally in Hindi and Urdu about 15 periodicals are being published from Bareilly, 4 from Bijnaur and from Basti about 19 weekly papers are coming out among then only two are fortnightly. At about 19 weeklies are from Bulandshahar almost as named accordingly with bravery talks. 3 weeklies are from Chamoli.

And a matter of surprise 61 weeklies and fortnightly are public alone from Dehradoon itself. One Frontier Mail is in English and another weekly in English is Green Vallies and golden fielder. It is a hill belt so it is mounted with weeklies in Hindi, English and other regional languages. Another is count score in weeklies and in fortnightly is Devaria where there are few in Urdu and maximum in Hindi. A sum of 8 weekly and one fortnightly is in Hindi from Etava. 1 fortnightly and 9 weeklies are from Etah District. 18 weekly in Hindi and one in Urdu from Faizabad mostly uttering the language of Ayodhya as such. About 16 weekly in Hindi and 2 in Urdu are being open out from Fatehpur District. Almost 7 weeklies from Farrukhabad, 8 weeklies from Firozabad itself. District Ganda is producing about 9 weeklies. Only two weeklies are from Gazipur is the lowest count from the U.P. itself. More than in count from Dehradoon at a rate of 63 weeklies comes out only from Gorakhpur. The last rope of these weeklies end up in Ghaziabad. Uttar Pradesh as 134 in number is the count weeklies only from this place which is a peak corner of Delhi and known for the political halchal day to day life-lifting with so many angles.

All these dailies, weeklies and fortnightlies in the row, should be countable under the press or outside of it, where it smells free breeze of open thought. I say useless to sense it even just because all these dailies weeklies and small size better of press but some where in its big influence imposing the editorial up on all the people concern. As everybody knows that two main remarkable strings taking sides in Indian Politics from the moment of freedom fighting after 1857's revolt which was crushed up by Britishers, further followed a tricky try to divide all Indians in parts, the main sour of sensing Hindu as Hindu of their own native and Muslims treating an outsider here, as they had feeling of defeat inside, where both of Hindu and Muslims joined hands against them and they captured and controlled over it by means of such. It draw a line parting in press orientation before partition Urdu press as Resala carried a responsibility of Muslim's and thought provoking of mushy sentimentalism in one corner of being a Muslim and in another side the country feeling and to see India free as Hindustan of their kind. He other side all Hindi Press took the burden of Hindu's and to Hinduism and thought to see India free as Bharat Varsh Singing Vandemataram, and the press outside with restriction under Britishers try to prove and gather saffronised view for Maa Bharti, the motherland.

Thousands of small newspapers, here I am not quoting dailies as Times of India or Pioneer, but to Hindu as with the name of it, had siding part to Hindus, terrified with conversations of religion forcefully and tactfully both, where Brahnism failed to control, due to its hard lifestyle of living studded with the whole day Karmkand, Yangya and Bali-culture. But the noticeable fact is that it was much pampered by Muslim ruler from the time of Akabar who divided Hindu in more small particle with the ownership of land ceilings. They were more prone to Yangya for their own welfare as a matter of surprise but it concern negatively my subject. the referencing at side view only meant to say about that thin line which divides Hindi and Urdu press at separation. But as a working outside for reader the urdu press and Hindi press both were little bit jumping much on personal issues on placing the moral values of the society which needed revolutionary reform to get rid of and superstitionism.

The result was unlike Congress the first political party to keep neutral in its views had flow of common press saving goodi goodi and with smiling soft editorials. The old credibility of English newspaper still stand today and for preparing tomorrow, using a twisting and refined language feeding classes to the countrymen to gentleman. The press out side without the visuals visualised the facts that no cast but class and culture of higher up does stands even to day in India. These group of press after political discussion took the society and its problems at a first priority. For them the religions is not to be smelled like sustains. Till I come to other side of media better confront with many other papers with the orientations, and lookouts of their own may be aligned or non-aligned.

Newspaper does have consent only upon news which people want to read day to day matters and in editorials at the edit page they want to read the views of the editor. The newspaper consists free opinion only on this front. The very point is always touched and fully inquired by the government and finding the actualized view it goes against the government sometime it checked in other manner. This untold hanging sward upon the outside forced the press person's to tackle in as and industry holding the pressure of the paper owner and beware of the press inside just to continue and run the paper regularly.

A newspaper from Hyderabad 'News Times' is totally concerned with news of all kind but the weightage to the side of politics now day or in democracy a chewing food material of all common people, just as Northern India Patrika as named covers the north fully taking big press type of news in politics and current affairs. Punjab Kesari even today is not free from that stupor condition the partition time it contains the news followed by the agencies as it is but viewing content is always full of nearest Urdu Press mushy sentimentality but keeps a high circulative area.

The Rashtriya Sahara keeps a highest circulation paper from Lucknow and in other places. Why so? Not questionable but to think about the under current affairs with current affairs up. The readers and the writers does feel satisfied only when they see an open of the present position not the gesture propagated not even manipulated or neither a symbolic gesture which is shown in paper of old credibility who play with politics side and guard the journalistic ethics at the other side of norms. So it images a person at a top fight being sometime under paid and through a folded abuse to image till damage some other person at the otheside which they are not concerned but according to norms of the paper they have had to cover it. No matter of liking or disliking as it is a news in full. But raising the issues of society and problems of a common man and elaborate to make it reach to reader that they should be fully able to sense and smell both for that point, person or to people, further the definition of persons personalities in matter of viewing them I shall discuss afterward.

Equally let me carry on the government may or may not consider it, but the Press inside the government always aware while walking the policies of popular government which changes with the changes of government and twisted by hand above Ministry of Broadcast and Information and carries the plan and promises to people, performances of directive and perspectives as an efforts in the directed directive.

So the basics Government Press in my opinion a Press inside have three dimension direction, like Plans Promises, Performance and Perspectives are the pillars of undeclared ethics for press of this own by that they produce, Magazine, Annual and Message for common people. Total abundance from analogy, politics and arguments. I can say it an open ivory teeth holding the shape of policy. But it rule under current from policy to polity keeping eye upon the press outside A peaceful patient watch upon those press who thunder on sensitive areas and weak nerves clutching the country welfare first. Press as a rule is considered to be totally country oriented but when it stars siding any political party or personality that shows doubt without any reason. Reason never disclosed under the ethics of journalism.

Under pressure are the whole in a freeflow of information, the story of the press outside. But the press inside if noted in Uttar Pradesh the most and ever a sensitive part of the country and normal deciding factor of often in India politic and pride of giving most of the Prime Minister Prime-Ministers from this place. So let have a complete information of this section, such as Press Information Bureau of Uttar Pradesh at a glance and few important questions asked during the period of doing footwork for this book where the idea of the subject dinched at a high of my mind.

Some reasonable restrictions are to be follow, be mainly putting the point hot ever and hiding facts from Press outside is a normal fear of leakage even those points and documental facts which may put a damage to the government. As a press outside need to maintain credibility of the paper here the press inside government need to maintain secrecy and credibility both. In some other manner Press and bureaucracy both combine at this spot. But the basic role of giving information is mainly entitled to Press inside as a matter of right.

But the specie matter of thought is just find that the press outside carries all sort of matters of International relationship and theory of today's problem. The matter of this kind is mainly conducted by few papers separate from other important dailies like Asian age, 'Sunday Observer, and also Observer of Business and politics, Statesman, Times of India, The week, than a monthly.

Have a switch over so called yellow journalism and I say why it is not blue why not red why yellow in colour or the meaning carrying it. I feel that the matter published make the person concern pale in face which clinches the heart to deep in blackmailing. At a time B.K. Karanjia started this kind of investigative journalism with publishing Blitz Magazine from Bombay (Mumbai) now this magazine is in hand of Mr. R.K. Kajaria. This is mug-paper which then and now still have a capacity of best seller. Matter published in Blitz were rising above the hype of any media. Karanjia's method of investigations were peculiar and same time it is always challenged but definite not therapeutic for the society. As the demand on an open press contains the thought to educate people not to sensationalise then till brink of horror. But even the credibility of truth considered were powerful than an other paper. The paper seen trains, in bases and in all sides of roads tells about its popularity. The Blitz broke through all laid-down patterns of journalistic ethics.

**Activities of News Agency**

Most of all these papers for news depends upon News agencies. The few in India and much in outside wing agencies from outside country also played a role putting non-aligned newspolls for newspapers. To be complete non-aligned in news although started in 1973 to decolonisation of information. Later news agencies started exchanges of news on an experimented basis. But the pool of news as such was formally constituted at a meeting of Ministers of Information and among the head of the news agencies mainly of Non-aligned countries in New Delhi July 1976. This idea was endorsed and supported by the Columbo Summit of Non-aligned leaders later in the same year.

The pool is not a news agency itself but an exchange of arrangement. The main logic to develop of new agencies will show that a supra national news agency is a distant ideal. There are no news agencies in the world which are truly supra-national. There some agencies whose main operation are international in scope but there root and orientation can be traced to individual countries. It is for this reason that the Non-aligned movement decided that an exchange arrangement based on equal and full participation of all member countries is the only practical thing for the immediate future. Even countries which are committed to a single ideology are not able to forge a common new agency. Therefore it will be all the more difficult for the non-aligned community which encompasses a wide spectrum of political system and opinions.

The experience of the past few years of the pools operation fully justifies the earlier, assumptions for a mere handful of participation in the pool now covers nearly countries. The wordage exchanged has grown for a few hundred to nearly 50.000 a day. Because of uneven development of media and infrastructure it has to help itself through resources within the movement and through help from outside agencies like UNESCO, to create infrastructure, for news collection and dissemination in the countries where it does not exist and also to strengthen it in countries where news agencies are in early stages of the development.

One more point considering in the dependence, truth and credibility of news. So one more point that the professional skills are another his problem area where institutions like the Institute of Mass communication are doing their best to impart training and raise cadres in members and inequality speedily. The information of the pool has encountered stiff opposition at the start from establish trans-national news agencies. It also at the time sensitised the world community to the need for giving the developing countries a say in the global commucative process.

Today this pool does not concentrate on spot news. While such news are not excluded, then to provide news of development and other field of activity as are excluded hither to from the view of the transnational media. In this one more unfortunate part they pool has no such head quarters and all the members name equal right and obligation. The costs of reception and transmissions of informations are not by individual news agencies at their ends. The centre operation is based an the principles of self reliance.

The India Desk of the newspaper operated by P.T.I. which about 12 satellite channels linking all cantonments well further expansion is under consideration.

There are four news agencies which provide 110% news. And of foreign news printed by word's newspapers known as United Press International associated Press Reuters and agency France Press popularised as wing four agencies. The coverage which these agencies provide is cheaper and more comprehensive than a spare network of own correspondents. But these agencies have their own faults, as an one incident that when Surname became free as an independent republic in 25 November 1975 and there was not a single reporter there's to cover the news in any such kind of four Big agencies. When suramin is Brazils next door neighbour. Its capital Paramaribo is within 2000 km of Peru and Equator in the west of Panama in North. It is to say that South

American Papers referred to buy a report of the occasion from United Press International (U.P.I.) a giant news agency with its headquarters more than 5000 km away in New York. To cap it all Brazils leading paper Estado shunted the report to an inside paper and chose the news jewel robbery as one of its lead story not the freedom of a new republican Surnan. We all know that the fifty per cent of all news published in the paper of South America came from main two agencies. U.P.I. (United Press International) and A.P. (Associated Press) and further 12 per cent from Reuters and A.F.P. (Agency France Press).

As a known fact South American newspapers is not an isolated one. Newspapers in Asia, America, Africa and in Latin America which cannot afford to own and maintain their foreign correspondents depend heavily for their foreign news on these big four. Each of these are carved out its where of influence from the old colonial empires. As in French Speaking Africa A.F.P. in Paris has its strong hold throughout. A P. and U.F.I. both U.S. based have extensive operations in Latin America and are even widely used in Japan, South Korea in Philippines, the areas of U.S. control in the post war period. And the British have maintained considerable influence in the English Speaking common wealth countries though Reuters. So according to its view no other single factor has contributed to so much to the maintenance of British Prestige.

I find the Third World which represent over two thirds of world's population and area accounts for only 30 per cent of reports from these 4 Big Agencies. Agency is the only and the mainlink to connect the press on its running ground from its outer world and the main means of sources. So since the agency or agencies are base in the west he major part of their news package is about events in the industrialised countries. A publishers of the Fight Sun Philip Harkness complains out his editors being snowed under the British Football results and other unusable organising from the Western Agencies. The exchanges of news between the West and Asia is typical of imbalance.

The news gathering priorities of the news agencies are reflected in the postings of their own correspondences. Some of 38 per cent are confined to U.S. While further 32 per cent are based in

European capitally and only 20 per cent Asia or Australia 16 per cent in Latin America, 8 per cent in the Middle East 6 per cent in Africa. A reporter posted in Delhi is expected to cover even from Kabul in the west to Rangoon in the land mass sprawling over five and half million squire kilometres.

Besides campaigning about unbalance in the flow of the news between First and the Third worlds politicians of the developing countries that there is western bias to the news about that printed their countries. People from Third World seem to make news in Europe and the U.S.A. only when they die to starvation or kill each other. Riots, deaths and the marriage scandals of any important political leader hits headlines of the news in the western press while the positive news about the development projects or industrial growth are ignored. Even the language used is reports is heavily leaded in favour of the Western establishment. Guerillas fighting racing regimes in Africa or Military dictatorship in Latin America are both described as the world 'terrorists' which was badly followed in India in concept of Punjab Ugravadi Sangathan, as terrorists and none in Kashmiri terrorists and further the Tamil Militants were also adopted in the very directive language form of imperialism covered under the democratic set up but influenced by all these press agencies as such. Back to see that not till the last years of war in Vietnam did the Western news agencies explain that the National Liberation Front enjoyed widespread popularity and was fighting what the Vietnamese people considered an occupying Army. Likewise the name of many independent minded nationalists leaders of the third world like Massadec Lende are invariably prefixed by terms like Leftists or Marxists. The leader is hardly described like a Rightist or capitalists why so indifference of opinion? The effect of the kind of terminology in its content use should not be underrated. It tends to reinforce storey types that have been built up over generations the Far East as an area constantly as bolt with revolts and the carnage. The Middle East meaning with Shaikhs and their hareems and Africa Teeming with strange animals. Such a bias mould to public opinion to point where Western military interventions in Vietnam or EL Salvador is made quite acceptable.

# Seven

# Commercialisation in Press

**Commercial Line of Media**

So the tailoring the news to meet the Western self interest often means cultivating. The idea of a threat from without, reporting on a meeting on a Third World bauxite producers a U.P.I. dispatch added that, some expert feel it could be the first step in the establishment of series of international curtails of controlling raw material essential to the industrialized nations, which could set 'United States' economy back more that 46 years. Such kind of alarmist reports create feeling that the industrial countries must defend themselves by obstructing such organizations of producers from the Third world.

So the foreign agencies like U.P.I. getting 100 per cent of the revenue from Western newspapers, it is not surprising that they look at the front page news as longs. American soldiers were killed but receded after U.S. withdrawal until events like famine barely got mentioned. So at a time when Kissinger attended a conference of, Latin American Ministers in Maxico, this same U.P.I. devoted 90 per cent of its coverage to Kissingers speeches out the same time the newspapers subscribers to the U.P.I. wire services in Equator or Guatemala had to book elsewhere for reports of their delegate's contributions.

This sort of superior technology and proffetional expertise have enable Western news agencies and journalists to provide informations efficiently. When combined with the best in a humanitarian liberal tradition these have produced some remarkable journalism. It is overwhelming trend of sensationalizing poverty and civil wars, damning and distorting the aspiration of ordinary people and ignoring the historical and social context of Third World problems that has marked Western Reporting about developing countries.

This the story of four Big may not be an essential guidelines for all kind of newspapers. I feel there must be a guideline for these agencies and I am putting a brief history of it as a rule. Associated Press was the brain child of six New York dailies created in 1848, which fought a long battle just to break the monopoly of the British Reuters which was once caused by Associated Press's Executive Manager of denigrating the U.S. in reporting American news of the world, a query paralleled to the charge levelled today by the Third World against Western News agencies. After the end of the Second World War with creasing American economic power, associated press expanded not only into Europe and Latin America but also in the Far East when American economic interests were developing. And today it is the biggest news agency sending out 18 million world a day.

Known as Paris praised A.F.P. is the only one which depends on the subsidy from the government usually through official subscription by government officers. As a result it is often regarded as the voice of the French Government. It network is spread over 168 countries. It is particularly strong in Francophone Africa base on French colonial government subscriptions of the past, a tradition that has been maintained.

The second in these agencies is the Reuter done by Bason Julius in 1828 thought of sending pigeons to carry economic intelligence faster than the mail train from Brussels to Achen, which he could not imagine that less than 140 years later his successors in the Reuters office in London would be using computers to book investment brokers into stock market prices. It has the highest income among the big four. And internationally it is more popular or the most popular than 80 per cent of income comes from foreign subscribers compared to 20 per cent for Associated Press.

The terror of newspaper's operation was set at its inaugural meeting held in India during Mrs. Gandhi's emergency rule hosted by a regime that impressed its own journalists attended by delegates from government with similar repressive, the pledge of the conference of Non-Aligned countries to provide objective and authentic information, could not help but sound empty.

Most member agencies are government controlled and

restricted to releasing news depend fabourable by their ministries of Information. Official handout about high agricultural production or speeches from heads of state dominate the non-aligned wireways. An earlier pledge by the newspool members to avoid criticisings each other has also undermined its credibility and conflicts between member nations have some time escalated into armed warfare and still not been reported.

Inter Press Service (IPS) began 1964 as a small co-operative journalists writing about problems in Latin America and distributing handouts to embassies. Today the agency has grown into a five million dollar international enterprise offering 110,000 words a day in three languages. This service is an alternative news coverage and by making its editorial and transmitting facilities available to other agencies in the Third World.

With its emphasis on analysis the West suspects IPS of getting most of its funding form left wing governments and is accordingly mistrustful of its coverage. So the Director General of Inter Press Service points out that the one third of their budget coming from foreign press contract includes agreements with agencies in countries as disparate as the United Arab Emirates, Austria, Mexico and Libya.

The story of these four 'Big' tells the problem is not the finding hard to find news from place or country but it is to questioned that how it could be implemented and here again it is a problem that how to divide the press inside some where it is through government agency and some where it is through agencies, under registered rules of government. Both the news from this part of the government get a press by paying a price to it but in an oriented manner or imposed by bureaucratic imperialism and either totally non-aligned, which looses the spicy-bites of the news the main attraction of the readers or vices or of listeners.

But now as Press and Media has captured the world market holding strings in hands it can easily walk tight ropes of news with the overage of International Relations Theory. There are so many bridging points through the agencies in India and in the world press market, which fill anyone of newspaper with richness of the news. As stringers and reporter of the place where a newspaper is based on these all kind of news services and even on newly mushroomed so many feature agencies and other news resources as such.

Obviously all are connected, and even contracted with the Ministry of Information and Broadcast. More or less a complete pull they have in their hands and even exchanges in the ministries of foreign concerns with the basic agenda of exchange of informations at international grounds. May the International Exchange of Politics Socio-cultural and some of putting the figure from the Third World countries to give a helping hands to them from all countries at a time of killing riots and against the starvation of much more poor countries. This is no matter of importance to deal with only Britain, now England, America, Japan and many others of Developed countries. As we all know we have come to the point world front face to face any kind of problem containing our own sensitivity of people and to mind with it the press outside works. But the press under government some time tries to hollow it up by drilling the weak financial resources, and often stopping the flow of information and sometime to check the advertisement to tighten up the corners of free flow of informations, which are the matter of Right or the Right to know the people, manipulated by the press outside.

So the International Relations itself need a free flow of information exchanged in a manner of adequacy to the government, mainly in political interactions and changes in Trades of modernity. So let me define little on this as a basic theory of International Relations today. Mainly what International Theory rarely accepts although there have been important and always marginalized exceptions throughout its history is our rationalization of the International Theory and what is relationship between the study of international relations and particular view of what constitutes international practice. The self some reason which rules over thinking also help again to constitute international practice. There are exceptions to this general trend most notably the work of many writing before the establishment of separate discipline of international relations. In short International Theory is indicated in international practice because of the way that theory in the main divorce via 'reason' separated from ethical and moral concerns. May claim is that the dominant strain in international has been one which sees ethics as applicable to the kind of community that international society can not be. Thus in the name of elightment and knowledge, international theory has tended to be a discourse, accepting of and complicit in the creation and recreation of this kind of international practice that threaten discipline and do violence to others, nuclear strategy and especially its treatments of arms races as natural phenomena is merely the most explicit example of this tendency, the areas of international thought confirm it. It is reason which is implicated in the recreation and re-affirmation of international practices of domination and co-ordination and through which the identity of others is legitimized.

The second the more fundamental influence on the aims of this theory that to use the writings on the archeology and the geneology of knowledge to illuminate what stories an international theory has told about itself.

So this way of thinking about international theory has been particularly important among those who fit within what is usually if inaccurately termed the 'English' that means a class-voice not for all through the press doing outside wings. This argument was best expressed in an influentional paper by Martin Wight in which he defined international theory as being a tradition of speculation about the society of states or the family of nations or the international community. In contrast to political theory which was concerned with 'speculation about the state'. His argument was not that there could be no international theory, rather that there was no body of international theory to rival the achievements of political theory. Not only there no body of the international theory before the 20th century to match the work of the great political theories but also what political theory had existed had been maked by intellectual and moral poverty. In connection historian could best explain, 'the nature of foreign policy and the working of the states system.'

One more point for keeping press outside is that communitarian versus cosmopolitan thought which the categorisation refers to a debate which has been particularly influential in the development of what is termed as normative theory. Although this is rather a misleading term since it implies that there is any such thing that is non-normative theory. The basic distinction is simple, communication theories has argued that the political communities are the bearers of rights and duties in international society. Cosmopolitan theories argue that moral arguments should be based pot on communities but on either humanity as a whole or on individuals. The debate between these positions have opened up considerable space both for developing normative international theory with wider philosophical and social science and literatures.

The main probable faced by the press outside is the catagorisation is that the vast majority of international theory has proceeded as it did not exist. So the central thrust of discipline in newspaper in connection with foreign relations emerges as a separate subject in the aftermath of the First World War has been to create an autonomous theory of international politics. This require treating the international as district from the other reference points of social and political theory, so let alone the obtuse debate within contemporary moral philosophy. The dominance of so-called realism furthered this tendency with its stress on practical and scientific knowledge and the consequent belitting of normative theory.

But for press as such the international political sphere is one of necessity, regularity and also a danger, which is wholly unsuitable for the moral philosopher. Moralizing belongs in the pulpit not in the classroom or in the corridors power. Taking normative concerns seriously would at best mislead the 'press' as to the real nature of international relations and at worst a court national disaster. The problems with this view points are three fold, first it is based on implicit assumption that non-normative theory is a possibility in the 'Press' outside. Second it assumes that the 'political' and the "International" are in same way a very natural categories, not at all the product of the ways in which we think about the social world, finally, it assumes that realism does not already adopt, albeit implicitly, moral principles. On this point in section of holding hand with open press that it is fair to point out that same classical realists of any country or society but do sometime speak on international sphere as one suitable for moral reasoning they also speak preponderance of power political considerations and warned against the dangers of a moral foreign policy. Moreover this strain of practical realism has been dominated by a more technical realism that lies at the center of the realism for Press with the utility first at the point. It is only recently that this dominant view has come under sustained attack most powerfully upon the press inside working under the government.

Nonetheless, the cosmopolitan/munitarian debate in an open press does have the difficulty that it places that the center of my analysis with moral and ethical concerns. This is also problematic for press outside because of the disciplines focus an scientific approaches which eschew concern with ought-type question alike in concern with official secrecy an official is being asked as under the judicial proceeding he would prefer to go to jail instead of uttering the facts, must be it is a question but definitely not be answered property. But when I send letters getting views from outside country, no flat refusal but a well managed talk message within time as contributed here with many terms of writing here and there. And would also refer the country of Press Information Bureau Uttar Pradesh giving the lists of newspapers as all other provincial services of its sister part equally contributed with the matter needed sending in time and properly. It is an off the time talk against subject.

But this could refer the differences in the services done to me here and outside India. By which I could content International material theory through which this all came out. Again talking about policy in outside matters as an international talk formation, which is for we still a problematic one with the questioned manner focusing on policy relevance. How can international theory be fare when the policy analysts wants the answers to day's problems? The worry is that the cosmopolitan/communitarian debate results in a marginalization of international theory. More important still is the worry that the debate is still rather too narrow, because it is based on debates within philosophy and political theory that are themselves coming under attack for what they leave for equation.

### Commercial Vocal Language

One more very specific point touching the ground of international concept and Indian relationship with the world, located completely though the press outside in columns which deals with the matters concerning international prospects and problems both. But most of the time unanimity of this kind is often a matter of suspicion, and, sure enough, further investigation does reveal all is not as it seems. The very point in Indian and International tone of language using the word 'community' is tough to decide for which, the community of whom? It is a deceptive and different notion to an International trade policy politics. But the same 'Community' used in Indian concept in printed matters is a rioting figure to even decide which community, as this word used most in the matter of casteism not communalism both are terrifying word in India Press market. Having noted its reference to a sense of common than community where the 'common' gather the community begins itself common identity and the classical contrast with 'society' as such very much formulized as a contrast remarks that it is a 'warmly persuasive' word, whether used to describe an existing or alternative set of relationships, what is more important perhaps is that unlike all other terms of social organization (state, nation and society) it never seems to be unfavourably and never to be given any positive opposing of distinguishing terms. The term 'world community' in newspaper, it is never employed with pejorative connotations. It may not be entirely clear that those press use it believe that the world would be a better place if it could be described as community. As with the diplomatic use of International Community, a related but in contrast to 'world community' — a related but in contrast to world community an essentially state centric terms which is always used in press section persuasively.

Now the matters of common interests looked upon in both section of press as such. The question remains on what basis this can be argued that there is a trend towards the development of ever wider common interest and deepening sense of common indentity? But here the world community variably use in printed matter sense wise the surrounding is important at the outset to make a distinction between trend towards it creation of community and trends which simply point towards the emergence of 'One world' not with community, otherwise it will be divided into 'communal' shape and need of so called 'Communal harmony' will stand as it is to day in all over the world it is.

The very easy to say now the press inside the government never and never use this word 'Community' aloof, in terminology as it will create a sensational points arouse each of the corners of the world, and divide figures separative movements every where. But an illustration of this point, important in its own terms can be 20th century's globlisation and going ahead 21st century as hoping this world community would not be use in press in the same manner as it would have been ever in this section.

There is a more general point to be made here. For community to begin to emerge there has to be growing awareness of common interests and identity, the creation of one world is a necessary condition of today which only press and media can float it to the terms of it. This is clearly so with regard to unifying forces of global economic interdependence, but perhaps less intutively, obviously, the point also applies when it comes to other unifying forces, including material factors such as common consumer goals. This contents when differ is various statement is press given in uniformatively combine with news and people's sensitivity of social econorms with political terms and condition given by them to feed back community or the common man, as ever quoted in Times of India' cartoon by Laxman, where a common man who is the part of community sees every events happening and known through day to day newspaper, look surprised upon. I see that number of countervailing forces in the modern world in the realm of ideas or technology broadly defined or of social and political action appear to act either promote or hinder this development but crucially behind the struggle, between these forces it is, I suggest generally assumed that there is an underlying trend guaranteeing, or at least making very likely a victory for the promoters of the community. And the press after independence in India has the only thought of political socialism to utter about for the welfare of common mans, in more which a convention of community, here the press has one more responsibility to open the window for liberal thoughts about community, which sometimes by the provocation of the promoters of the community does provoke this same common man towards the communalism a permanent dangers in society. So press has to have a watch upon that, for the permanent communal harmony this word, 'community' should be used in newspapers in a very much guarded manner which should never create any communal feeling till the sensitivity of mind, which might figure out rioting and other mob violence. I have already told to mind that the press as such under the government and in radio or television never use the 'word' 'community' or communal as such. Because the norms of this press is basically constructive and in force not giving any lead story to it, may be it is a defusive factor, but the government press and government media always try to avoid it for betterment of the society and people, but the press inside and all media under government, always believe in 'one world' community even spreading the new, picking from the places. But the norm and ethics in producing them is their own.

But beyond that after 1936 a kind of progressive press with small and medium newspapers were who float the concept of Marxism which carries the concept of holding Masse in hands for a revolution in the society and it also fought for casteism, communicism in India, and with the help of an opinion towards the masses and to all others, but these kind of all oriented press tried to revolt against that system which was base on fundamental disharmony in the society based on cast and community basis and of the interest between the people of its component and its core, semi-periphery and periphery. For the time being, for this concept that there is no word like community as base under inside press this stood at a base of Marxism and communal separation of thoughts and views.

**Economic Role of Advertisement**

Press to day holds a partial part in contributing in the world economy as not only through publishing advertisements but keeping a full page on finance and so many trade magazines are published in a manner to fix norm in financial setup through newspaper keeping underhand policy to show the welfare of the common masses. But in India under differential economy it was thought that the advertising about economic plan should be property propagated for siding masses and that common man, which Times of India put in figure done by Laxman.

Here coming out of this let me discuss about the political

economy and our relation with international figure, at which my point is only that the political tides that gave legitimacy to great deal of that sort of work which kept in financially afloat are already receding and may do so still further in future. An alternative focus on these economic, corporate and inner state, underlying the regimes, rather than the regimes themselves would give better results. But the inevitable bias is towards order over equity, value and equality toward inter government, bargaining to the exclusion of other bargain, either those within the states or those between the government and enterprise or with other social groups. There is also in regime analysis a certain bids towards state analysis of organization which may remain in being long after their sustaining bargain has collapsed in economic theory of today world market and when our press opens this issues, it is but natural bias on its own countries policies and favourable figures to sooth with shock of loosing their country's currency value in the world market in ritualistic actualized manners in outside press after politics, the finance is getting a second lead of the newspapers so long. I can count it as the increased integration of national economics in the world market economy but leave affected India time to time. The change affects countries states but originates outside the states in all four of the basic structures of international political economy but mostly in the increasingly intergrated structure of credit and finance and in the increasingly transnationalized structure of production. So the result is a marked reduction in the autonomy of the state, a reduction that other social scientists, the anthropologists, the sociologists, even the geographers, have shown themselves rather more aware of than either the economists or most political scientists.

Once a very powerful said economic natured person Dr. Man Mohan Singh treating India's best economical policy to prevent the gold smuggling from others nations to India, was situated in Newspaper as a best "Golden policy". But at that time, The Times of India published an article times before written by a small boy Abhigyan Prakash "The policy which was never golden " showed the prosperous and little danger to Indian Economy. Today is conceptional views to implement Swadeshi is hankering thought as stated by one of the minister that 'Swadeshi is not about boycotting foreign goods or xenophobia', but one of the minister that 'Swadeshi is not about boycotting foreign goods or xenophobia', but it is a humanitarian concept, puts a symbolic gesture and doublespeak standard of a person.

With the time when multinationals introduced in India some of the newspapers specially launched in this field to keep a tight hold upon world economy and the world market. Evidence is there for all to see and no longer any country or any state today can afford to opt out of the global market economy. As for instance the successor states of the U.S.S.R., (Burma) Myanmar, the peoples republic of China. India, Iran, Vietnam and South Africa have with more or less reluctance accepted the fact and acted, accordingly to invite foreign owned firms to invest in their economics, to liberalize their protected national markets in order to make producers more and to allow more competetive through press and media to allow world market prices to act as realistic signals to the private sectors. This all is prepropagated by the press in print media which can not be dealt with any one of other media. You can not discuss it in Radio or Doordarshan. But the advertisement of production show the meaning of it to popularize their products. It may not be profential and inconsistent with the analysis of production power and world order, although the special emphasis has been given to international market which is widely interchanged by Indian market. But in between the intervening variable social forces and other outcomes which separate the security of the market structure sustained by the system of states from the financial production and knowledge of the structure is in debate like the paper Sunday observe of Business and Politics, Business India Economic Times and so many of others in India and outside world.

Each and every Newspapers have a column for their Business page mainly to analysis the facts and surrounding of economy all over the world and so on with the experts in Indian and international economic policy, through placing debate in newspaper and periodicals. But through the press outside the purpose should be to arrive at a clear analysis of the outcomes also in a global household and how they were brought around and about. The outcomes involve both distributive outcomes in that who gets what and those concerning the mix of values in the system as a whole. Does the way in which international political functions continue to favour the production of wealth over the provision of justice? What room does it give for the exercise of autonomy or freedom to chose? This all is being directed to traders and all people who are commercially involved in things of their choices and look for a canvassing market to handle their business, are taught by the Economic press outside with no concern with or without any government.

Any countries' economy is the backbone of its structure, after that any other problems. After Independence press outside had only the opt of fighting with common man for the need of his and as I see that after imperialism only thought left for fighting with capitalism to handle the new economic situation with the press outside with its economic frontage, and footage both of much stability and security does it provide in the long run as well as in the short run? And for each of these value, there is destructive question, but for whom? It is for the so called customer, who believe in customs of buying and selling and for which social, economic, ethic are religions groups does the system provides most wealth, most security, most justice, or most freedom to chose the thing of the choice like banyan tree which puts its roots in follow-ups or in following traditional sale or purchase stands with norms of old Britishers patronage entered here through economical flow for setting trades in India. The world trade continues its meanly with further going known as tradition. The trade gets in to traditional, carries the economic credibility of their business of their chosen field, what suits and follow their stars, tailored by astro advisers. So much of this mean to say and how it is all concerned with the press talk does require to say that even in the very first newspaper was launched in India by a Britisher for getting the new of ships and of shipping trade's know-how for India as the British India company was established in India, established first in Calcutta as the most luxurious city of that time, which was much ruled by Indian traders instead of based Bengalis, they were also, in two parts at that time surrounded with 'sovereignty Zamindar', small and Big kingship or poors as 'Prajajan', so the trade took a part in its most important stabilized shape and carried its best to bestowed that tradition to ahead. And the press outside even at that time played the part of advertising through the newspapers.

So the going back to the beginning for me means starting with what used to be called that there is not moral philosophy in trades accord to Britishers. Although I see the concept of expressing thoughts of manusmriti as "yah Arthah Shuchi Sah Shuchi", where the meaning is pious that contain purity-Artha-Money-Artha, the meaning which accustomed with 'means' means to live that money should be earned with good and pious means when found not possible at all the system 'Byaz' on 'Mool' was kept at sight to run the trade or business , and profit after 'Spended money' was advertised through that times hankering media. But against it the Britishers placed the thought as a meaning of prosperity, with 'Pros' perity—defined all kind of saleability and publicising for that can bring prosperity in House to run it. The shape of publisystemetic publicizing is the only way of media till today stands through the trading press as today the press itself is in the clutch hold of trade centres and in the hands of industrialists as such. So it does keep no meaning with the moral philosophy in trade at all.

The horizons of morale philosophy as the social sciences no longer ends at the frontiers of this country. There to start with morale philosophy is exactly a powerful safeguard against the nationalist not with traditional traders it is a bias to business sectors by the Britishers as they entered in Business India Company which started the first press started in India. Although Jesus started first press for publishing Bibles theory but it was only to spread messages of Bible in India which was first translated in Hindi as Hindi was full language itself there were regional languages for all, not in one fold, but in spreaded identity of Indian people. So we can not consider it a press for knowing and communicating base.

It always be considered that in India a trade journal introduced by the Britishers was the first journal with informations of trading ships. I don't feel that how far to go to beyond analysis to the prescription of pressing ways rotating a complete news circle which is a rather subjective question, so source of individual may think upon the concern of press with economic track, but for me to say in an stable manner and in normative motive, advocating the purposive promotion of a different mix of values and a different distributive outcome of particularity in trade news, beyond the advertisements done in all kind of papers today. Other my be concerned only to make an objective and accurate analysis of trade in press and journals of the arrangement and managements with the structure of production, finance security and knowledge and also that how they have come about?

Here again I come to main theory of Press with my own point of view that the basic purpose of the press is simply to discover "how and why things are as they are" and also in a shaping guideline to the rulers, and to advise them how to survive with outer community even fed it by them but the middlemen and media-men do wrong in informing the proportion of facts and factuarity, the plain talk to define the relations with others. For reasons which should now be plain that my feeling is that the study of international political economy today needs more favour and fewer of press in the need of accuracy with pointing out towards the trends of financial economy touched with golden policies of the government, with international relationship to boom the business of Indian traders and stabilize the economy of India comparing with international market and with current economic world affairs which really affects the value of Indian currency in the world market.

As Indians always keep a kind of 'security seeking behavior' but they carry security dilemma justified by one state as legitimate security enchanting measures are likely to be perceived by others as a threatening. So the Indian trade person normally face international anarchy; through domestic order in pattern of business and its directionality, so in connection with they normally never use the plus points of press to deal with the flowing wave of the market of the world.

And these assumptions about the nature of the international system and the so called security seeking behavior of states fit with realist analysis of the behavior of the great powers in the post-second World War period. This was the time when traders ramped in race of business on the top only by pushing news from current newspapers and periodicals.

These types of statements given in press sometimes defuse the trade policy of businessmen who see the leader of the parties concern for chose and to feed for their development of their business. The traders wings of India always look and watch that who is going to feed their own accord which may support this community is opening a window for this noted so called Indian Business Community and put them if not in a hike but keep them running in the open world market and catching the rope through media. And they always keep one eye upon their business and one eye upon the press outside dealing with the subject matter in finance as directive solution and so many other eco-political matters relating to their trade and benefits.

So they never like to see a dreamy budget but not even very strangely nationalistic one also as to the man of the street and even to a millionaire the tests are a sign that India has at last come-out of the shadow of western powers and they want to them now on their own. Have an eye always upon the finance minister and ministry in India, the today's trade person does like that to slash taxes all round and trying to carry favour with foreign investors an others as I told it earlier that our finance minister did in 1991. Instead he produced a budget, call it Swadeshi which was even followed by in Lohiawadi concept unlike in hands of B.S.P. Government which mainly looks after the interests of India's first just as the nuclear tests were staged to safeguard the interests of India first.

Advertisement in Newspaper-radio, and television are very highly paid by the advertisers who see the product to be launched and reined in the market through media and are about to get good results of that in the pool of market money in the hands of traders.

The others section of media as a audio visualization may not be pressing but to taste all kind of expressively communicative thought clicked by radio, as a constructive media now setting a trend to the norms of Indian government and even other broadcast media working upon news in all other countries. But first I must see a little History of Broadcast media from the very beginning which is still the first and a giant chess board of information and knowledge both.

As I would like to say that the broadcasting brings public life in to private life and private life into public life for pleasure and enjoyment as much as information and education. The many voices in this domain, the broadcasters themselves, public persons and private people amount to a universe of discourse. The totality of output of programmes in Broadcast media is not the part of 'normal' range of the needs and interests of the audiences or listeners as in the sum of its contents. To make this point is to underline the importance of trying to think of broadcast output as a totality and always to register what it excludes as well as what it includes. The crucially sensitive 'boundary' topic for Broadcasting with this general viewpoint let me have a glance at first at the beginning of Radio as a broadcast media in India with its history and with so many other developments.

Just because the broadcasting and its services was addressed to the whole of society in its programmes. I do not think to imply that this was simply or easily achieved then or now nor do I underestimate the difficulties of middles class and so others. As I have already defined the history or Radio as powerful medium in India even after growing influence of television.

To compare the section of news only with print media as such after which as we all know it very well that the Art and the literature and all kind of other performing arts would be considered as an expressive media, come under the one section of journalism, who feeds the feeling of senses and non senses of people's thought. As Radio is much more known to people as an entertaining medium.

But a very popular world service known only for the blunt news in the British Broadcast Corporation, which very first think in norm to be kept for journalists to have something which the audience wants information. They want it because it is new, important and relevant to them. But however much they may need it, that they will receive it only if it is presented in a way that is interesting and entertaining. At times broadcasters will be required to tell their audience not simply what they want to hear, but what they need to know. In newsroom parlance, not every story is spicy and 'sexy' with instant appeal. Some have to be worked at to draw out the point of interest.

The goings on in the common market debate in the Common

wealth or Congress all is dealt with click without taking any time for listener's mood. Now it may be found that the broadcast news with its quick fire deadlines and lack of time for checks and balances, sometimes falls pray to the most elaborate of hoaxes. People ring up claiming to contracts who are knowingly the station such as police inspectors and offer phony information. B.B.C. News services also depends upon the same 'big four' as defined earlier. So it is not to be repeated again.

Here I am discussing about the radio news first at a glance. In an imaginary pattern I see that the radio certainly go for the voice of the steelwork the clashing of metal and the voices of people at work. Like many countries our radio also uses 10 variation of news in 10 codes. Instead I say Fight in Progress for example an officer might say 10-10 progress followed by the location. Each force may have its own version of the code where the number mean something different. Some of the key messages in one variation of 10 codes are alike I-Crime progress 2-Man with a gun 3-Emergency 4-Riot 5-Major-crime alert 6-Accident 7-Hit and run 8-Notify Corner. It all said for this that whatever is heard over police must be checked before use. Frequently police get called to emergencies only to discover a storm in a tea cup.

**Disadventage of Broadcasting**

I feel in the matter of broadcasting, on automatically go and get a ministry then somebody from the opposition. All these people do is give you party political statements. I find that boring and can't believe the public learns anything one already knows that political parties are going to say, which I can't I see where any of that does a damn thing to improve the quality of there understanding. Even in radio's which a complete government media not a press outside as such but even then the local politicians are a prime source of news for a local newsroom. Like all other in newspaper they are happy to oblige as this raises their profile and may win votes. And a reporter should be wise to that and make sure legitimate, news rather than vote catching, rhetoric gets on air. Every radio journalist should know the names of the area's representative in both local and national, government and should have contact numbers for them at work and at home.

Radio watches agencies that when politicians are not making news themselves, they are usually good for comment or reaction to stories that affect their constituencies towards. Political comment is cheap and readily available and this type of reaction, can be overdone, and lead to accusation of political bias and live a bulletin sounding as dull as party political broadcast is normally used very much sparingly.

At a known fact this a more formal and often takes the shape of a news conference. As when the town planners announce their three lane highway which they do show with a lavish presentation. Every time the whole media is invited to a conference in the chandilered opputance of the town hall may be in India or any other country's in a banqueting room where the drinks are "laud and the buffet" provided but the news as such is missing for the government media like radio, there the press may catch the crowd of the gathering even in hush-a-hush. See the same when the reporter have been wined and dined so the talk of their journalistic sensibilities is as a rule submerged beneath a stupor of alcohol where the mayor and other senior officials are intensively ceremoniously if invited to make their presentation in news or for newspaper, there in the print media it can be done with other person helping hand through but not any way possible in radio to read or to produce any kind of news. This is one very common problem for presenting news as such.

The road scheme is flourished with neat and convincing rhetoric about better traffic flow, reduced accident figures and positive, affect on trade in the town. Not for radio but it is for the cameras there are stylish mock-ups of the road and artists', impression, which radio covers but what of that? This can never be either for the news and coverage of print media nor for radio, but the Television can catch the expression of it also here the value of news and views both fails to click any of this kind of movement to hold on. Here for all media like on very such occasions press packs are provided with slickly written articles which the organizers hope will be published unaltered or will be broadcasted as it is by the news readers. But the key speakers or the newsreaders are available immediately after the presentation for photocalls and in even interviews but in a damn manner. All this is usually staged for publicity is not very much concerned with the news of radio with no credibility nor the news values are there for good broadcasts.

As seen each morning editors in broadcast newsrooms have a pile of mails dumped before them at their desks, like an editorial table at a newspapers. It is a very normal scene that most of the items posted will, media will end up in the waste paper bin after scarcely at a second glance. This is just because so much is irrelevant and of a very little interest to the listeners. Even the money matter are also not listened by people, like an instance of Middle Eastern countries have been known as to send regular bulletins on their economic progress and international politics just to small town radio station in England. It is compared in India where the radio is never going to entertain such news in for studio even with its own norms and ethics in producing news for. Even by the editor a copy tasted mail is that to still the wheat from the chaff here it must be scrutinize again and again with each of the item very carefully yet it can take hours, so each envelop is ripped open and its contents hastily scanned unless.

Some of radio news releases carry embargoes which means they are not to be used before a certain release of date. Public relations people use the embargoes try to control the flow OS the news, and prevent stories from being run in what they would regard as a hapzord fashion, on the plus side the embargo gives the news room time to prepare its report by giving the advanced warning of the event in radio news specially. This kind of news may be somebody's Birthday, some of the reward being given at a time of that chosen day, may be preserved for the radio news and for the press media but it will never work for the television as it covers the abstract visual through camera at a spot or make it a live telecast at the very moment for its settled spot not time fixed before the date as in radio or in television.

This is a good example of embargoed material. The sent list of embargoes to radio by the teleprinter well before the official announcement. All local stations can then produce stories about people in their area ready to run the moment the embargo in lifted.

In radio among the daily plethora of unsolicited material

which arrives in the newsroom may be very much a number of recorded interviews sent by agencies if in India like U.N.I. P.T.I. Bhasha and in outer world taken story or the news all established 'Four Big' agencies of a very old time but still continued in all corners of the world sector, and them a sent by public relations companies in radio. They all are often available free of charge and usually have some of time bounded advertising tie-ups.

This is more sophisticated variation of the news releases which appeals to producers who are slothful or obstreached and who may be grateful to receive something for nothing. But as the saying goes and there is no such things as a free lunch. Here I see that P.R. Company hopes stations will find a slot for the tape and play it an air united. Radio uses in this way, syndicated tapes are simply free normally unadulterated publicity oriented news.

At best, syndicated tapes are normally harmless, even useful fillers. At worst they can be scarcely disguised adverts or propaganda. No unsolicited taped should be used without checking for violations of the advertising code, and that journalistically and technically the tape is up to standard and its relevant to the audience, but no use of it to be technified by radio for its news, but even they are most useful tapes for the record.

Items from tipsters cannot be given the same weight as tips-off from bona-fide stringers or correspondents: the information is not from a trained journalists, the source may be unreliable, the facts confused or even libellous. Also every station has its time wasters and hangers on who phone in or call round out of sheer self-importance. Worst of all these Tipster may be malicious and the information a hoax.

In radio what are the advantages and disadvantages of using stringers. The stringers are cost effective because they are often paid only for work that gets used on air.

They enhance a station's ground cover by using local or a specialists knowledge to get stories that might not be available to stall reporters. They can be commissioned to cover stories that would be too time consuming to warrant staff coverage. Experienced broadcast freelances can fill for staff members who are sick or on holiday.

But there are disadvantages also, but more than the

advantages. Stringer copy is seldom exclusive as their living depends on supplying news to as many outlets as possible.

Copy is seldom in broadcast style as many stringer are normally newspaper journalists more familiar with writing for print.

Stringers have to sell their copy to make a living, so stories may be dressed up to make them more and more marketable which looks obvious.

Stringer are less accountable than staffers who can be more readily disciplined for their mistakes.

These all kind of deference in between Radio reporter or stringers from radio all are in two main directions one in Press inside in Radio, which speaks of and another in Press outside which tells and writes about, what should be known to public, but both in equipmentive manners never touch each other in motives.

As news in radio is always have a base of constructive figure to tell people it should to be listen which may not provoke them in any manner to the term of sensitivity to be increased unnecessarily. But as about the newspapers it is a sellable matter which term out to the circulation of the newspaper, so if news are not of spicy bite they will be lull and dull to be read out with no kind of interests.

To categorize news for radio is to be believed that if in doubt please check it out. The only sure and certain kind of protection against the news of a hoax is a set of sharp wits and the common sense to check the information. If someone rings up claiming to be a regular contact and does not ring true for some reason get his number and check it against the known contact number. Even if it matches ring him back, ring him back to make sure that he had not simply looked up the number in the phone book. So if the caller is genuine, he should not object to the core with which his information is being checked. In radio there are phone calls one duty to obtain news and even for those programme who have to be entertained as in All India Radio, Hello, Farniesh Programme as a popular programme of Film Songs, made to be listened to people on their demand as such. And in radio news mainly in emergent news bulletins there are such quick news matter voiced over by any one of the reporter, stringer or even news editor.

So in radio occasionally, a tip-off will yield some useful

information but for safety's sake all tip-offs, whether they appear genuine or not must be checked before running even it does mean the missing deadline. In the end of this the accuracy counts for more than speed if doesn't check out-check it out.

A very logical point in radio and in other news services is one side of presentation and on the other side it is there the news to write with systematic catagorisation putting Banner headlines, lead story then departing news one by one with the importance accord. But in radio news does need to be serialised by the newsroom editors and it goes to reader to read in a systematic manner.

Yet one logical step from relying on the resources of agencies or free-lances is for broadcast organizations to pool their news stories and programmes. This yet produces economics of scale. If five stations take the same programme then the costs of that network are spread in five ways. When stations work together more cash be can found to produce higher quality programme. Material which have been beyond the reach of a small station may now he made if available under a pooling scheme. This is the principle behind the networking.

This kind of need in pooling and picking does have in print media but the news desk of an editor is authorized part to do it in a manner instead the lead and banner may change here not unlike radio.

As the news of communal disharmony goes on an outside press will be or may be sometime a headline but it will certainly not work in radio, it will be broadcast in the last with very little words used and when thought to be needed, not a necessary part of it. Generally playing with the head of policies, the world commonly to community and then to 'communal' is orderly used in newspaper, but it is never used in any government media like radio or television as a rule. As if a news of riot is open with recent happenings, paper may give it as a lead story but with same said restricted norms and radio will try to avoid the broadcast of such news, and they will broadcast the appeal to public with massages of important ministerial authority and local authoritative body to maintain law and order. When a newspaper story will define it with details causing the riot without pointing out the name of any section of community.

So the radio networking can take place in a loose federation, as with independent radio as in Britain which fresh and free terms are not still used in All India Radio even with the talk about Prasar Bharti. In Britain each station is an autonomous company or in a formulised system where all the stations are owned and regulated by a single body such as B.B.C.

So in America the first national network came into operation in 1928, even to think beyond in India, it had fifty six stations under the control of National Broadcasting Company (N.B.C.) This was to later spawn the American Broadcast Company (A.B.C) with four separate news and music services, where other include C.B.C., M.B.S.and N.P.R. National Public Radio. The listed form is only formulated in writing above just because with thought provoking comparing with All India Radio to see it as one step ahead or one step back, in concern with the standardisation of news, and the openness of the news in India broadcast system, where it looks upon constructive points to through upon the listeners, and try not only to make them know but to educate them also, not like all foreign news services who mainly put the news "as it is " or with the imperialistic angle if the news is a broadcast of B.B.C.

In Canada where the Canadian Broadcasting Corporation operates twin radio Network and one T.V. Network. Then the Australia has public and private radio and T.V Networks while the publicity owned Broadcasting Corporation of Newzealand controls two T.V. Networks and more then thirty community radio station and two non commercial radio networks. So in Africa also the retains control over T.V. and radio both.

All India Radio is totally regulated by government and broadcasts in more than 90 different dialects. India has also developed a satellite T.V. Network. But it is beaming mainly educational programmes to its ground stations for distribution across the country. Many of their networks feed their strings of their local stations with National News from centralized newsrooms, and those stations which is turn set back reports of major stories to the network.

In London an Independent Radio News is a wholly owned subsidiary of L.B.C. London Broadcasting Company. It provides independent stations with news bulletins on the hour and a teleprinter and an audio service, so they can take the National News live or assemble and real their own versions of the I.R.N. bulletin.

Some station in remote regions such as Scotland prefer to compile their own National Bulletins which can be angled to suit their Scottish audiences rather than settle for news with London emphasis. Network station pay for the I.R.N. Service with a fixed percentage of their revenue. This means prosperous radio stations pay much more and then subsidize the smaller ones.

The B.B.C. Network service and a General News Service provides copy and audio both but it does not after a live bulletin which stations can pipe in on the hour.

In United States regional networks ranges from groups of stations who exchanges the tapes from regular basis to sealed down the National Network with a centrally produced bulletin piped in on the hour when a station switches over to take the network news, this is called 'opting-in' to the Network. The process of switching back is called opting out.

Where opt-outs are used, bulletins will end with a readily unidentifiable such a time check. Which is presenters que for switching back, to local programming. Many radio stations follow the National News with a local bulletin and some of the others proceed with local news to Network section, this kind of news give to its basically known as mix, news bulletin. Many of the radio and television stations produce their own regional news and mix it with National News Service on their network.

Local T.V. and Radio stations will also be expected to contribute to the pool of news stories available to the network. Material is supplied to and from the Network along a contribution circuit stations with similar interest may install there own contribution circuits and supply with one another material operating like a network within a network. I feel it to explain like this which is an interexchang programmes to follow within time limitations. It can only be possible with radio or television news just because the voices in broadcast media and visuals of Television can separately be dealt for preparing the news and its camera visuals on television.

But in print media journalists take a professional pride in beating their fellows to a story. Most of news editors monitor the rival media or press of others angles just to make sure that they are ahead with the news to see if there is any thing which they have missed.

One of the news editors in press out side is the first tasks each day is usually to go through the national and the local papers to see if there are any stories referring to the area which need to be followed up. Following up a news item means checking and developing it to find a new story angle. This is different from taking a story from newspaper and rewriting if for bradcast. That would be plagiarism, stealing somebodies work. Facts may also be wrong and errors repeated.

There is no copyright on ideas, however and journalists often feed on another for their leads and inspiration as in the actual example.

In any visual or audiovisual media broadcast suppose 20 minutes are counted in to the programme and all that still remains is the weather and the headlines. Here the story counted as a main story, may be called father of news which still not found and time for news is running out. The producer takes over the story. He gets through to the father even as the closing headlines are being read by presenter. Here director quickly tells one of the presenter through his earpieces that the father is on the phone waiting to be interviewed, here the presenter has 45 seconds to ad-lib the interview before the programme ends and transmission returns to the network. The very important factor is that it is strictly not possible to overrun by even a second.

Now it was a story of a businessman's father's who at the time as considered the father of the news as missing and caught with interview like this.

# Eight

# Changing Role of News Media

## Broadcasting of News Media

Here the director counts down the closing seconds while the presenter thanks the father for talking to him and wished the viewers a calm good evening. Thus the programme ends the bang on time and as coolly as if it had all been planed from the start. Here our Doordarshan has led the way on this foreign story but the B.B.C. got the better story so it is why, the answer is the making of missing time preparation was little left and late when father businessman was not there.

At an international level news services frequently buy and exchange reports with one another to enhance the world wide coverage and from all country's broadcast systems.

Here the press outside exchange the news but it is always reedited and rewritten for the cover prints from newspaper headlines. But the talk of radio is going on so let me talk about news editors are to broadcast journalism what generals are to warfare. They set the objectives weigh the resource and then they draw up the plan of campaign. And under their command are the officers and the troops on the ground.

Some of news editors of inside press like radio prefer to be in the thick of battle directing the action from the front line, while in the same situation other favour a loftier perspective set back from the heat of the action. These will oversee strategy but delegate a number two to be responsible for tactics. In larger newsrooms, this may be the deputy news editor, senior producer or bulletin producer, working to the news editors plan of campaign he/she will kept in touch with news as it develops and arrange coverage.

In a view to my subject as it is all being talked about Broadcast media which is in India totally regulated by Indian government in comparing with all so other in the world Radio visions of their own picking up the section of news and finding. The solution when song of the point are missing under presenting the news, and why it so, and how it was cope it up. As about India radio which is in my way of thought is under the government and mainly it is considered an entertain media first than to section of news. As if literate or little literate even they prefer to read newspapers first as with their awakening the morning. In our Indian systems itself it has become a kind of morning pooja without the newspaper tea in hands.

Radio news is always listen to catch the time being accuracy and promptness of the news as such, to very recent happening as it catches the news before the time when published newspaper normally next day issue. Second good of radio news is stated that doing any kind of job you beat with the promptness of news without wasting your time to sit for reading or watching visuals in front of before the television news so on.

So let me see for holding power with the responsibility to it as in our Indian broadcast media with comparison of other countries and further the popular programmes produced by radio's day to day routine.

As there is a weird power in a spoken word, which is able to win people for more by the spoken then by the written word and that very moment of his globe owes its rights to the great speakers and not to the great writers.

So framed and hanging in a prominent position on the wall of a commercial radio station is a poster depicting a wildeye better dressed revolutionary clut ching a micsophone and shouting slogan across the airways.

Came the revolution point, every radio and television station becomes a strategic target. The poster may have been aimed advertises but its message is universal; even in peacetime, who ever controls the media has the whip hand in the war for people's hearts and minds.

But it is a frightening thing with television not with that one has this enormous power to produce the news if at 10 O'clock, it is not to be forgotten the news at 10 at a sharp. So no wonder at media control, its accountability, total kind of impartiality and at vexed issue of censorship, which have been featured so largely in debate, and this kind of debate is permitted after such a long battle of Prasar Bharti Bill in recent time but the implementations of it still not under full consideration in the Press inside as it is not even used to it or praned to it as such.

At the heart of this issue is the question of who should hold this reins the public of clutching outside press or the press under the government media as radio and television or but and mainly first started broadcast media. Although it is free media, which has its full responsibility not to politician as the press outside has its first proposed baseline for Indian politician's day to day game of power and tussels both as a frontline hold of news even in front page covering for but the radio or television is committed to its listener and audiences only. It is another problem in the world media not anyway possible in Indian media so on, that it uses or use its liberty to determine the esteem in which it is held by those services, that esteem may some time even in the press inside the government media like radio may prove decisive in whether the balance eventually tips towards freedom or control.

**Restrictions of Newspaper**

Regulation of Indian television or radio and British radio and television operate under more restrictions than there newspaper counterparts. Newspapers can back upon that which political party they choose, but in place of that the broadcasting is require by law to be impartial and balanced in its own outlook.

So in composition the purpose laid down for the B.B.C. and mainly in All India Radio that it should be first well connection and well informed itself and then it should inform people and to educate them and than all other rest of the time to entertain them on which I shall speak on later upon this subject. For B.B.C. and All India Radio in their independent services alike, a premium was placed on the breadth and quality produce by the radio for programming. The B.B.C. is governed by a royal charter and All India Radio is governed by the government itself and an independent radio and television by the government so it is the party in power which mainly controls the purse strings.

As it known that I.B.A. awards franchises to radio and

television station which it has the power to remove. The I.B.A. in turn is licensed by Home Secratry. So it is once again a party in power has even the final say to say towards people's commitment. At a time of writing one has the plan to except and expand and finally it comes to deregulate that very radio sector and even to shift control to a different body, but upon one which would be appointed by the government.

To see that in United State of America that its regulatory body is the Federal communication commission. Mainly this composed of seven other commissions who are appointed by the president. So the F.C.C. here formally holds a looser rein over radio and television both than its counterparts in United Kingdom, it also issues, renews and it also has the power to remote the licences when the F.C.C. as such has on power to censor station output with no direction to control over the networks.

Many U.S. stations also subscribe to the voluntary code of the National Association of broadcasters which tries to maintain the standard of fachial fair and unbiased reporting as well as with balance and good taste.

The complaints and comments both done by sending letter which is read by programmer in radio and television from listeners and the viewers also play their very important part in shaping output of radio and television as such. In Britain the Broadcasting complaints commission adjucate the complaints from out intellectual and individuals , who believe that they have unjust and unfair treatment or unwarranted infringement of secrecy in privacy attacked by the press inside like the press outside in and under controlled government media.

Instansively the Australian broadcasting is regularly regulated by the broadcasting act and also overseen by the Australia where the Australian Broadcasting commission and even the Australian broadcasting tribunal which mainly are the statutory bodies of the government concerned of country so one.

With an establised facts of the Press outside is that the reporter in both side of press are nothing but the puppets so they are simply respond to the pull of the powerful strings.

As in Britain the government can step into prevent the programme going out on air. Here the Home Secretary had the power under the licence granted to B.B.C. to require the corporation not to broadcast a programme. But the I.B.A. even has similar powers over 'independent' broadcasting.

Several other of major questions are even lie at the heart of the censorship issue such as by censoring what basically government want and a listener or a reader or even a viewer see or hear or read. Is it that the government exercising commendable responsibility in sparing less well educated viewers from "harmful opinions" they may not have the mental capacity to judge even for themselves which is still question mark of today's game or I see that government is trying to display a paternalistic arrogance that underestimates and even same time patronizes its citizens? Then again to think that is it wise and responsible government to ensure that a tool as powerful as media is used as a positive force for social control and, national development and the common good? Or is political censorship simply a cynical way for the government to preserve its power by silencing the more outspoken voice of opposition?

Here I find that the conservative M.P's took a lible action against the corporation over a panorma documentary which portrayed them as extremists. The conservative party chairman publicly accused the B.B.C. of bias and unprofessionalism over its coverage of a U.S. bombing raid on Libya. A programme is aptly named secret society series about plans for a British spy satellite was deemed to be in breach of the Official Secrets Act and was banned. Special Branch raided B.B.C. promises and took mastertapes, cocuments and notes. Days after a special branch raids Director General of the B.B.C. who was asked to resign. Before long most of his top management had also been removed. But censorship and government interference is no more rife in Britain even now than in many other nations. Britain 'half free' press as it has been called as a good deal more freedom than its counterparts under some regimes where freedom of speech is something it would be wiser not to discuss.

The reason is, that after having a long discussion about Prasar Bharti implemeation over All India Radio not to come out of the strict regulation see the issue of media control in a different light to the West. There government often seek to use the media, which would otherwise become a powerful rallying point for the opposition. Failure to do so, it is argued, could lead to destabiliztion in country which may already be suffering from unrest, famine, political or religious strife.

For broadcasters in nations governed by single party system with no concept of a loyal opposition, the task of providing an unbiased and factual account of events can be fraught with danger.

As a matter resulting with growing influence of Indian progressive developments upon the world map and gradually topping towards the global side, all big dominating countries in International world. History tells that India had ever been in others eye and facing envious voice from all sides.

This made neighbour to insert the kind of disturbances inside the country. First it was noticed with disturbance in Punjab, further which was and it is a convertible problem like terrorism which basically destroyed the economy of Punjab disturbed the country totally. Later it shifted to Kashmir and then to other interior section of country itself. Which time to time made India weak and weaken.

How the press outside suffered and in the sense specially radio reporters who were very much lively to plan their work for country oriented prospects which opened the truth and the hands behind it. It is noted that thirty years or so more or less the reports of the reporter are mainly showed their calculative formulation to prove reports on reporters that in the average of ten years along journalists and most of them radio reporters have been assassinated by the secret police. Mainly upon the insistance of not coming to open area of news have to been the fear of life and killing has led the individual jounalists to the self-censorship instead of to feel implemented by the government censorship as such. Investigative journalism is almost impossible or getting to be impossible in all over the world, mainly in developing countries the most hard at Guatemala.

The said facts opens an eye-view that in one year alone more than 30 journalists were killed world wide and some how half of them only in Philippines and about 110 imprisoned, all about 13 held hostage or disappeared so and about seventy six bombed, beaten and wounded and badly or interfered with. As I know that this kind of increased censorship was reported in Zimbawve,

South Africa and areas of South America and while censorship was relaxed to some of degree in Nigeria and South Korea.

But here the burn of topping sense is again a clinching point towards that very freedom of Press, the denated freedom here is always a siding fact about the press outside. But when the radio-reporters and cameramen of television are killed, tortured and stepped aside the den, who is after that I can say definitely not our government, then who, and why?

Here the world of internationally biased with the develop of India or that very developing country which is crossing the figure of being back-seaters, raise the ear of those who's money in the shape of loan is feeding the humanity kind, and places the storm-wind of this very thought that they have no right to live till we are working for them as such.

B.B.C. has no editorial opinion of its own. Not to take is an obligation now and a duty to reflect all main views on a given issue.

And this very selection of the news reported involves bias.

**Commercial Line of Communications**

As the world policy of inner and untold soverignty has the mind of all developing country so that very formultive tint of being some be highlighted beating others head on feel of the money which is the day lunch and breakfast of all such developing country. With the thought of today Clinton is nearly supposed to know about America for having Pakistan with keeping power of Nuclear Power Energy, and was papered and even tailored for exposure and for exposure both to just let see India. And now in the matter we should provide to say under current all party persons important joined hands with full force of feeling of country-orientated. The pride of self here went on seat back with the lord question of that 'Party or country' which should be at the first? The country Saviour is the priority of all beings to day.

Nearing inside the facts all others joined hands for all good of this country which frightened one again to that world of market which business the thought and feeling of all developing countries. This if see in India nurtured by the Vajpayee government keeping the further thought that will it be the forthcoming talk for all such concerned that is it. So that after Shri Atal Behari Vajpayee than 'No Bhajpae' Bhajpaies always tucked up to those clinches which are not mainly the objects of the country at least at the points of entering to 21st century. But my point of view is only to keep the press outside make the issues alive at a base to see the country to be seen completely undisturbed.

After India got free and when first parliament was constituted in 1947 Nehru itself never wanted it to be Congress-characterized and his thought to place Patel as first person of the country and then he did formally decide to bring Dr. Shyama Prasad Mukharji as a second persons in his list who was the president of Hindu Mahasabha at that time just not to put any whole in Parliamentary section.

But in the hearts of men of the origin as Hindu it pointed that after independence they have been left behind and the favour of heartial sympathy flewed to those so called person who were parted from the place of their own at the time of partition. But the arising part of todays Hindus and other sects which was never connected with the problem of Media itself and for the press out just because it objectively sensed that after a long struggle got freedom set by the builders of India. So the press totally regulated by the government and the press outside media with even little but with the freedom of press maintained by a hungry man alike ruled over it as a top priority and it was never sensed even to say by the press outside with any clutch of power, does not matter that whoever it may be so on.

This is a very rare point which never seen by this angle openly but it is total under control either with norms and ethics of newspaper and this under current covering upon these topics. The newspaper under any pressure normally carry all kind of contrasts with their given statements. Here they contrasts the statement above using the world "ought to' "may be", "should be" to defuse people to say with statment of how things probably are.

For any press outside a complete impracticality is like perfection: an ideal for which many will strive but none will wholly attain. Even the most respected journalist can only be the sum of his or her beliefs, experience and attitudes, the product of his/her society and culture and upbringing.

I can firmly say that no one can be free from bias, however hard she or he may try to compensate by applying professional of objectivity, for objectivity itself, subjectively apprised, must by nature be an unrelable yardstick.

I even see to see the journalists duty to recognize the inevitability of the bias without ever surrendering to it. Here may be talked about the B.B.C. is world service claims to deal with the problem of personal bias through a combination of professional integrity and an exhaustive system of check the balances.

One told fact that people do have their politics, quite definitely but they are very good at keeping them out of the news. They would never get through any ways, because there are too many checks and balances, too many people asking questions. There is always a dual personality which is said by as a journalist that they are not an observer, this is not their talking of politics, but they just talk about and from both side of the politics to which they are not directly involved. So they are telling people that what is happening outside.

The process of eradicating bias begins by recognizing that every argument has atleast two sides and that truth most probably lies somewhere between them. The journalist must stand back and view and the argument from all sides, before scrupulously drawing out the key points to produce as full, balanced and impartial a picture as possible in the time available.

We find here one another of the Journalist's dilemmas, that there is never enough airtime to point the masterpiece he/she would wish. Even the fullest report of an issue can be at best at a sketch and at worst a caricature of events. That is why Alexander Cockborn has defined the first law of journalism to confirm existing prejudice rather than to contradict it.

The inside media of American broadcasting has a tradition of five commentators: reasoned journalist who tread the margins between factual information and well reasoned opinion. It contains very thin line in between reporting as such and opinion based thoughts. This path was established by some American journalists and was followed by All Indian journalist in the section of press outside as they were little free to talk about, but it did much to haul America out of distractive intorspection an era with its fanatical witch-hunts against public figure with real or imagined links with communism.

I have basically defind that the word common when enters into the section of mars it comes in collective manner as community as such and but when this communitry sets itself in a form of communism it is real danger to society. Society is never so called community. Society gives a socio-ecological for like behavior but community does not concentrated at this point, but it creates a figure of a tested sect which evokes the thought of public of their oriented sect which evokes the thought of public of their oriented sect whether you are put to be bound as in bounded form of a lively insect which needs a sect to be organized by others, and depends upon the teaches of the community Head. When society is never with sectwise combination as to form a gathering. It is well-versed combination of togetherness so on where the difference of cast and community wiped out with other challenges so it contain, almost no clash of thought or opinion which could harm anybody at a crucial time of individual tussel to read out by the Press which works beyond government bothering or less bothered to see at one track.

As the word community is informally used by the press in open side but any kind of media with the control of government or formally regulated by the government like All India Radio, Doordarshan never uses the 'word' community as such even giving the reports of riots. It is but aggressively used in the press outside but which are much prone to yellow journalism like 'Blits' of Kanjias and than after Manorama, from Allahabad, and in so many daily, eveningers. But not in radio and television.

As our press sectioned opened in British India so could not thrown the possiblility of being away with British ideas as the British news tradition tends to shy away from the projection of personality, preferring to aim for the factual approach that permits viewer and listeners to make up their own mind. As times change, press concentrated on print media and gets in focus upon the audio and audio-visual media, with that there are signs that the pendulum may be swinging towards a more personal style of 'telling' rather announcing the news, but in India it still the news is being read by untrained news readers. So this can be seen most clearly where factual reporting crosses over into interpretation and analysis which is often presented in a very personal way by the reporter.

**Journalism Effects on Media**

Another section of press does mean that the campaigning journalism. Here in Press outside not in the inside media, the campaigning, or commited journalism must by necessity be biased journalism, yet it has its place as when you talk about famine either in Ethiopia or in India here, being biased is a firm necessity to file a logical profile siding with the problems containing faminity in world by shaped figure with having margin to fill it with their thought-wise versions.

The reason why that so many magazines fill the market with eager thirst to all about their insidings. But no magazine were such problems to shown with based thought to feel a man's world. Now some of our non government channels provoking this though with the support of this, as 'Purush Kshetra'. It is considered that in all over world as made oriented society, they aptly have no such problems which might be considered as a bias to the section men.

Same with children, and mainly of those children who are poor and are being kept away from all kind of necessities of even a very basics of life and also a need for anyone's livelihood. But it is not such a point to be bias we talk about child labourers who have no right of education, hygiene and other section of need. Here the bias is a necessary action done by press and media, even in aggressive matter if it gives a weightage to their problems and the hopes of getting them benefited.

Although both the points here are "unashamedly emotive" to feed any kind of feministic issues. This bias is a 'weapon' supplied to this feminstic world's up and downs by the press outside, there the press must have the untold full freedom and privilege both for emoting a famine on media hype for the upbringing of this class, I quote here the press officer of U.N.I.C.E.F. (U.K.) for him "It seems though he was no longer merely reporting but actually experiencing something. I feel that it should also be quoted by I.T.N.'s chief editor that in scenes of great tragedy and conflict a reporter has to be touched by what he's seeing. It is not to think that the reports would be as valuable as if one didn't get a feeling of involvement and concern on behalf of the reporter.

For press outside impartiality a must whose strongest test of media impartiality comes at times of international division or external conflict. Here nothing nails colours to the mast more quickly than a good old fashioned war.

The more free press like B.B.C. even of being undercontrolled by the British government as its independence has been challenged at critical times oftenly. So it has principle that had always survived.

The most pressure which have even been under was certain during the wars. The time normally communication are well controlled by the Ministry of Defence and this meant that they effectively as such because the section of Ministry would cut the line of communications with correspondents until or unless the reporter told the lines and agreed to delay stories. On some the reporter or correspondent delayed for as long as 24 hours which the correspondent never think it is anything which would ever agree to again with hindsight.

As remembered at a reading that during the Falkland war, B.B.C. Panorma presenter was removed after presenting a programme which ran an interviews opposing British Military action. These were not the adherents of underground organizations or unhinged or irresponsible fantacies, but with elected members of the British Parliament M.Ps.

In an open press the very responsible kind of reporting is needed, not so called table journalism settled in India by non eithical journalists. So it is possible for the very presence of reporters and camera-crews to create news by making a tense situation more worst. It is a set back of mainly in Indian reporting which may be called a reporting discorder as the reporters are the only spot on lookers what they bring to editor it is normally dispatched to press or printing as they produce with skill of twisting of angles ahead. In crowd the demonstrations have been known to liven up at the first sign of a camera, and there will always be those who see the presence of the media as an essential weapon in their particular propaganda war. It can be difficult to distinguish where the coverage of an incident becomes incitement. So many of the reporters must have been tempted to ginger up the coverage of demonstration by encouraging the crowd to start chanting as they begin their live report.

Another danger in the presence of cameras may be of press or televisions is that they be seen to be seen legitimizing or endorsing what is happening and encouraging that to continue. And as every camera person will know has ever had a good shot laid to waste by someone's converting are yelling then the mere presence of lense can bring out performer in most of us.

The media and outside press is not always welcomed by anyone or every-one when a person is of suspicious identity or the place where there is definite disorder, especially when it is coupled with violence and crime. The presence of a camera or recorder on the streets may be seen as threat by those who fear for identification if the recording or reporter both from press and audio-visual media turn towards authorities.

I still feel sore about whenever and where ever asked question's from the concerned authorities, all replied that you give it in writing and we shall send you the answer, and the answers never answered by those authorities even the very questionnaire from all such departments concerned with. Even if answered it was a waste to listen and quote both. Here it all was covered under the official secrecy which again I would like to define later with a comparative study of both.

Here let me little discuss about the radio with its all sections which prode news-views so, literature and many other things produced in a shape of entertaining people world wide with. It is not in India where radio has two section one commercial and the other one for government regulated one A.I.R. here but no separate commercial radio's are here in some of other countries with standard equipments and with all other features needed for studies any commercial radio stations having a separate complex to make all adverts to meet the challenges of government owned radios which usually has comprehensive mixing desk and adjoining talk studios. These talk studios are very common in countries minus India. These all talk studio has a visual contact with the main studio and it make a programme easier to survive at a point where the main studies are filled with bulk of activities.

The contribution of these studios are for that where the news may be read from the onair studio or a contributions studio. For the former the newsreader hands the technical operator (TO) the carts or tapes and possibly copies of the script. The news reader can then concentrate on the presentation while the T.O. in the audio. In so many other countries newsreaders sometimes operate their own studios with equipment while they are reading the news. This takes place in a small contributions studio, with a simplified control desk, which is sometimes called a news both where audio inserts will usually be on cart. It is good idea for out broadcast system which is much more helpful for getting the news standard better at performance. Here the interviews and reports to the main network station will be sent from the contributions studio.

Some of radio stations serve areas which are too large for the reporters to be able to cover the stories and even get back in time for deadline, or for guests to be willing or able to travel to the station to record an interview.

Recording everything by phone is quick and cheap but at expense of quality. Remote studios are a better solution. These are often small rooms rented in well placed larger buildings such as city hall. They contain a microphone, mixer and possibly a tape deck. The remote studio is connected to the radio station by a studio quality line which is rented from telephone company. Guests can go there to be interviewed and reporters can use them to send reports.

This all is a suggestion for the betterment of the All India news services for more accuracy and promptness to the news service.

Now let me come directly to our All India Radio, which from early in the morning till night at 11 O'clock at night has constant view upon the pulse of listeners which remote senses of people who opt to listen Radio news, Radio talk, Radio interview and all other entertainment programmes hits like Vividh Bharti and other section of this part.

**News Presentation**

Radio news in India any province may not have a hype of sensation like in news of any newspaper as to be in highlighted manner. But the proximity of All India Radio new service is but a most credible punch to listener with faith of being it touched to pointwise division of news with it but only for the public in common.

The reason why told in other countries this medium as a public service broadcasting the practices of which associated with it have changed considerably since the earlier decades of the century. If broadcasting today is defensible as a public service it can only be a service to the public. And yet what the world public means in the context of broadcasting remains remarkably undermined in debates about the social role of radio and television now and in the future. Here we find that either regulated by the government like in India or outside media broadcast with its own broadcast service the broadcasters for their interpretation of public service they normally remained unenlightened.

So where to revalue the broadcasting's social role against its devaluation in arguments that regard to primarily as a form of social control of cultural standardization or of ideological representation. In India even the dominant ideological educational system through the government regulated body as All India Radio has been that the media which is manipulative, audiences are beguiled against there better interests and the involvement and also disinterested role of education is to teach critical awareness of how these manipulations take place almost behind men's back.

Some of the newsreaders normally rewrite their stories just extensively to make certain the style suits their voice the best way to familiar with a story is to write it yourself.

As I am not concerned with the set up of newsreading but have to find out of all good which deal with all good stories of news to be produced. But with suggestion I can say that the newsreader should engage his brain before putting his mouth into gear-think before he speak. After newsreaders have rehearsed the bulletin, they should try to insist for a few minutes piece and quite before the programme to read through again, but it is only for radio broadcast this can be vain hope. In the end the performance is the everything whether in television but in radio there should be well voiced and the newsreader should not be stumbling through an unrehearsed bulleting bursting with up to the minute stories and failing to make sense of it as a very smoothly polished delivery of material that may be ten minutes old but complete sense.

The policy of All India Radio for the news that the essence is to get over what you understand to be the truth of the matter and the essence of that is to completely understand what you are reading before you open your mouth. Provided you understand it so your listener will understand it. One does hear a lot of reading when there is great deal of wrong way stressing and it just shows that the person hasn't comprehended what they are reading as being a newsreader.

So the intelligence in reading is a very important factor, because the listener has only one opportunity to hear the news in what you are saying, he can't turn back the page to read any of the difficult sentence again, as he can with a paper.

In the section of newsreading normally confidence come from experience, from being in command of the bulletin and thoroughly familiar with the material. In experiened newsreaders should spend as much as time as possible reading or re-reading the stories 'aloud' so when they go on air they are on familiar ground. This also highlights phrases which clash and jar, mistakes, unfamiliar names that need a practice, poor sense of punctuation and the sentence that are impossibly long. But all these problems are easily missed by the eye but are likely to be picked up by the voice.

Some newsrooms operate a gate to give a change to compose themselves. This is a bar on new copy being handed to the newsreader later than five or ten minutes before the bulletin. Old hand may scoff at this but they can pick up a pile of scripts and deliver them sight unseen without batting an eye-lid but for the less experienced reader, a gate can made the difference between a smooth performance and wishing the studio floor would open up and swallow you.

(I would like to file here a joke of British Newsreader David Dunhill-who had said that The worst disaster that ever happened to him was when I was smoking during a news bulletin and set his script on fire, I tried waving it about but it only made if frame up more. I got it out some how but it as a bit distracting, I dare say anybody listening attentively will have realized something has gone a bit wrong. I don't think I said anything just carried on British tradition.)

The worst mistake any presenter can make is to swear on air do not even think it, otherwise you will probably say it. The commonest problem is the taped report that fails to appear. The introduction has been read the presenter waiting and nothing. Next swearing a broadcaster's second deadliest sin is dead air. Silent air space is worst in radio. On television the viewers can watch the embarrassed situational expression but what on radio. If an item fails to appear in radio the presenter should apologize and move smartly on the next. But in T.V. the presenter will usually directed what to do by the control room. Up to three seconds of silence is the most that should pass before the newsreader cuts in. No vices often make the mistake for pausing for ten or more seconds in the hope that the technical operator will find the fault and cure it.

The problem can be compounded by confusing the audience with technical jargon like : I am sorry, are the worst to face for audiences. So they must practice that what they are going to say when something goes wrong until it becomes almost a reflect action. When that report eventually does arrive the audience will have forgotten what it is about and presenter should reintroduce if by re-reading or re-paraphrasing the cue. Where readers stumble over the word or a phrase they should judge quickly where to repeat it. If the sense of the item has been lost they the sentence should be repeated. If the mistake is a minor one let it go, chances are that the listeners will forget it where as drawing unnecessary attention to it with an apology will only make it worse.

Newsreaders face few greater threats to their credibility than that corsping on air. Corsping may not be literal occurrence but it can feel much the same. It means to dry up, grind to hault or worse burst out laughing.

These are signs of nervousness and panic, such laughter is seldom, sparked off by genuine humour, it is a psyche's softy valva blowing release tension that has build up inside the reason "Anything incongruous or even slightly amusing can trigger it off. The listener of the radio never like jokes at a time of news, especially at that time the laughter erupts through a serious news item or of a tragic news. Where the professional self control is in danger of collapsing the realization that untimely laughter can bring the untimely end to a carrier and that of substantial part of the audience may write you off as an idiot. Unless you pull yourself together can often have a same salutatory effect as burst sousing with a bucket a icy water.

Self reflected pain is another second line of defence. Some newsspresenters bring their mirth under control by restoring to personal torture, such as digging their nails into the palms of their hands or grinding the toes of foot with the heel of the other. So the key to the confidence that marked out the top-flight professional is the ability to be in command and at the same time relaxed. This can be a tall order under deadline pressure and the spot lights of the studio.

Another problem is that in the news in radio by the presentation of a newsreader that beginners can sometimes literally dry up. Tension removes the moisture in the throat and mouth and it becomes impossible to articulate. A radio news presenter the relaxation helps and a glass of water, sipped slowly to prevent the splutters will usually by sufficient to moisten the lips, mouth and throat.

For a reader a word of warning that drink nothing containing sugar or milk. Hot sweet coffee is out. At the time of reading alcohol should be strictly avoided. Same goes for eating food just before going on air. Any kind of eating bread an butter and its tray particle cause excess saliva and there is always a risk of going in to bulletin with a fit of flatulence.

Tiredness can also ruin otherwise good newsreading. Boadcasters often works in shifts and have to cope up irregular sleep patterns and for early birds and semipermanent fatigue. Weariness can drag down the muscles of the face, put a sign in the voice an extinguish any sparkle. So much of black coffee and without sugar may be one answer limbering up the face by vigorously consorting the lips, checks and mouth may be another. But do not let anyone catch up.

Here I talk about news by editor to be produce which is read by a presenter. A routine task is for a producer is that first get-up, listen to Radio and read popular and quality newspapers, then arrive for work and check a wirecopy. Conference with editor in chief have a conference with editor in chief. To produce draft list of prospects only half may end up in programme. Monitor the A.I.R. news and news to afternoon. One can have something on desk and think the ideas for graphing the news. Discussion with script writers and graphic artists, Allocate stories, Revise running order, Consult editor over possible running order. Meeting with personal involved in programme. Rewise running order give running order to programme director. Look at every story that is to be put on air. Supervise programme transmission in control room. Off the air, this is followed by radio station to proceed further for the news.

About getting programme in the air with planning in well advanced, the task of making if happen on the air falls to the director and the news reports that go to make-up the programme. The news is briefly rehearsed at time before. Aspects of these news preparation bears more than a passing resemblance to that depends largely on late reports still coming in. In the studio the newscaster can hear everything going on the controlroom though the ear-piece. This constant chattering into the car can be a blessing or curse depends upon the newsreader mood and view both.

The opening sentence of the programme the 'bongs' still fall in between as it is rather like having to write a headline in a newspaper is under discipline.

In radio news main sources are the reporter, producer, directors and then the presenters, all have never been more tested then they are today. Now the challenge now facing the programme makers is to push back the frontiers in the most complete way possible by further dismantling the borders between news and current affairs even with national boundaries.

My point to drag the show toward all kind of those hauls which are created with the sensation of newspapers but not in any government regulated form as in All India Radio. It is better for me talk about out All India Radio as a most powerful medium as such. But with the news produced by All India Radio and the news take up by so many other means to serve the purpose of right to information. Right to educate and so much of more to be seen.

I would simply like to compare the news value's facts with television and with the newspaper. So the television story should be a prior certainty pull up the subjects's view points. There is always a book for the reporters either in newspaper or in radio either in television, this is not for engineers but the most news organizations would be happier places if reporters had atleast some idea that how their equipment worked and a little sympathy for the struggles for their hard pressed colleagues who are often more at home in silent contemplation over a soldering iron than attempting to describe in lay person's terms the technical limitations of satellite receiver.

I see that the T.V. reports has to spent many long hours on the road co-operating with an attempting to win the co-operations of colleagues in charge of lighting, sound and camera equipment. A little under standing of how that equipment works will even up the chances in an argument an might save the reporter being blinded by science.

I am picking up a small history of television with this just to locate those very particular from each others. In process I see that world's first true television pictures flickered into life in a solo antic in the autumn of 1925. Where a reluctant office boy by the name of William Tayntor grudgingly accepted half-crown bride to become the first to appear on the small screen. You see it today in vice-versa now brides have been accepted by the media maker to give a break to anyone of the person, which is sometimes good and mostly bad as things happen further as a discreditable shows shown in television and people had to bear it just. They can do anything for this, only to make criticism in their talks and walks. But good in a manner if they select the person and brush them for any virtual appearance which have been probably missed just because of some timebeing's disordered facts as a boy who may be a genius failed in exam's interview because he got nervous and lost his vision to express the way it was wanted to be. Here a mediamaker if tries to pick the talent peeping inside that missing point and just covers it up for the good of the media not for the good of his/her or of his own's.

Further the story process begins with one of Scottish engineer and one time soap manufacturer and even an inventor of the absorbent sock was ready to unveil his new discovery before time with critical gaze of members of Royal Institution of Great Britain.

So we find the first television programme featured a dummy called Bill. The newspaper The Times described the image of the Bill as fainted and often blurred but instead it was recognizable. The experiment was a success.

The first experiment was a success as a Telephony wit vision and television. The breakthrough which made it possible had been made in 1818 with the invention of the photo electric cell, a device which converted light into electric current. The stronger the light the greater the current it produced. If a light can be turned into electricity then the electricity can be turned back into the light, which is one of the basic principles behind television.

Then the invention of amplifier to boost those weak electric signals to the point where they become usable, brought the dream of television closure to reality picture. The development of the way of scanning a picture line by line so each line could be sent by wire to a television receiver. The process was reversed at the other end and the picture reformed line by line into an image of the original. Its original camera divided the picture into thirty lines. The technology has moved on, but the principles remains the same. It is an one of the evidential technical facts of television but as I concern the media as section of press which provides a pressure point to those who are to be touched and through the press have the vision of underlined story material for.

But the press inside the government does not have that eye which cuts the boundaries of those who offence the criminological sociology to find an open story material to feed the public and fill the newspaper with even little controlled by its own ethical norms. But as concerned with media under the governmental regulation they produce news or any kind other programmes.

So little touch with television news is essential to part with the subject. At this I am not going put any technology of the audio video camera but the total clutch hold upon the views and all other programme produced in television or in radio and all it for whom and why so, in what number.

The facts of news is tugged up with the agency blow as it is the weak point of press of both sides where they are totally dependent upon reporters and agencies what they feed up to them. They systemtise the figure of news when brought by the agency or by the reporters of the pass. Whatever information, scoop or so many of clinch reporters but on the desk, the editor is bound to select things in between without any other choices to find more or so. Here television is in a rich terms with having their visualized camera shots of sports taken by them to follow the news so.

**Photo Journalism**

Television where there is free flow in the sense of the popularisation which monks money to high the radio seem a poor relation technologists have had the incentive to come up with new ideas to satisfy the never ending demand for faster news.

Immediate replay means that the camera person can check difficult shots by running them back through the viewfinder and can retake them if need be. There with film he/she will have to wait until the prints come back. A further advantage is that video pictures can be repeated. So the good shots from a report can be used at headlines at the start of the programme, where the film shot can be used only once. The trade off is that video-tape editing is less flexible is difficult to correct mistakes once the reports is finished you can not cut out a sequence or insert an extra short in middle of a report without having to relay all the shots that flow with film you just snip a section out or cut one in.

The technology which is developing too rapidly for there to be any single worldwide standard for television equipment some T.V. companies are sticking to film, while others with more money to lavish have reequipped with electronic news gathering, so a further complication is there are different types of electronic news gathering, all of which makes it possible to speak in any other than generalities. So generally speaking a typical, a typical news crew using film or electronic news gathering would compromise two or three staff, a cameraperson, a recordist, and for shooting indoors or in poor light, a lighting technician.

First the news in happening should be immensely questioned that if it happened then how it happened 'How' is a base line of news performance and 'why' is the backbone of the news but ever followed or I can say it never followed even by the newspapers. So in radio or in before the camera shoot presented by any of the presenter is rarely answered in the manner where 'why' is the 'key' for happened news. The predicted in reason out the factuality of the news. But as these kind of all news handled and taken teleprinters given by all spreaded agencies in India and in the world of few I have already discussed before in earlier part of my book. Normally in every newspaper the news has been sent up by 'Bhasha' in Hindi and then the U.N.I. P.T.I. to send and further follows the news events.

For television clipping up by video camera views and for newspaper the still photographs are the only source of visualized capture for using them to make an happening illustrated.

But this both is never a possibility in radio and but it is first flashed and credible section because of the hard but constructive rules and regulations of a A.I.R. Secondly Television has to clip up the whole show with visualization of Video Camera shoot which needs a bit time factor. So sometimes the camera movement is little back and news a Radio is first flashed as soon. It leads and with very conceptional thought of news as a fact or a truth but when it is blown to A.I.R. by agencies the truth is with them and radio carries it with their tools and machineries to be read and to be listen even.

Some of news reports need only natural background and fore ground sounds which requires the expertise of a recordist. Camera person and recordist may from a close working partnership, often permanently fully assigned together and usually travelling in a company car which has been kitted out to take their equipment. It will also have two way-radio to keep in contact with base.

The reporter may travel to the story with them or meet the crew at the scene. Four in car would be too many and especially with bulky lighting, so that the lighting technician will usually head for the news separately meeting the rest of crew on location.

Some organisations for the all in one approach and go for a higher profile, sending crews out in mini vans bedecked with the television companies name and logo in foreign television not in India's. But in Indian set up the government should be more and more helpful for this because the advantage of travelling separately is it offer the assignments editor greater flexibility. He/she can mix and match reporters and crew who may already be on location. Here the cameraperson is kind of reporter who handles the scene with informative news as they are always work without a reporter to get rush shots back to base. Commentary can be added later after the pictures have been studied. Sometimes a crew will be sent to record material for library shots general views of scene which can be kept on file for later reports.

Some newsoutfits used in these covering which was originally intended for amateur use. Experienced camerapersons will have a well developed news sense of their own and will often take fledging reporters under their wing. But in the end it falls to the reporter to act as the director says where he/she will have to pull together and write the script so should have the last world about the story treatment. However the very shrewd reporters will quickly find that tact and diplomacy are better means of persuasion than dictatorship.

The news camera operators are paid to be artisans rather the artists. There filming is direct and to the point. Long evocative zooms, sweeping pans, and shot filmed at artistic angles may go down well in the movies, but are guaranteed to give an editor apoplexy when it comes to assembling a news report. How do you cut into a pan a zoom and how do you follow a short booking up an interviews left nostril.

But for the T.V. news that the editor wants is a sensible selection of angles and sequences of long shot, medium shot and close-up. So that he/she also wants a minimum of film to sort through. For a news report of about two minutes, there can be no justification for using half an hour of tape.

The best way to be taught is to use the camera like sniper's rifle not machine gun. Every unnecessary shot is a waste of two people's time, the camera operator's and the editors, so every shot is made to count with the aim of filming on a ratio of better them the last where one in a final reports.

As still we carry the system of U.S. news, which in practices is often to do away with the recordist leaving the camera-person to setup and monitor the levels, occasionally aided by the reporter. This approach towards the section of news in T.V. and now has been rejected in Britain which India follows, where a combination of Union insistence and even the quest for its perfection have safeguarded the role of the recordist for the time being. The recordist is generally regarded as a vital part of the team. As well as adjusting and monitoring levels, he/she is traditionally the teams fixer, who the arrangements and get the right doors opened at the right times.

The recordist and reporter usually stick as close as possible to the camera-person. There is more to this than the more clumminess. All these are often linked with cables, which can make the going difficult in a fast moving situation such as a riot.

If the crew is recording film and sound separately, the recordists kit will include a portable reel-to-reel tape recorder. To be certain recorded sounds match the movement of the lips, the recorder will be synchronized with the camera. Where background noise only is recorded the sound track is referred to as wild track just to put a natural sound on film.

The recordist will usually pack with wide selection of microphones, where mikes are susceptible to wind noise, when even a slightest guest across the top can be transformed into roaring hurricane. Outdoors mikes will be protected by a windshield, which is usually made of acoustic fame.

Here the directoral rifle mike is standard kit for location recordings. The recordist can stand or kneel out of vision and the mike will pick up sound from the direction it is pointed across the narrow angle. It can even isolate individuals within a group. The recordist aim has to be good. A couple of degree out and the gun mike will pick-up the wrong person or background noise instead. Another drawback with the gun mike is that with its cover off it can look, little two like its namesake, so it is best avoided in battle zones. See original unless the recordist wants to become a target. The alternatives for interviews out of doors is for the reporter to hold a stick mike with a winshield similar to those used in radio.

## Role of Satellite Communication

Indoors, where wind noise will not be present, a pair of tie-clip or neck mikes (liveliar) are usually favoured. But it all is not a matter of talk of my subject but still as we know that the satellite T.V. began as dream of science fiction writer Arther C. Clarke whose imagination was fired by the war-time rockets used by the Germans which was figured out with a spacecraft the equator of which would keep race with the earth's rotation and appear to be having stationary above the planet's surface. All these could be used as a mirrors to bounce communications signals half way round the world. If this could be achieved the technology would revolutionize broadcasting. From there to now many satellite was launched a giant reflective balloon knows a ECHO. Two years later after a huge leap in technology telstar was put into orbit, relaying black and white television across the globe. From that time many satellites have since followed ringing the world with communications chain sending back colour T.V. pictures, telephone calls, radio transmissions, navigation and whether information and host of other data.

The benefit to satellites have brought television to remote areas where reception would otherwise have been impossible especially regions outside the range of ground-based transmitters and away from T.V. Cabling projects. Here our India is installing more than a sum of 120,000 community viewing sets in villages across the country television for the first time. India's own satellite INSAT IB first was put into orbit in 1983. The scheme is being widened by relaying satellite pictures across the surface using ground based transmitters. Some of 73 per cent of country can now be reached by the T.V. and India's satellite programme is all continuing.

Late (Prime Minister) Mrs. Gandhi said that when INSAT began 'India is economically background today-because we basically missed the industrial revolution. If anyhow we miss what is happening now in the new advances of science, then we haven't got the ghost of a chance of making up for lost time.

# Nine

# Influence of Television in the Society

## Telecast of Programmes

This very saying is again an alive fact of today's set up where to see eagerly India at a world map—the present Prime Minister Mr. Atal Behari Vajpayee, who want India as strong deck in the world politics and see it economically free and very less dependent upon World Bank's banking.

As with a confidence the blast of a nuclear test was hounded the Clinton's mind with the head open. But he dealt it diplomatically. As Clinton knew it but had quiet attitude about the facts. The time before Minister of Defence statement that war food preparations by the scientists need to be appreciated the Vajpayee government, which definitely clicks an intelligent mind that Ministry of Defence at time before thought of getting in handful to see India sound for the warfears. I am leaving this tugging point here and I shall discuss it when I came to compare with all section of press to force those sensitive news for then being tough to make either any banner or any kind of lead story. Here the television is mainly at my view and vision point.

What is going on in our Indian Television as Doordarshan followed by terms of 'Akashwani'. These Hindi names in setting the tyrant tradition to think back that we are going to have same such thing which is definitely going to feed our cultural mindset. With the prompt accuracy of news flow Doordarshan speak off but shows the show of factual vision but as not termed up with the outside press it will be totally rehearsed programme to be shown to them who are only see it from a distant point like Door Ka Darshan. Here the 'News' are a complete exception as they are an adoption of agency set up and are followed by television camera to visualize that which is termed to be an eye-opener to the viewers.

The inquisitive viewers or mainly those kind of people who are aware of around the clock situations.

The programmes of Door Darshan like Ghar Angan for women, Phulwari for children and Chaupal for peasantry section and discussion on health social problems and so many of other hangs. Ballets and some of soap opera like most public touched first serial in Lucknow Door Darshan was 'Bibi Natio Wali' and the same sort of soap opera serial 'Hum Log' written by Shyam Manohar Joshi towards those close cuts which tell about small family fighting but for nothing living as they are totally suppose to live, which is not taken a pride by further generation, seeing mother a dumb women. All these children of the family started seeking there was of life outside world and get confused and away how by the superhead of the family to brought them at one bench.

This all was experimented later on first at one beginning. The only and one 'entertainment' programme was after news ad some other local programmes under theatrical help 'to perform the set and set on that for Door Darshan'. One Thursday it was 'Chitrahar' base on the film music and one Sunday's big and bump attraction was for audience the Hindi films.

Sand uppers are usually short. There static nature can slow down the action and the reporter's memory may not be very good. Memory aids include a clip-board judiously help out of camera. Key words are chalked on the ground, even a portable prompter which can be set up beside the camera. If all such of the techniques would have been followed by our radio or television then all such programmes no more a fascination to people had not been reduced the interest of people as for good one point that the it has not be horrified by other competitor as no other broadcast media is on the front face of All India Radio.

Most of the television sets were purchased just to see a weekly film and enjoy the weekly film music. This phenomena was nothing but the follow up by Vividh Bharti a most popular programme produced by All India Radio. But even after all the only one and first credibility of news broadcasted in under regulated from of the government. With its own norms which entirely dippers with the print media a most circulated media to people with thousands of scattered small and medium kind of news papers all over, with increasing under of literacy. But where the T.V. news camera I again come to that point there the piece to camera may be used at the beginning of an item to set the scene in the middle to act as bridging link two threads of the story and the end as the reporter's way of signing off; T.V.'s equivalent of radio's standard out cue.

But Door Darshan has such a face where it has to face variety of channel introduced in a media market. At least radio is still one of the most powerful media and even most credible. But with its visual illustration Door Darshan eventually gets a kind of popularity.

But the techniques used radio for the news show is another useful trick, when to write the news script and record it on a cassette recorder. Where you can listen to through a concealed ear piece and take your prompt from that.

So if none of these solution is available and there is too much to remember in one take. The commentary may be split over two takes if in television and joined by cutting from a long short to close up. I see at times the reporter may have to voice the entire script on location. This can happen when the deadline is close and film or tapes, depends upon that it is for Door Darshan or for (Akashwani) have to rushed back to the studio. Where voice-overs (VO) are to go over natural sound on film or tape the VO should be made in a quite location such as a hotel room or inside a car. It they are to go over a portion of silent film, then the background sound in the V.O. should closely match the sounds behind the stand upper or other items, to prevent a stop-start effect in the background. This may mean recording the VO in the same location.

Here the full scape planning is a luxury increasingly reserved for the world of T.V. current affairs. This normally differs from news in four respects : Subjects are usually covered in more depth, larger crews are required to put the longer items together, there is more time at their disposal and more detailed planning of coverage is necessary if television's expenseive resources are to be allocated as efficiently as possible.

A researcher will be dispatched in advance to investigate the subject, explore locations arrange interviews and gather back ground material. From the researcher's findings a draft script will be prepared listing the main shots that will make up the programme. This is the treatment. Plans might change later, but the treatment offers a rout map to show where the team is starting from, where it is heading and how it plans to get there.

Producing a treatment gets your ideas out in the open where they can be examined instead of waiting until you start filming to find they do not work. Once they are on paper they can be knocked into shape. Anything that has been left out can be added, sidetracks can be sidestepped and blind allays avoided. You can also see if you have got enough good ideas to sustain a programme.

But here the news crews sometimes dispense with these under pressure of deadlines instead the reporter will return with these under of deadlines, instead the reporter will return with he tape and talk the editor through the footage. Even then the camera person will usually have made same record of his/her work be it only a hastily scrawled note on the videotape box. For longer items like documentary, this information is vital if the team is to keep track of all the material.

Once the shooting is finished an editing script can be produced listing the takes that are to be included in the final programme. T.V. stations lay out their scripts according to house style, but for the sake of clarity, visual and narrative information is usually more separated into two columns. Visual on the left and script on the right. The information in the left hand column tells the director the visuals that will accompany the story. These are placed opposite the point in the narrative where the visuals begin.

For a tell story where only the newsreader appears in vision, his/her name will be given in the column at start of the script. Where the presenter is out of vision "Out of vision" is written visuals used to illustrate a story are marked alongside the script showing it clearly where each begins and end.

The inwords are the first words on the report, which can be referred to make sure the correct report is being played. Supers are the captions and titles which are inserted live. The times given show the time from the start of the report when those supers should be displayed. They will usually be left on screen for a few seconds and faded out.

Graphics and animation these will usually be complied in advance of the transmission and recorded on videotape, his all covers the embarrassment of the production team by giving them the chance to rehearse and correct mistakes off-air.

But the caption information should be kept as brief as possible to avoid overloading the viewer or the screen and should be displayed for long enough to allow even slow readers to take it in.

Unseen by the viewers the back of the set is a coloured backdrop of lurid blue, yellow and green. This colour is switched out autonomically by the vision mixer and replaced with a picture or visual from a second camera. By using the studio set with its bright blue drape can be transformed, for example into an attractive backdrop of graduated wedgehood blue created by a graphic machine. This image can then be replaced with a full frame still or moving shot, of a news story, or supplemented by a windows in the top right or left hand corner showing a picture.

The only problem is when newsreader decides to wear the same colour as the one switched out by chromakey. If the newsreader's tie is a very matching shade, that to will disappear leaving what appears to be a hole punched right through him to the photograph or scene behind. So no self respecting newsreader wants to be seen on air with troops marching across his chest or politicians draped across his midriff, so care it taken to avoid clothing which matches the chromakey colour.

Bright brow eyes may also trigger the effect, but in practice the shade chosen is so unnaturally vivid that the problem of accidental switching seldom occurs.

**Effect of Pictures**

An older alternative which has largely been superseded by electronic picture insertion is back projection, where a slide or moving image is projected from and behind the set on to a translucent screen. One seen can be replaced by another using a second projector.

This is less expensive also but also lesser flexible than the electronic system and requires extra studio space for the projector.

Here the front projection saves mat space but the image is projected into a well bit studio and may appear to be less bright. The lighting also has to be carefully set up to avoid the newsreaders shadow falling across the screen.

Other alternatives are to project television pictures on to a large screen behind these newsreader, or more simply to display pictures on a monitor which is in vision, through this can cause problems with colour balance where chromakey and electronic affects are not available it is possible to create visual effects mechanically using the inlay method.

To produce a wipe, where one picture is wiped off the screen to reveal another these cameras are required camera one views the seen going out on air camera two looks at the second scene while camera three is focused on illuminated ground glass screen. A sheet of cardboard is placed across the scene blocking out of the light. To create the wipe the cardboard is simply pulled across the glass screen, travelling and revealing the light beneath. As the light is revealed, the image in front of the camera three changes from black and white.

The light going into the camera operates an electronic switch activates camera two. As the cardboard begins to move, the output of camera two is displayed on the T.V. alongside that of camera one. Camera two's image occupies the bright area seen by camera three. As the cardboard is pulled across. The image on camera two takes up more of the screen and the effect is one of seen wiping the others off the screen. Cardboard can be made up into many different shapes to provide different wipe and overlay effects.

The camera is mounted on a pedestal and the head can be raised, lowered, tilted or swivelled or panned. A panning handle is used to adjust its position. Fitted to this is the zoom control which is similar to motorcycle twist grip.

The camera may be mounted on a lightweights tripod or heavy weights dolly which can be remote-controlled. Between these two extremes is the pedestal, the camera mounting most commonly used in T.V. studios. It can be operated by one person and is normally adjustable for height. The studio floors are carefully levelled to allow the cameras to move smoothly across them without jumping or bumping on the screen.

Some camera have preset control which allow the operator to select the appropriate short with the zoom lens and programme them into the camera's shot box. Instead of adjusting the lens by hand he/she can then go straight to the shot at the extreme of button.

When a director puts a camera our air an indicator will glow in the viewfinder, and a red cue-light on top of the camera will light up to let the presenter know the camera is live. The camera person can line-up the picture with another by super imposing the picture from the second camera into viewfinder.

Each camera has its own intercom, so the operator can hear and reply to the director's instructions.

Pictures from the different cameras are selected and mixed in the control room. The vision mixer or technical director can cut directly from the camera to another or can use variety wipes, fades and dissolves to gradually change between pictures.

The last section of Television as such I have taken it as in little detail to show the inner vision of the press as media in and out to be seen by audiences, who may or may not judge the thing as whole sum. I draw it as a picture scene as 'Thick padded doors and walls, anything from two to five cameras looking hungrily for something to shoot a flock of technicians waiting behind double thickness glass (some occasion a bullet proof one) for the producer's every word (and even every mistakes).' All this could just as well be a torture chamber as a television studio. So once you know how to do it, directing a studio can become addictive, an exhilarating drug which can stimulate you to a high it takes hours to come down from.

The clean uncluttered lines of the T.V. newscaster's desk and incasing decor of the studio set are as much an illusion as the tasteful graduated blue chromakey backdrops favoured for many newscasters.

Walking into a news studio is like stepping into a barn or factory. It will either be many times smaller than it appears on screen or cavernously large. The first impression is one of disarray and overwhelming untidiness. To the first time visitor, the news studio is a bewildering array of lights and snakes next of cables. Ceilings are high and incredibly cluttered with lamps of all shapes or sizes. The floor is the man-trap of wires and the cameras bristles with flex and book as brutal and uncompromising as ship's engine. Even the set which appears. So swish and urbane on the screen, looks uninviting in day light. The illusion is all in the lights and the tricks of the camera.

The news programme may have its studio or it may share a set with the rest of the T.V. Station.

Sets vary in sophistication. They may have elaborate desks with panelling behind giving the impression of an affluent sitting room, or be incorporated into newsroom itself, presenting a back drop of hustle. Alternatively, the background may be a picture window which appears to be looking out on a local scene, but is in reality a picture projected from a slide. Increasingly, set sophistication is giving way to electronic illusions created in the control room, offering full screen graphics, windowing and chromakey backgrounds. Behind the desk the backdrop may often be nothing more than a set of pointed wooden panels or highly coloured cloth.

Where several programmes use the same studio, sets may be constructed to fit inside each-other, so instead of dismantling one to make way for the next programme, another may simply be placed over it or around it while the boards behind, known as flats, are turned round to reveal surface of a different texture of colour.

On the desk in front of the newscaster but out of view of the cameras, will be a pair of lights! One read, the other green. The red tells the newscaster he/she is an air, and the green is for rehearsals.

Built into the desk will often be a microphone, clock and a monitor to show what is going out on air. A second monitor off camera may show a perview shot of the next item. Plenty of space is left on the desk for scripts.

**Flexibility in Programing**

Besides newscaster may be a hotline for the sub-editor to give instruction live into the programme. This is used only in all emergencies. Another phone sits the desks for conducting live telephone interviews. Instead of a bell which could interrupt broadcasts. It has a light which flashed when a caller is on the line.

A third telephone may be kept behind the in case the newscaster needs to contact the producer. This equipment is duplicated for each newscaster and the assorted clutter on the desktop is concealed from the cameras by a raised lip at the front.

So each news programme will require its own particular array of lights to provide illumination which best suits the camera work used on the programme. When different programmes regularly use the same studio, permanent lighting rigs for each will be kept in place. This results in duplication. But saves having to reset all the lights for each change of programme.

Some lights are floor-mounted. But most are suspended by cables and poles from framework of girders across the ceiling called a light grid. They range in power from a meagre 750 W to searing 10 kW. The lighting director fades them up and down from control panel. In some studios the lights can be programmed to function automatically. Flood lights bring up the overall level of lighting to within the operating range of the cameras, large squire mat fillers provide defuse light to brighten up the studio, while spotlights act as the keys, lighting and modelling the subject. These have 'barn-door' style flaps which can be adjusted to alter the spread of light.

Backlights pick the newscaster out from the background and add sparkle to his/her hair and areas that other lights might have missed, such as the top of shoulders. Additional lamps may be used to illuminate the set and add sparkle to the newscaster's eyes.

A typical T.V. studio will have between two and four cameras mounted on mobile pedestals. Each will have zoom lens which can shift the picture from long shot to big close cup without having to move the camera closer to the scene. Another knob or lever adjusts the focus. The operator sees the picture through a view finder on top of the camera. This displays a black and white picture, even on colour cameras as a monochrome image is clearer and easier to focus.

T.V. news programmes are usually presented from a mixed set, with the newscasters in the same position each might. This means the camerawork is fairly predictable. To streamline the chain of command from director to cameraman, some stations use one or more remote-controlled cameras which are operated from the control room.

The walls of the studio are acoustically treated to eliminate echo and provide a natural sound. Three different types of microphones are commonly used. Newsreaders will usually be fitted with a personal mike which can be dipped to the tie or hung round neck on a cord. This means that if newsreaders turns to one side to conduct a live interview the microphone will move with them and there will be no danger of going off-mike. A desk top mike will usually be in position as a back up.

Where the presenter is likely to move around, a boom microphone will be operated by a sound engineer or the presenter will be fitted with a radio mike. Both these solution do away with problem of trailing cables. The boom mike will either be a microphone on the end of a pole, known as a fishpole, or a more sophisticated sound boom which can stretch up to 6 m and be adjusted for length, height and tilt.

The floor manager a cross between mine artist and racecourse tic tac man. Here with combination of hand signals and gesture he/she acts as the director's tink person and makes sure that everything runs, smoothly on the studio floor. In the run-up to the programme the floor manager sees that all the props and equipment are in place, and during the programme guides the presenters and instructs the studio crew. He/she hears the director's instructions through an ear-piece or headphones and passes them on by means of hand-signals.

Newsreaders never work without a script on the table, though they may seldom to refer to it. Few things look worse than the top of newsreader's heads as they glance down to read the script, and the more professional T.V. stations get around this problem by using prompting devices. The most affective of these are machines like the autocue or teleprompt which display the script on the screen in front of the camera, so the newsreader is always looking straight at the lens.

The script is typed out in large print on a long narrow strip. This is run over a roller in front of a small camera. The picture of the moving script is displayed on a television screen which is reflected on a glass sheet in front of the studio camera. This is invisible to the camera lens which looks right through the glass sheet at the reader.

Correction and last minute changes to the script are made by sticking gumed white strips of paper over the words and the hand writing the changes on tap.

The speed at which the script is run through the machine is regulated by the operator who matches is as closely as possible to the reading speed of the presenter.

The hi-tech alternative is to produce the script on computer and display the computer screen in front of the camera, scripts boards held to one side, and roller prompters on top or to one side of the camera.

The control room captain is the T.V. Director who sits at the centre of the control desk, cueing the cameras and calling the shots from the studio. The red light for action station is the read transmission warning. A bank of monitors dominates the wall in front of the director, displaying a most bewildering variety of pictures than most television showrooms. Each image and sound that makes up a programme all the camera pictures and pre-recorded news reports, slides, graphics and titles, are fed into the control room gallery where the director reigns supreme, deciding when each picture report or caption should go to air.

The transmitter monitor shows what is correctly on air. Another displays the picture the control room is working on. Beside that the next shot is lined up ready to go. A fourth monitor displays a caption to be added to report. Another has a graphic. Three more show what each camera is looking at in the studio. Several more display countdown sequences each tape and telecine machine that has a report standing by ready for transmission. On another is the picture called up from the electronic still store. A black and white monitor repeates the transmitted scene to offer a clear image for checking the focus. Another shows what the network is seen so the director can tell exactly when to opt in and out of network with the programme. And to make sure the station is keeping up with the opposition another monitor reveals what is currently going out on the rival station.

The director tells that the telecine and video and videotape operators to stand by located in a prominent position is a large and accurate clock. In the background the programme sound is being played over the speaker.

Each picture on show can be switched to air. The director has to keep on eye on these and remain in constant verbal contact over the talk back with cameras and crew as well as acting on split second decisions by the producer about the running order of the programme.

Presented with need to have more heads than the one, if only to keep watch on all those monitors, the director on larger T.V. stations forms out a number of responsibilities to other personnel. The Production Assistant (P. A.) or the production secretary keeps one step ahead of the programme. Some scripts are numbered shot-by shot. He/she calls these shots and cues in items on telecine and video-tape (V.T.) allowing five seconds for these machines to pick up speed. The P.A. knows exactly when to cue them because before the programme began he/she worked back in the script and marked every word which fell five second before the Picture was due on air. As soon as that word is uttered by the newscaster, the P.A. cues the machines to roll. Five second later the newscaster complete the cue and the pictures are up to full speed and running.

The P.A. is responsible for copying and distributing scrips and for the timekeeping of the programme. He/she has timings for everything from stories to stills, knows exactly how long the programme should run and can tell from the stopwatch at any given time whether it is running over or under. If the times mismatch items will have to be cut dropped or added in. At sometimes the P.A.'s tasks falls to the assistant director, on others the production assistant directs, and the time keeping is carried out by the production secretary.

Where a script has to be altered, the chief sub-editor will whittle it down or pad it out with extra sentences or lines, carrying out a constant process of fine tuning to make it fit. Prime targets for tinkering are the recap at the end of the bulletin. The chief sub has a telephone link with the newscaster to pass on any emergency instructions.

At the directors command, the vision mixer, (switcher and technical director) fades, or cut from one shot to another, punches up outside-broadcast cameras or plays tricks on the screen with special effects. Where effects are used extensively a second vision mixer may be on hand simply to operate those. While this is happening, a constant check is being made on the circuitry to make sure there are no technical hitches. This is carried out by the technical manager (operation superviser; senior engineer). At the first hint of he/she on the hotline to the engineers in master control. Meanwhile the vision controller is checking only adjusting the quality of all the pictures.

In an adjoining room, with visual contact through a plate glass window, is the second controller, who regulates the sound levels of all the microphones in studio. These used to be kept on the sound effects records and any sound effects records, hence the title grams operator but increasingly effects are being stored either on tape, compact disc, or computer.

From a panel in control room or an adjoining room a lightning director and his/her console operator work the studio lights. The lighting 'plot' may be keyed in to a computer which will operate the lights throughout the programme according to the pre-set plan.

If the programme is introduced by an announcer, he/she will sit in an adjoining announcement both (presentation area).

Personal and their roles will almost certainly differ from station to station.

With so much material to be co-ordinated from many sources, the director and his/her team could not be expected to rely on their memories to guide them through the programme. As much as possible is scripted, though news programmes are fast moving and likely to change as stories come in. Every item will be on a separate page so pieces can he dropped or added as needs to be. Each page of script will include details of camera shots and visuals such as stills and graphics, as well as duration for the item.

Each item and the lead is timed. Here I see ad-libs are mostly discouraged. The programme may opt out of the network to offer regional news or may supply national news to the entire network. Either way, split second timing is essential. On television and unscheduled two second delay can feel like infinity.

**New Concept of Broadcasting**

Each programme will have a running order but with 'eng' making instant updates a possibility complete running orders becoming a something of rarity. More often it will be unfinished and smothered in hand written additions and corrections. A new lead may arrive a five minutes before the programme is due on air, stories may be cut to make way of others, an extra item may have to be included just to make up lime. This is were a short copy story has yet to arrive a blank sheet known as a skeleton in inserted into the script, to be replaced with the story as soon as it is finished.

The producer make decisions about the content of the news Prógram, the director makes those decisions work on air, with news the problem is seldom one of having to fill; script: scripts may have to be edited and shortened even while the programme is going out. The nearest the director may come to rehearsing the show is the prerecording of the title sequence shortly before the programme begins. That the news programme ever gets on air without a mistake seem little short of miraculous to an outlooker. Infact when the mistakes do occur there is always an inquest to find out how and why and to prevent them happening again but, with shrinkings world's news coming in thicker and faster that uncomfortable sense of teetering even closer to the brink can only continue to grow. It is a tribute to the team's professionalism that somehow it never seems to show.

This is all about 'Newspaper' 'Radio' and 'Television', its history base lines of general techniques and the informations as such including our Indian Press Information Bureau has been taken to edge the points which have already been in notices of people in common. Now let me see the press outside and inside both deals with art and culture.

As television in findings are getting on now, and I have already defined as how it contains the content of news. But the news divided and take into stride in all these section is little more difficult especially when talked about the polity and policy to touch the world field and where the press suppose to market the politicians this will also be taken at the end of this book. Here I see the television and radio both deal with cultural commodity in this era. As it works within an economically capitalists economy, but when we have said that about it as I have said that what mainly television delivers is not programs but a kind of semiotic experience. And this is characterized by its openness and polisemy. Television is not a reading or listening process and even is not a quiet and type of do it yourself meaning kit but even not a box of a readymade meanings for sale. Although first of all both radio and television is mostly considered as an entertainment media. So it works within cultural determination is also offers freedoms and the power to evade, modify and challenge these limitations and controls. All texts are polisemy but this polisemy is absolutely central to television's textuality. With this it has a financial economy within which wealth circulates through adds and sponsorship and a cultural economy within which meanings and pleasures circulate and the relationship with them is not that deterministic as some of the theories have proposed. In the financial economy television means the programmes, advertisements, news with discussions and views not textuality. In the television a programme is a commodity first produced and them sold to distributors but in our Doordarshan it is sold to government. So in distribution its role is changeable and then it becomes not a commodity but a producer with his production in whatever ways is a new commodity, the audience which is then in its turn sold as a commodity to advertisers. The very ramifications of this financial economy are fascinating but this is not the topic of my writing. I only want first to concentrate upon cultural economy through radio and television then to discuss all kind of cultural programmes. First talk about the role of financial commodity then the cultural aspects of cultural economy in media. From where the role shifts and under gone by the programme in the financial economy that from commodity to producer is now undergone by the audience, whom I left as a commodity and becomes a producer, but a producer of meanings and pleasures and it, at this moment stops being an audience and becomes different materialization of process that I would like to call it a viewing television.

While in my opinion the metaphor of a cultural economy is a productive one we must not let it blind us to the differences between it and the financial meanings and pleasures do not circulate in the cultural economy in the same way that wealth does in the financial. In the First term there is exchange of money at the point of sale or about the prospects of consumption. Though television appears to be free, however it may actually be paid for. But here the payment has no direct relationship to consumption, people can consume as they wish and what they wish with no thought of what they are able to afford. Watching a serial story, an opera open and a concert or any movie, costs no more than a quiz show or a rerun sitcom. This liberation from economic constraints frees the viewers from the subordinate role in the market economy, that consumer who by definition by more than he or she receives from television programmes. The crucial difference between the television commodity and other material goods in the market-place foregrounds the considerable freedom won by the viewers in the shift from consumer in the financial economy and producer in cultural. Meanings and the pleasures can not be owned or bought and sold in a way that grants in a propriatorial rights over them to some but denies them to others. The basic theory of cultural capital works mainly for one section of the intelligentsia and it similarly to the way that economic capital works only for the business section not for all. Normally it works to maintain power in the hands of the powerful one and advantaged minority whether this kind of power be expressed in economic or cultural terms. We need to add to this notion that of a popular cultural capital that puts culture under constant pressure.

This kind of freedom make the audiences to make socially pertinent meanings and pleasures out of television is essentially considerable. On the other hand the middle class section found purposive meanings that supported the system and placed all the blame upon the failures of the individuals. For them were produced by the socially derived discourses of class, education and economics that they brought to bears upon it.

The scatological versions of the television commercial jingles produced even by school children provide an extreme example of this 'rewriting' process which is itself typical. The most viewers of course do not need to rewrite television to this extant to find pleasurable meanings in it but these example demonstrate that the freedom is there, they are not a distinct form of pervers or abberant viewing but an exaggerated and so an explicit example of the normal process of making meaning and pleasure from television.

This model differs essentially from the underlying political economy stressing the relative autonomy of the cultural economy from the financial to which this political economy traditionally grants considerable, if not totally determinate power. The political economy model is thus enable to progress beyond seeing audience as a commodity or in defining it other than in market terms, those of demographic head counting equally it can not conceive of the text except as the free lunch that catches the audience for the advertisers, of course for television the audience is the main commodity. But political economy can not conceive television audiences as being socially diverse and therefore capable of producing different socially pertinent meanings from the same commodity nor of convincing of these productive activity as pleasurable. Thus it cannot conceive of the cultural commodity as text that requires reading and thus capable as serving the contradictory interest of both the producers in the financial economy and of the viewers in the cultural, it can not conceive of the text as a sight of struggle for the power to make meanings or of the notion that what finally determines the meanings and pleasures provoked by a text is the social situation of the viewers reader, not the interests of the producers and their ideological investment in consumer capitalism. It leads to another crucial factor in the cultural economy which political economy is unable to take into account and that is popular discrimination. Here people choose to make some text popular and some not and this process of choice is essentially a popular one, however hard the industry may try through market research promotion, advertising and scheduling to influence popular choice, its failure rate is enormous. It has thus been forced into producing the television products from which the public is invited to choose. And really does not know which of these products will be chosen as shown now in partial discussion like 'Tol Mol ke Bol' a product from outer T.V. channel but which is never possible in our Doordarshan programme as regulated by the government. As so many questions arc facing kind of progressive critics may now need reversing the rather than asking that how it is the culture industry makes people into commodities that serves its interests, we should now be asking how it is that people can turn the products of the industry into their popular culture and can make them serve their interests through media.

**Television Effect on Social Life**

In television serials the social differences are produced by the social system, but the meanings of these differences are produce by culture, the sense of them has to be produced constantly and reproduced as part of the subjects experience of these differences. A viewer driven meanings made from texts of the production of a television programme and subculturally driven meaning made of social experiences involve the pleasure of producing rather them the subjection of being produced by them, and make it possible to maintain the consciousness of those abrasive, uncomfortable social differences that hegemonic common sense works so hard to smooth over.

Television plays a crucial role in, it though this is produced by the same culture industry and bears within it the lines of hegemonic force it is not by the tactices of the every day. If I cheque to self that social power and power to make meanings that serves the interest of dominant work strategically, that is that the work in a manner of an self-occupying army in massively organized structure of power. But they are not by the tactics of guerrilla warfare plan, but which exploit the particularities and possibilities of each tactical moment. People deal with what they have, and in a heavily bureaucratized and industrialized society of late capitalism, what people have is what is provided for them by the institutions and industries of capitalism. It is though these that the social strategy is put into practice, but its affectivity must not be read simply from its intent or from the strength of the forces ad its disposal. So what we need in a television programme just to investigate that provocative theorizing, is the everyday tactical and therefore pleasurable uses of these cultural resources.

I can say that the links between seniotic power, resistance pleasure and the maintenance of seristive social differences the role of television in this and the part that all this can play in social change are theoritically arguable what I would like to see is the methodologically daunting project of tracing actual instances of these links being made of these process being actualised of the delineation of the multitude of cultural process at work in the different moments of viewing television.

Another big bust of today is racial and religious ideology in today's media, mainly named as 'Racism in Media' or Racism and the Media which touches directly the problem as nothing but an ideology placed upon era-wised society since the media's main sphere of operation is the production and transformation of ideologies. An intervention in the media's construction of race is an intervention in ideology terrain of struggle. Here as I am using the term ideology just to refer to those kind of images, concepts and the premises which provide the frameworks through whicl we represent, interpret and understand and make sense of some aspect of social existence. Language and ideology are not the same linguistic term 'democracy or freedom' can be deployed within different ideological discourses. But language, broadly conceived is by definition the principle medium in which we find different ideological discourses elaborated.

The Three important things are need to be said which is used in Media language about ideology in order to make what follows intelligible. First ideologies do not consists of isolated and separate concepts, but in the articulation of different elements into a distinctive set or chain of meaning. In liberal ideology freedom is connected or articulated with individualism and the free market in socialist ideology freedom is collective condition, dependent on, not counterposed to equality of condition as it is in liberal ideology. The same concept is differently positioned within the logic of different ideological discourse. One of the ways in which ideological struggle take place and ideologies are transformed is by articulating the elements differently. There by producing different meaning, and breaking the chain in which they are currently fixed, and establishing the new articulation.

This breaking of the chain is not of course confined to the head, in takes place through social practice and political struggle. This is a conceptional show in media. Second, ideological statements are made by individuals, but ideologies are not the product of individual consciousness or intentions within ideology.

They normally predate individuals and form part of the determinate social formations and conditions in which individuals are born. We have to 'speak through' the ideologies which are active in our society and which provide us with the means of making sense of social relations and our place in them. The transformations of ideologies is thus a collective process and practice not an individual one. In the productions of television it has been taken for granted as a little boy like playing rough games and little girls however are full of sugar and spice is predicated on a whole set of ideological promises though it seems to be an aphorism which is grounded not in how masculinity and femininity have been historically and culturally constructed in society but in nature itself.

Third ideologies 'work' by constructing for their subjects individual and collective positions of identification and knowledge which allow them to 'utter' ideological truths as if they were there authentic authors. This is not because they emanate from our innermost authentic and unified experience but because we find ourselves mirrored in the positions at the centre of the discourses from which statements we formulate make sense. Thus the subjects can be differently constructed in different ideologies.

An example of this kind of racist ideology with an important distinction to between what we might call overt racism and inferential racism is covered in television in locked mob fighting or in riots. By overt racism I mean those many occasions when open a favourable coverage is given to arguments, than in television, where the regulations of Balance impartiality and naturality operate.

By inferential racism talked in media which I mean those apparently naturalized representations of events and situations relating to race, whether factual or fictional proposition inscribed in them as a set of unquestioned assumptions. These enable racist statements to be formulated without even bridging in to awareness the racists predicates on which the statements are grounded.

Both type of racism are to be found in different combinations in Indian Media. Open or overt racism is of course politically dangerous as well as socially offensive. The open partisanship of sections of the popular press on this front is an extremely serious development. It is not only that they circulate or popularize openly racist's politics and ideas and translate them into a vivid populist vernacular, it is the very fact of such things can now be openly said and advocated which legitimates their public expression and increase the thresholds of the public acceptability of racism. Racism become acceptable and thus not two long after 'true' just common sense what everyone knows and is openly saying. But inferential racism is more widespread and in money ways more insidious, because it is largely invisible even to those who formulate the world in its terms.

It is probably made by a good and honest and liberal broadcaster who hopes to do some good in the world for race relations and who maintain a scrupulous balance and naturally when questioning interviewed for the programme. The programme will with a homely on how if only the extremists on either side would go away normal blacks and whites, or in India Hindu and Muslims, Shia Sunis would better be able to get on with learning to live in harmony together, yet every word or image of such programmes, are impregnated with unconscious racism because they are all predicted on racist premises of this kind. It undermines there professionals by suggesting that they have been partisan that they have supposed to be balanced and impartial. It was an affront to the liberal consensus self image which prevails broadcasting. Both responses were infact founded on the profound misunderstanding that racism is by definition mutually exclusive of the liberal consensus where as in inferential racism, the two can quite easily cohabit, and on the assumption that if the television discourse could be shown to be the racist it must be because individual broadcasters were intentionally and deliberately racist. Infact an ideological discourse does not depend on the conscious intentions of those who formulate statements within it.

Racism has a long and distinguished history in Indian and British culture. It is grounded in the relations of slavery, colonial conquest, economic exploitation and imperialism in which the European races have stood in relation to the 'native people' of the exploited periphery.

Three characteristics provided the discursive and power coordinates of the discourses in which these relations were historically constructed. Their imagery and themes were polarized around fixed relations of subordination and domination. Their stereotypes were grouped around the poles of superior and inferior natural species. Both were displaced from the language of history into the language of nature. Natural physical signs and racial characteristics became the unalternable signifiers of inferiority. Subordinate ethenic groups and classes appeared not as the objects of particulars historical relations. The slave trade European colonisations the active and fast under development of the so called 'underdevelopment' societies but also as given qualities of an inferior breed. Relation secused by economic, political and military domination were transformed and naturalized into an order or rank ascribed by nature. In Britain as considered white mulla to and Black as in India is a four rank of man Brahman. Khatriya, Vaishya and Shudra as nominated division in the society is still an identity, men as they are taken of formation to build a thought of being in the society. As defined in Manusmiriti they are defined with their work sections and even today they all are identified with the same longshot as if they are characterized in all kind of socialistic culture based television serials, telling the story of gain and suffer according to their cast basis thought evoked by the same society. All kind of human stories in all of these newspapers and in television news stories in some of events and all other socio-cultured dramas and where it is a dramatization of the men as superior and inferior of the society, so all these characterisation in all part of the world depend on each other and rising in a proper climax of subordination in which the white holds the highest in Britain and the superior called Brahmans in India hold the highest place.

Often it is forgotten degree to which in the period of slavery and imperialism all popular literature is saturated with these fixed negative attributes of all kind of colonalised races in all other countries but in India it is tribals, scheduled castes and in open view even our all sort of such minorities are not even being today considered with a class of the society except the Parsians but they so suffered without house range of people in the country unlike our most emulgated Muslim class feels it away. I feel they have arised the question like Indian Muslim and the Muslims as a sectwise people.

**Educational Value of Telecasting**

Media took it all up with the regional channels to television and in all kind of regional newspapers. The differences of all such I find them diaries observations and accounts the notebooks and ethnographic record and commentaries of visitors explores. Missionaries and administrators in Africa in India the Far East and the Americans. And if even after something else, the absent but imperialising 'white eye' the unmarked—are made and from which alone they make sense. This is the history of slavery and conquest, written, seen, drawn and also photographed by the such supercast and whites as a winner.

They can not be read and made sense of from any other position. The 'white eye' is always outside the frame—but seeing and positioning each and every thing within it.

Telling the sequences either can be found in early films of the British Raj in India with the sources of endless radio 'reminiscences' and television historical show pieces to day like 'the great Maratha' 'Tipu Sultan' 'Jhansi Ki Rani' 'Dilli' and in legendary shows 'Mahabharat' 'Ramayan' 'Sri Krishna' and with first fiction in serialized with ethics made around the oldest Asian City Varanasi a place of Shiva with great mysteries inside, named as 'Chandrakanta' by Neerja Guleri visualizing it todays story in television. The Chandrakanta was the first book serial upon Indian mistries written by Devki Nandan Khatri from Chaukhamba Varanasi.

Unlike the cast head ethical legend 'Manusmriti' called as at first man or 'Purush' in between two women creating a world with life flowers and tears and side by side Manu defines the rule and regulations of the society with the formation of castes with its divided work culture, which brought about a drastic change in our polity after independence.

This has been even taken an inspiratory part in creating a poetry literature in Hindi in recital from the same old city man Jai Shankar Prasad in his write up 'Kamayani' which was totalatised in form of 'Chhayawadi' Hindi poetry.

Kamayani has ever been a loveliest theme of tablo drama in India theatre like 'Chandra Gupta' and 'Dhruva Swamini' a play write the save written by Jai Shankar Prasad as such.

My point was to point out all about that where it race with concept of dividing humanity in races and how it is dealt with television radio and other press outside and inside both.

But to me assumption of effortless superiority structures every where, when the positioning in the frame the fore—foregrounding of a colonial life mainly touched at tea-time talk on the plantation, the background of native bearers. In the later stages of High Imperialism this discourse poliferates through the new media of popular culture and information, newspapers and journals, cartoons, drawings and advertisements and the popular novel. Recent critics of the literature of imperialism like 'Raja-Ram Ki Kahani' have argued that I simply extend my definition of nineteenth century fiction from one branch of 'serious fiction' to embrace the popular literature of today's. We will find a second, powerful stand of English and Hindi literary imagination to set beside the domestic novel, so called formulized concept of any society as the male-dominated world of adventure, which takes the empire rather than the 'middle march' as its own microcosm.

Once I read about a graduate student working on construction of race in popular literature and culture at the end of the Nineteenth century coming to me in despair-racism was so ubiquitous and at the same time it is unconscious, simply assumed to be the case that it was impossible to get any critical purchase on it. In this period the very idea of adventure became synonymous with the demonstration of the moral, social and physical mastery of the colonizers.

In the modern media this concept of adventure one of the principle categories of modern entertainment like old fictionary adventure 'Chandrakanta Santati' as I referred earlier moved straight off, the printed page into the literature of crime, espionage, children's books and the great Hollywood extravaganzas and so many in comics. There with recurring persistance as they all still remains. Many of these older versions have had their edge some what blunted by the time. They have been distanced from us apparently by our superior wisdom and liberalism. But they still reappear on television screen especially in the form of old movies of course continue to be made. But I can easily grasp their recurring resonance better if we all identify the base images of the grammar of race.

See it here in a foreign movie for an example the familiar slave figure, dependable, loving in very simple and childlike way the devoted 'Mummy' with the rolling eyes or the faithful field-hand or retainer attached devoted to his master. The best known extravagance of all-Gone with the Wind contains rich variants of both. The slave figure is by no means any way limited to films and programmes about slavery. In Indian concept of this kind of selling and purchasing concepts are defined in old history where in Vedic period when 'Kauri' as a means of currency was used. But in case, one cow was sold in one kauri, a man was sold in one an half kauri and a women as costliest was sold in two kauri as at a consumer's need and it is the start of an instantial slavery era like all other countries.

So the some Indians and many of Asians have come on to the screen on this kind of disguise. A deep unconscious ambivalence pervades this stereotype. Devoted and childlike, the 'slavey' is also unreliable, unpredictable and also undependable capable of turning nasty or of plotting in a treacherous way, secretive, cuming throat one's his or her Master's or Mistress's back is turned inexplicably given to running in the bush at the slightest opportunity. Where the whites can never be shown that this childish singleton Sambo is not mocking his master's white manner behind his hand even when giving an exaggerated caricature of white refinement.

Another base image of these 'native'. The good side is portrayed in turns of cheating and further out, savagery and popular culture is still full today of countless savage and restless natives and sound tracks constantly repeat the threatening of drumming in there might the hint of primitive rites and cult. Cannibals whirling derrishes Indian Tribesman, garishly got up are constantly threatening to over-run the screen. They are likely to appear at any moment out of the darkness to decapitate the beautiful heroine, just kidnap the children burn the encampment or threatening to boil, cook and eat the innocent explorer or colonical administrator and his lady-wife as well it shown in the Films and television everyday, but it is not the story of any radio or newspapers as such. This is a typical thought—In newspaper it is being described when a self in two party races or riots among them—or even sometimes. The film should 'native' always moves as an anonymous collective mass-in tribes or hoardes. And against them is always counterposed the isolated white figure 'Out there' confronting his destiny or shouldering his burden in the 'heart' of darkness displaying coolness under fire and an unshakable authority, exerting mastery over the rebellious natives or quelling the threaten uprising with a single glance of a steel blue eyes.

A third variant is that of the 'Clown' or 'entertainer'. This captures the innate humour as well as physical grace of the licensed entertainer putting on show for the others. It is never quite clear whether we are laughing with or at this figure, admiring the physical and rhythmic grace, the open expressivity and emotionality of the entertainer or put off-by the 'clown's' stupidity.

One of the most noticeable fact is about all these images is there deep ambivatence—the double vision of white eye through which they are seen. The primitive nobility of the aging tribesman or chief and natives rhythem's grace, always contain both a nostalgia for an innocence last forever to the civilized, and the threat of civilization being over-run or undermined by the recurrence of savagery, which is always lurking, just below the surface or by an untutored sexuality, threatening to 'breakout'. Both are aspects, the good and the bad side of primitivism. In these images primitivism is defined by the fixed proximity of such people to Nature.

It all this so far away as we sometimes appose from the representation of race which fill the screens today? These particular versions may have faded. But there traces are still to be observed reworked in many of the modern and updated images. And though they may appear to carry a different meaning, they are often still constructed on a very ancient grammar. Today's restless native hordes are still alive and well and living as guerilla armies and freedom fighters in the Angola, Zimbabwe and the Namibian 'bush'. Blacks are still the most frightening, cunning and a sort of glamorous crooks. This all is televised in so many movies and serials in television.

The image of a racial brand is on the television sets not or never in radio either in any newspaper. In Hindi films a character like 'Mugambe' and so many dances all displayed in film mainly a chorus are shown with hooing shrouds with the tribals, who are black and bushy in look all the time teasing a princess like girl on the stage. But on the otherside in today's beauty contest, the same black own once considered as 'slave girl' now are getting to be special admiration in beauty moving on stage in sqinned gown and supported by a white corceus line.

Black man, black tribal and white man, superior and inferior man all are the subject or media outside vision to be seen and dealt in manner it even clinches to day at the differentials of the races, but with the effect of mind you language.

After that one more aspect is introduced with their subject of serials and play's and then movies is 'Adventure' just after race, or it is the world which is encountered by rape, without being confronted with racism of the perspective in use of this word power. And after this subject it is entertainment. The most prompt word which is conned with media. In our Indian television there is strong counterposition between serious, so the informational television which we watch because it is good and also presentable and pleasurable both. And the purest from of entertainment television is in a comedy. By its definition television is a full licensed workers and disconnected from the seriousness with no danger it is all good and clean fun for media in Hindi mainly. In the area of fun and pleasure it is always forbidden to pose a serious question. Partly because it seems paritatical and it also destroys the pleasure of switch registers. Yet the race is one of the most significant than mainly shown is media literature or the literature in media described. Some of the thing always defended on good anti racist grounds the appearances of black alongside whites in situation of comedies, it is argued will help to naturalized and normalise. Their presence in any society and no doubt in some examples it does function in this way but if you examine these all kind of fun occasion which are more closely, you will often find as we did in our two programmes that the comedies do not simply include high and low, but they are all about the 'race'. That is the same old categories of racially defined characteristics and qualities and the same relations of high and low, superior and inferior, provide the pivots on which the joks actually turn. The tension point which moves and motivate the situations comedies in television shows the comic register in which they are set, however, protects and defends viewers from acknowledging their incipient racism. It creates disvowal.

# Ten

# Development of Programmes in Mass Media

## Role of Sensational News

This is even more so with the television stand up comics who is repertoire in recent years had come to be dominated in about equal parts by the racist jokes. It is sometime said again in their defence that it must be a sign of inferiors acceptability.

Two other erenas relates to the harder end of television production news and current affairs. This is all the places where race is constructed as problem and the sight of conflict and debate. There have good examples of programme where blacks have not exclusively appeared as the source of the 'problem' and also where they have not been exclusively saddled with being the aggressive agent in conflict in television and our Door Darshan programmes. But in general tendencies of running a programme in this area is to see low and inferiors to see the mere facts of their existence in numbers as just constituting a problem for so called high society problem. Where they normally appear as law breaker, prone to crimes as 'trouble' as the collective events of civil disaster or disorders.

In the numerous incidents where black communities have reacted to racist provocation, or the police harassment and provocation the Media have tended to assume that right lay on the side of the law and have fallen into language of 'riot' and the 'race' 'warfare' in visual media. In all such questions the All India Radio has nothing to do except the covering to new occurred at the place of riot only but in other section of media it feels such kind of existing stereotypes and prejudices. The precipitating conditions of conflict are usually absent. They are either missing or introduced so late in the process of signification that they fail to dislodge the dominant definition of these events. So they testify once again to the main disruptive nature of blacks and Asian people as such. The analysis of the media coverage of any country or place provider the media with the authoritative definition of the event. All these in turn shaped and focused what the media reported and how it explained and what transpired. In taking their one from these authoritative sources the media reproduced and account of the event which with certain significant exceptions translated the contact between racism and anti-racism into a contest between, Asians and Non-Asian, the context between two kinds of 'extremism' and so called 'fascism'. Think as a left and right alike.

At the moment our country is mainly suffering with these two problem in first in Punjab with exremism Kashmir with terrorisms and Fascism at every trade sector. But this all is selective or turned vision with a vengeance.

Sometimes just as a good example that how the real causes of racial conflict can be absorbed and transformed by the frame work which media employ can be found in the nationwide coverage of on the day following the events. The two interlocking framework of explanation governed this programme. First come to fascism which is dealt with media had the effect of downgrading to the problems at the centre of the south-hall affair the growth and growing legitimacy of the extreme right and its blatantly provocative anti black politics of the street and the racism and brutality of the police even in always in news on Television, Radio and in Newspaper. Both issue has to be forced on to the agenda of media by a militant and organized protest. Most of the press reports of the South hall were so obsessed with the embroidering the lurid details of roaming hoarders of coloured youths chasing young whites with a carving knife a touch straight out of sanders of the River though a so far uncorroborated that they may failed even to mention them the death of Blair Peach at an intensive power. This is selective and tunnel vision with a vengeance.

A good example of how the real causes of racial conflict can be absorbed and transformed by the framework by the media amply can be found in the nationwide coverage of south section even in India with day to day. Following events as I see the first conflict is seen in conspiratorial terms of far left against the extreme right in any kind of any league against the nation and to the national fronts.

This is the classic logic of the television where the medium identify itself with the moderate, consensual, middle-road average viewer and sets off in contrast extremism on both sides which it then equates with each other. In particular exercise, 'balance', fascism and antifascism are represented as the same both equally bad because the middle way enshrines the 'Common God' the 'most need of today' under all circumstances. This balancing exercise provided an opportunity for national front to gain access to the screen to help set the terms of the debate and so spread his smears across the television screen under the freedom of airwaves.

Let a thought go to the same tale-talk as I have already discussed earlier as for a man in common unlike the cartoon of R.K. Laxman's figure out a 'single poor person' tooking with scratched head to all the 'going' and from that community then to communism and then to the communistic sense of the give to us through Marxism. The various sorts of communist, raving with Marxists and others which assorted left-wing cranks, and for further to be handled by the press outside as good-knot-about stuff, and then after a linking passage—southern lookout to the second framework, rioting our Asians vs all other big countries monopolitechnicalities towards India, and all is watched television with certainty of longing thought of the country identity, so throwing a brick to begin a rioting situation in India at the moment should well caught with 'reason why' by the television if possible further. So I say to all to the press even if underpaid that don't start making those arguments, as a growth of an organized political 'racism' and the circumstances which have precipitated it were simply not visible to nationwide as an alternative way setting up the problems.

Sometime in media and as I say that the press outside tries to illustrate the inferential logic at work in another area of programming, even in B.B.C's 'great debate' on the immigration. It is even not necessary to start with any kind of preconceived notions least, and of all speculation as to the personal view on race by the broadcasters involved, though one can't expect either the B.B.C. hierarchy or to believe that. But in outside press in India have now simply to look at the pragrammes with one set of questions in mind. But at my viewpoint here is a problem defined as the problem of immigration as in India after 1947 and onwards which made any Indian to feel it that our country does have a real 'problem of immigration' in terms of open outside press and media, ever raised but in a hidden mannerism.

I would like to open it up and leave to you all that 'what is it'. How it is defined and constructed through the media and press programme? What kind of logic governs to its definition? And where does that logic derive from? I believe for me at least answers are clear. The problem of immigration is that in foreign countries it is the problems of black and whites and in our country it is two religions overlapping with forceful emulgation done by the outside visitors and then by the temptation to poor and weakend sections of the society which could get a boost from the press outside just for siding the origins of older wings of country to thrash a brain holder to pamper those logs who are big in counts not in intellectuality or in any cultural set-up who can be taken in stride which breaks the integrity of the country and disturbs the unity of self. And a feeling of and for the immigrants to 'send them home' is the only tough teach to the society and the main concept of 'racist logic'. It comes from a chain of reasoning whose representative in all respectable public debate and in person on the occasion to day might be a forceful agenda for the press outside and for media world.

Where everytime presenter wanted to define the base line of the programmes which shoulder this 'racist' vision thought and others should also feel it about as the press or media representing it. Everytime it strayed for from the logic to question and underlying premises.

So it certainly does not follow the old fenetive line to agree with that kind of government which seeks security in democratic set up by exploiting the sensitivity of people to divide them into 'races', 'castes', 'creed' and 'religions' as a matter to hoard the party and defuse the country.

But the bias on this should be of a kind favour when 'others' and 'envious' 'neighbour's take priorer part in all kind of problem in our country not holding the job of their own developments.

Here press might be pressing to hang the organs working against the country feeling no matter who ever it may be.

If a party leads any Mr. Such and such say that they know nothing about it or to do with the problem of 'race' or say absolutely nothing about the views on race and immigration' is a false say this I can claim. And here we should not make any judgement on such leaders view which are irrelevant to argument.

**Communication Gap**

If the press and the media function in a systematically racist manner it is not because they are run and organized exclusively by active racists! as this is a category mistake. This would be equivalent to saying that you could change the character of the capitalists state by replacing its personnel. Where as the media like the state have a structure, a set of practices which are not reducible to the individuals who staff them. What defines how the media functions is mainly the result of a set complex where one can not avoid the bias even if he/ she wants it or not? So often the role of an outside press is a contradictory, social relation, not the personal inclinations of the members of the press. The main sign fact cause is not that they just produce like the problem of Hindi and Punjabi , tour the place a terrorist of Punjab and 'rival racing' of Hindu and Sikh as indifferent identity was nothing and even 'no problem' but it was pampered by the press outside like Jagjeet Singh Arora and so many literature written all by the Punjabi writers writing in Hindu and so the press elaborated the problem of Hindi and Punjabi to Hindu and Sikh just to sensitivise the media hype.

Before the birth of Bangladesh, I see Punjab and West Bengal and then Kashmir the target of oriented to a specification of verbal thought tugged up in common man to revolt against their own country, could be very easily now be assessed to all of us that who is behind? And who is pampering and for what, I think so with an envious touch of not seeing India at all happy and 'one country' in with no division again after Pakistan and Bangladesh.

The racist Baluch Pathan's as Nazis in Germany they all surpass the action of Nazis as it occupied in. Europe and the one parallel army of Punjabis also made an indulgence in atrocities which mainly in heinousness which could surpass the same brutal action in Punjab itself. Press outside has always made it a day to day sensations that point where country is at a biggest damage and people in common are terrorized, children are kidnapped, women are molested and so much of the government money is spent to control the situations.

So I see here the press under the government do think of constructive work and give a boost towards the country but one of the minus point to when even after that get the transfers as punishment for holding a good job to the country they feel to be shaken with thoughts like that if they would have been accepted the terms gold at that time instead of being scraching head under government polices, where they are not even inspired or even warded with good shot of upper boost work even so they feel oppressed for even being a country oriented feeling person. This was narrated by one of the fellow person of All India Radio.

The government media like All India Radio stations stepped at the most sensitive places and which are the main target point of opposite country hitting constantly at our country feeling here these government machinery is first taken into charge to get to be attacked, and just by hitting it as they are proving that they are quancured the country.

During the first Pakistan war, radio stations filled with war awareness simply made the other section confused where Colonal Niazi failed with brain hammering, when our radio station was bombed, it was a fake attempt and Pakistan had to surrender India. And the boost should go to our All India Radio Station wing to hold that courage to conceal that brain. But after in all other sensitive area all the centres of Government of India was a hit point by all other enemy neighbouring.

I am not depress with thought but see insight that if nor the press inside and neither press outside are at a balance towards the country feeling, how will it be any way possible for the person like who is most uncommonly touching both end to bring them at a pace for country's good and went to raise a debate on that of the same situation where we all need to balance if prepare it retain our independence.

These type of problems are suffered to all the countries

which are mainly Islamic oriented. And with oil revolution the flow of money turned this sect in Tijarati Violence with money and flesh of Indian poor humanity. The 'race' complex haunted hear as the black and white in beyond Asia. So I am not going to in details but to say at the time of as even I feel as I heard from my father in at my childhood, like he used to tell the stories of past and present unlike all other legendary stories as heard by him only before sleep which is new like 'jewels' in my hand and mind filled up with so many memories of his versions toward the country.

The only big fight for keeping tunnel vision that we need another big war for retaining our freedom. The problem is not of our country good but all the such of countries where Islam is a prime religious conception with a subtle ideology and feeding back the terms on self-supplement. I remember an article of Hindi giant 'Nirala' who wrote about the relationships of Hindu Muslim, that the Hindu can change his religion for his/her muslim lover or beloved but not a muslim even if he/she think such the section of community or the race as such never permit it to them for it.

But it was questioned by a Sheikh of Arab Emirate's that we have no crime rate like your India and if we bring girls from there, we marry them. But our media to disclose such original facts to raise these questions over today in free India.

Why 50 years, press is not pressing such point instead elaborating them to the level of Punjab, West Bengal and Kashmir. The answer comes after independence the feeling of journalism as a missionary job has been switched off. And it turned in to brokership in between suffer and those of being the cause of it.

Here the press inside under the government regulations have no such as interests, even Prasar Bharti also has given a privilege to the artist, writers and all other intellectualities concerned with Radio television and the press and magazines under government.

So the paper which are so called anti-established are the only media source of underground development in term of keeping a constant danger on the heads of their own. But I shall discuss it all later on as now the point is to talk about the race tussel dealt by the press outside and mainly in the television.

So what is significant is not that they produce a racist ideology from some of the single minded ideology and unified conceptions of the world, but that they so powerfully constrained, spoken by a particular set of ideological discourses the power of this discourse its capacity to constrain a very great variety of individuals and racist, anti-racist, liberals, radicals, conservatives, anarchists, those who know-nothing, and the silent majoritarians.

**After Freedom**

All is being faced by Indian as we are not being able to cope-up with the pain of partitions and terms of riots Punjabi Muslims, Bengali-Muslims and Indian-Muslims, Pakistani-Muslims outside Muslims, then Hindus divided in Brahman, Khatriya, Vaishya and Sudra after that thousands of communities which are the results of caste and creed emulgation in during wars and attacks and after that the unawareness and short sighted views of our leaders. As in my opinion I still seek no cause of declaring partition it only as hurried unbalanced quest for reign of our that time leaders, which made them to decide it and leaders who could not deal with 'Jhiman's whim of not being ruled by Hindus, was a false concept as he himself got unsheltered in Pakistan even being a builder of Pakistan.

In fact our country needed purely an Indian built Prime Minister not the Nehru and not even Jinnah as our all hastied decisions made it a 'now question mark upon' and it should need a rethink when we are celebrating our 50th Anniversary in a free India. The question mark is again on focusing the media as where is that press which keeps a hard eye upon the country goings as Mr. Atal Behari Vajpayee asked to press just the third day of his Prime Ministership. Even I wrote in one of my editorial articles when to raise a debate as that the voters wants in democracy and what the press, presses at this point.

But before that I would like to say that the partition of the 'races' in 1947 clinched into the minds of people who really never wanted this kind of freedom and but to say that all the press men could not raise any voice against this, when they were spreading news of riots, killing, bloodshed and so much lights on new ministry, leader, but almost no news of that nucleus for which partition was made possible, on which ground it was stated, and probably group of Hindus could assert the further situation as

R.S.S. was formed and one side on the 15th August when Union Jack was made down and our Tiranga was raised in air, a single person with very few of the followers flagged a saffron colour flag early in the morning at 5 O'clock two hour earlier to Tiranga hosting and the man was non other than Nathuram Godse and 4 newspaper of a very small kind only flashed the news of this and they were stated to prison in just free India, but for what and also by whom as Nehru was quite aware at the time of forming new ministry is just free India, that it should not be Congresstarian so he gave an important post and force both to Dr. Shyama Prasad Mukarji the president of Hindu Mahashabha.

So again about the credibility of the press outside in India however has a tough time about discourse of the problem television was true, despite the hurt feeling of particular individuals and demonstrably so. The premise on which, the 'Great Immigration Debate' is built and the chain of reasoning it predicated was or is a definitely a 'racist' one. The evidence for this is in what was said and how it was formulated to people and how be sensed that about and how the argument unfolded. If you establish the topic as the numbers of race fights are getting high to higher day by day and even the problem is breeding to fast, the opposition is often oblige and even constrained to argument that these numbers connected with riot, crimes, disabilities in the society are really not as high as they are one way represented by our Press outside which really has a responsibility to solve the problem of nation and society not to discreet it like dead body as nation is an alive fact of truths.

But briefly it can be said that this view is always opposed to the first priority but it is also imprisoned by the same logic of the 'race' and number game in the society or in the country, where the tug of war established by the press, the numbers are divided in creeds and communities and the cast just to cast the vote in party political polity in the country's policy. And chase of the press outside runs behind to gain the games of their life uplifting to gain and win the circulation of newspaper owed by their 'Maliks'. Is it not true to say that who and why produces such kind of utter hurts disturbances in the country.

But the activists, liberals—antiracists, even indeed raging

revolutionaries are in contribution 'freely', to this media debate and indeed are often to do so, and not to let the case go by default, without breaking even for a moment the chain of assumption which holds the racist proposition in place. However changing the terms of the argument questioning the assumptions which holds the racist proposition in place. However, changing the terms of the argument questioning the assumptions and starting the points, which breaking the logic, this is a quite different, longer and more and more difficult task as I find to say about. Now I again come to that section where I left time before talking about the race war setting Bangladesh a close up to the leader what they did and the press how it followed further.

**Aspiration in the Society**

As I feel no bias against but the fear of 'race' acceptance in mind made our leaders horrified and stunned that whom they fought the battle of freedom thus could India may be free. But here I see that Nehru wanted congress as anti alive joint of polity of India ruling with and above who may stand at one platform with him to rule a very free-India. Here also a 'racial concept' was there in his mind, he touched the heat of such of broken communities for ensuring them to give an upliftment of there and conceived theory of old Indian cast system of all four castes and an extravaganza to those who are at the moment feel insecure in India counted as 'minority' in political language and took the society as new patternology and all it was provocated by the press outside who found the no mission India self politics introduced by the Congress. Now the newspaper and radio are followed by the strategies of government, which can be taken as press inside but speaking outside for the government. And not even that post independent as many of journalist already smelling the power further turned into politician. As all others lost their mission which was still needed for retaining freedom.

In the same section I would like to quote Mahatma Gandhi launched 'Harijan', with this a story comes out a depressed section which really needed an upliftment, and later the word 'Harijan' pinched a punch upon the self identity of those who placed themselves in the society, disliked to be called Harijan, the claim was against Gandhi as they say that our community does have better work culture survive in the society they do not like to be back bencher or may not liked to be called with name which displaces their own 'self respect'.

Even I say 'naming' any 'race' and separate them from the commoners in the society, is real question to be think upon as today B.S.P. leader stated that we are prepared to force the world of power on our own. Politicizing Harijan a schedule sect in the new organized society did really could turn in to a big bang of vote cast point when I look that all of our Indian political scenario has been based up upon the Muslim and Dalit votes, and now both section has understood of their being so far. Here the press has taken the 'racism' in their own stride to think of those tunnels under which our front seat of politics is laid down. So 'Harijan' naming race of depressive unit of India was and even is a question mark?

Now let me come to a narration as a whole to our broadcast and television with the follow up to a commercial entertainment, cinema is overwhelmingly a narrative fiction medium non-fiction films have always had a precious place in the commercial cinema and nowadays they are practically non-existent. Broadcast television on the other hand carries long amounts of non-fiction, news, documentaries, announcements, weather forecast and various kinds of segments that are purely televisionlised narration would have to give pride of place to this division of television products between fiction and non-fiction, where as the classical narrative model and basically fiction model, basically fiction model still underlies our assumptions about the entertain film, it would seem that no such generalized conception of television narration would be possible. In fact, this does not seem to be a case, quite the reverse, the non-fiction and fiction modes of exposition of meaning seem to have converged within T.V. under the impulsion of the characteristic broadcast T.V. forms of the segment and the series and the pervasive sense of the T.V. image as live. This has produced a distinctive regime of fictional narration on T.V. which owes much to its non-fictional models. After all, the first true use of the open ended series format would seem to be the news bulletin, endlessly, updating events and never synthesizing them.

The mode of narration of T.V. does not have to be divided into two distinct models one appropriate to fiction, the other to non-fiction. Instead one model seems to be enough, a model that is capable of inflection by fictional or non-fictional concerns. This explains the case that television has long since have producing the programmes that are ambiguous in their status, the documentary drama, or the drama documentary forms that seem to have existed in the late 1950 in Indian and even in B.B.C. The divisions between fiction and non-fiction exists at another level to that of narration. They are chiefly concern with the origin of material used in the programme.

It depends on the conception of the broadcast output and that of segment following, segment and segments which by no means always have any .connection between them. It depends on the counterpart to this segmental process, the programme series with its distinctive forms of repetition and fovoured forms of problematic. It depends on the conception of television as a casual domestic form, watched without great intensity or continuity of attention. If assumes the ideology of television as a medium which transmits events as they happen even though especially in Britain this is virtually never the case. It is worth repeating in this connection that although the overwhelming mass of television output is recorded it still carries a different sense of imidiacy from the cinematic image.

**Impact of Film on Television**

Broadcast T.V. is capable of adopting a filmic mode of a narration as a kind of borrowing from an already established medium. This will almost always be announced as such by the form of the television movie or by the designation of the programme as a prestige cultural event. This tends to men that the programme will not so much have been made a film as made within a cinematic mode of narration. In this sense T.V. acknowledge certain inferiority to cinema. Cinema for T.V. means the culturally respectable the artistic text. The designation film for a T.V. transmission indicates that this transmission is to be viewed despite T.V., it is not to be segmented, interruptions in terms of advertisements breaks or viewer attention at home or to keep be kept to a minimum. The film transmission on T.V. will then proceed to construct a more cinematic narration. The vast majority of such events indeed are cinema films which have already been exhibited in a cinematic context. Cinema is currently not capable of a similar borrowing of broadcast T.V. forms., however the collective exhibition of T.V. material is still a novelty or an aberration.

Cinema narration has a strong internal dynamic, a movement from an initial equilibrium that is disrupted towards a new harmony that is the end of the fiction. Broadcast television narration has a more dispersed narrational form, it is extensive rather than sequential. Its characteristic mode is not one of final closure or totalising vision, rather it offers a continuous refiguration of events. Like the news bulletin series, the broadcast television narrative is open ended, providing a continuous update, a perpetual return to the present. Since closure and finality is not a central feature of T.V. narration, it follows that the hermatic nature of the cinema narrative with its patterns of repetation and novelty is also absent. Repetition in the T.V. narrative occurs at the level of the series, formats are repeated, situations returns week after week. And each time there is novelty. The characters of the situational comedy encounter a new dilemma, the documentary reveals a new problem, the news gives us a fresh strike, a new government, another earthquake, a first panda born in captivity.

Television news itself works very hard at strategies to win our taste and trust both. It scorns the crude editorializing of newspapers presentational techniques which suggests natural and balance. Whether audience actually accepts the television's presentations of itself depends very much on what beliefs, experience and information they bring to what they are shown. In his sample, some people clearly accepted the television account. But others adapted parts of the massages and change the key elements of news with its meanings. As for example some believed that the strike was mostly a violent figure just because what they had seen on television and blamed the police for provoking the trouble. they could be quiet aware that television news has not explained the origin of the violence in this way. The disfunction between what they had seen and what they believed was explained by saying television only showed violence from minors not police.

In such an example what is finally believed results from news images being interpreted through beliefs about both the police and television.

Mainly the process by which people understand a television massage depends in parts, on this beliefs which they bring to it and crucially and how these beliefs are utilized. There were cases among amongst the groups where people had a critic of television latent beliefs. They stated at first that they thought picketing was mostly violent and then moved away from this position as they began to comment on the nature of television as a medium, with its tendency to select and to focus on the sensational news. For the instance, if a happening in the country is being stated by the ruling party as a matter of credit but the other side the opposite party contempts it otherwise manner just because of no reason it will not be definitely a sensation of the new. But when the ruling party handles those terms and conditions which was to be challenged in protest the ruling party government as they could any how able to know all about, and the opposite party is not able to state any word against, it is a polical polity with no news but a silent new—no show of television, no radio racial, it is only covered in the newspaper with this opening thought. In these case, the exercise itself seems to have provided the stimulus for the emergence of this view. But it is important that the belief about picketing had in sense rested with them until they were pressed to just explain it.

Here the fictional stories and series, too repeats a basic problematic situation week after week, like the news and current affair, series and situation comedy, the crime drama and hospital series all turn to stability of the basic dilemma at the end of the week's episode. There is no development across the series. The serial makes along show narrative movement toward the conclusion, but often the conclusion is tentative or incidental. The situation which provides the study core is state of permanent semipermanent relationships between a stable and but antagonistic group of character, which is most fully development in the situation comedy. As in Doordarshan "Dekh Bhai Dekh" or 'Yehi hai Zindagi" and then the crime drama like 'Ahat', 'Mohandas B.A. L.L.B.' so may others than the hospital series all return to the stability of the basic dilemma at the ends of the week episode.

There is development at tall across series, the serial marks a long slow narrative movements today and towards a conclusion, but often this conclusion is a tentative one or incidental. The situation that provides the study core is a state of permanent of semipermanent relationship between a stable but antagonistic group of characters. This is mostly or fully development in the situation comedy. As I see stepole of son may well hate each other and they also love each other, and a repeated threat of the said character to leave the father never a serious one. In any play this situation is exactly the dilemma that situation comedy deals with, it normally repeats and represent the so on conflicting forces or emotions that can never be resolved. Hence the series situated highly suited to present a particular state vision of the family and of work relations. What is particularly marked about the situation series is the characters lose all the memory of previous weeks incidents which the television never learn.

But here of course the film were not made to be interrupted accept the interval in this way, as films are the most powerful media of expressive communication but it should be discussed later on. But in television people register who watch it still register some of these items as 'interruptions'. I remember first noticing the problem while watching films it not Indian as some of them have no sense of acts but to those British commercial television. For even an institution as wholeheartedly, commercial in production and distribution of the cinema, it had been really but possible but indeed normal as remained to watch a film as a whole in an undisturbed sequence. All films were made and distributed in this way though the inclusion of supporting some of the films and short features in a package with appropriate intervals for an advertising and for the planned selling of refreshment began to develop the cinema towards the new kind of flow. Waiting the some films on commercial television made the new situation quite evident, we are normally given some 20 or 25,minutes of the film, some of commercial gain, and so on to steadily a decreasing length of the film with commercials between them or even them between the commercials, since by this time it is assumed that we are interested and will watch the film till to the end. Yet even this has not prepared me for the characteristic American sequence.

Suppose on night in Miami or in Kashmir, may give a thought of producing 'Roza' or 'Bombay' or even a kind of such, but outside India is dazed from a week on an Atlantic liner, so I for the subject I started watching a film and at first I had some difficulty in adjusting to a much greater frequency of commercial 'breaks'. Yet I feel this was a minor problem compared to what eventually happened so on. But I feel as media expression the films were not made to be 'interrupted' this way. But this flow is planned not only in itself, but an early stage in all original television production for commercial systems. Indeed most commercial television 'programmes' are made from the planing stage with this real sequence in mind. In quite short plays there is a rationalise division into 'acts'. In features there is similar rationalised division into 'parts'. But the effect goes deeper these is characteristics kind of opening sequence meant to excite interest, which is an effect a kind of trailer for itself. Unlike an American television and Indian television has also picked up from that after two or three minutes, this is succeeded by commercials. The techniques has an early precedent in the dumbshow was the play or the seen may be an Victorian theatre on any of the Indian legendry cinema. I mean say that here what followed as a dumbshow was the play or the scene may be an Victorian theatre on any of the Indian legendry cinema. I mean to say that here what followed as a dumbshow was the play or the seen. Here what follows is apparently quite unconnected material. It is then not surprising that so many of these opening moments are violent bizarre, the interest aroused must be strong enough to initiate the expectation of sequence. Thus the quality of the external sequence becomes a mode of definition of an internal method.

At whatever stage of development this process has reached and it is still highly variable between different broadcasting systems it can still be residually seen as "interruption" of a 'programme'. Indeed it is often important to see it as this both for one's own true sense of place and events and as a matter of reasonable concern in broadcasting policy. Yet it may be even more important to see the true process as flow, the replacement of a programme series of timed sequential units by a flow series of differently related units in which the timing, though a real, is undeclared and in which the real internal organization is something other than the declared organization.

This meant to say in a long story is that the 'press outside' where it affects on the film to tell or not to tell is the matter of concern in the press policy, just as all other medium of press films are also a telling media, it is not only entertaining figure but a vision of society, history and also if in India Puran, Mahabharta and Ramayana all are the subject of cinema and television serials. Few more categorisation like I see, there is a further specialisation and predominantly musical programmes are briefly characterised, by wavelength, as 'rock', 'country', 'classical', 'nostalgic' and so on. In one sense this can be traced as a development of programming, extentions of the service have brought further degrees of rationalism and specialisations.

Be such kind of development can also be seen, and in my view needs to be seen in quite other ways. There has been significant shift from the concept of sequence as programming to the concept of sequence as flow. Yet this is difficult to see because the older concept of programming the temporal sequence within which mix and proportion and balance operate, is still active and still to some extent real.

Leaving it here I again come to the press and its main section of news which is dealt in credibility of news and also it has been said that the reader's, audience's believe to the news is only criteria to judge things concerned with news is the landmark of newspaper, radio and television. As we all know that the press and television sometimes accuse of selectivity in their reporting. The sheer scale of the events meant that there were many stories and of different types and the incidences which could potentially be highlighted. It is important to grasp the magnitude of the events in order to see how such process of selection can work. As we see that political and economic events which surrounded the strik resulted in conflict on a scale which had been unknown for many years. The police had a pivotal role in this and were seen as directly antagonistic to the strike by those who were pursuing it. But it is a relentless focus on these by television and the press accompanied by the comments on escalation and the "new records" which establishes for many of the audience, the belief of the news is that of violence was a persistent feature of most picketing. As there was a remarkable unanimity of belief amongst the groups in this sample about what had actually been shown. As I find in general sample about 98 per cent believed that most picketing which they had seen on television news was violent. And the remaining percentage either were unsure or believed that the picketing was 'shown' as 'an in timidatery' rather than physically violent. But perhaps what is most remarkable is the number of people who believed that these television images represented the everyday reality of picketing. There was occasionally a fear expressed of even going near a picket line because of the high levels of physical fighting which were believed to be going on. As the source of all such beliefs overwhelmingly given as television and the press with the emphasis on T.V. because of its immediate and more dramatic quality. Some people also, indictated how there attitudes had altered as a result of what they had seen. For example one of the secretaries in the solicitors office as in Bombay wrote that someones opinion of the police had improved because of the saying as one do not realise what they have to put up with. So for the news some clear elements and which are key points of belief were being provided by the media. But it would be completely wrong to see people as being totally dependent on such massages, as if they are siinply empty vessels which are being filled up by news may be at 9 or at 10.

To except and believe what is seen on television is as much a cultural act as the rejection of it. Both conditions, the acceptance and the rejection are conditioned on the beliefs, history and experience. As for a high degree of trust in the B.B.C. and also in All India Radio for example might result from a knowledge of it history and it peculiar role in British society as an authoritative 'national' voice.

In the matter of seeing and believing the most credible sense of news is mostly seen in one case as sample where the acceptance of the television message was underlined by indirect experience. I must say that the people there had a very 'them' and 'us' sort of talk analysis. This had led him to accept the television portrayal of picketing. This was most obvious in the case of people who had been at picket lines, whether police pickets all other observes.

I see in general sample almost 44 per cent believed that picketing was mostly peaceful and when it comes by giving reasons about these based their belief on the experience of knowing or having met policemen or minors. And his effect of such experience could traverse class and political culture.

The second major reason for doubting television news is the basic comparison of it with all other sources of information such as the quality and local press or any 'alternative' current affairs programmes and radio. About sixty per cent of the general sample made such comparisons. There comments were sometime linked to remarks on tendency of television to exaggerate and focus on violence to the exclusion of other events. In the general sample 16 per cent of the people made this criticism and gave it as reason or rejecting the news presentation. This is a relatively low proportion given that it is sometimes thought that beliefs about the tendency of media to exaggerate are generally held in the population. It might in fact be that they are. But what is significant about this result is that even where such beliefs existed they were not always used to discount what was seen in the news. It was also noteworthy that where people relied only on this criticism to this criticism to reject the news account, there was a tendency to estimate the level of violence as being very high.

The criticism of televisions as a medium and the comparison of it will all other accounts were made by people with varied political views. Bill there was another strand of criticism which saw the focus on violence as a conscious attempt to denigrate any case.

This view points of the news has been criticised by the trade unionist as they have commented that the media has picked out the violence so as to get the majority of people against the owners. Union leader have criticised some more aspects like of news presentation, such as a 'big thing' that was made some of being knocked over and the focus on violence instead of support groups.

**Radio and T.V.: Images for Viewers**

There was a strong belief amongst them that news in television take one side view not the cause in a generalized manner, but in a bias shot of camera.

The assessment of what was in the news most could also be affected by direct involvement or I can say that a close sympathy with the dispute. Generally people are cynical to view the media and many saw the news emphasis on the breakdown of the strike as an evidence of bias, against one side view. As to the mob one side is shown in public retuning as coming back to work is more a better to be shown in television. But the images were clearly also very significant in their own memories, because of what they represented in terms of the failure of the news. This was very apparent in the case of the print media workers who get involve with the problems and then they make the news of it which is never possible in radio or television where the news comes from and in television it is televised in camera shot it is only that which is seen only in front but they can never cope-up with that which cause the news base. Radio and television never have a clear correspondent in between these two dimension. Some respondents made clear distinction in between.

New with views of experts and, its pro and against opinions both have taken a part of making news at one pace. But wherever we see the thing on show of a television or even broadcasted in words uttered both are normally but even properly well rehearsed before the stage or before the broadcast.

As I feel to say that in the following of the news the reporter must see the basic cause of the news as he is the key person who sends the news to newspaper and agencies and local correspondent pick the news for radio sometimes.

Under the section of the press outside I take even the advertising as a most powerful medium of expression. I am not going in the section of that advertising, which is the backbone of media to be run financially so in the first place I sees the press out side and inside both is bound to feel a clutch of advertisement which pays a good perk to survive and to rotate the cycle and circulation both in connection to run a newspaper or an entertainment programme or in television,then the sponsorship of the programme made for audience and to listeners but they have to bear it sometimes those advertisements as they don't want to disturb in between the programme or news.

Normally A.I.R. and T.V. both carry news very seriously

even newspaper but for the financial liveliness they have to see it in a favoured slap just to carry on what and where they see or find it to be. Advertisements from the government section and from the Industries to launch their products and carry it on the page or the places in radio and television as it is decided by the programme and the news editor is to decide it where and how it should be placed as such.

In the first place let me say that the advertising is an industry which wields a considerable power within Eastern and Western capitalist society. But to say that it is tied in more directly to economic structure than any other section press or in media forms being linked into the chain of marketing practices which function to sustain the flow of goods on which the economic system depends. It also exerts the economic force upon the Mass Media structure themselves.

I feel that it acts mainly as a 'connected subsidy system' to whose demands the mass media must be responsive. A whole consideration of its relations of the production, therefore must deal not only with its internal process but with influence it exerts at this level upon the media system as a whole. Secondly advertising has often been seen within its cultural theory in which it has become so all persuasive. The high class people always keep away from their self advertising so they considered that any type of advertising is an 'inferior job' and some of declared it as a 'minority job' and also termed it as a minority culture.

And the Marxists pervades where it is a persuasive culture which was similarly argued as 'mass civilization' and under it the advertising is a culture industry. Again by the snobbish society 'advertising' epitomized as the exploitation of the cheap response which characterised contemporary word as I used it earlier 'mass civilisation' it has also been subsidized as a cultural media or the 'ideological' media which turned its culture into 'assembly line' whose standardise products it furnishes with 'well rehearsed' artificial differences in politics. For the contemporary theories too advertising function in the embamatic way.

It was argued as it invade 'every thing' and both public space and private space and the separation between them disappear to be replaced by great screens on which are reflected atoms, particle, molecules in motions in the era of hyper reality. I canside that for these all theorists, advertising functions are the key reference point rather than an object of sustained study in advertising.

Further I see the parts of marketing industry, advertising has conducted its own audience research. Now this marketing research has at times being closely identified with audience research produced within the mass communication tradition, by the critics it was termed the "dominant parading" of American media-sociology, makes this attack on their traditions.

As we know that it is no secret that the mass communication research descends directly from the development of sophisticated marking techniques, the theory of 'effects' was first developed for the direct, explicit of broadcasters and advertisers, and continues to be used mostly in those circles to grow more and much sophisticated there.

The conclusion that by its complecity by its advertising industry. Our Indian the Media sociology has functioned to legitimize a mid century capitalism is one echoed from elsewhere within the critical tradition of media research. It was considered with the thought approached though advanced imperilically grounded and scientific was predicted on a very specific set of political and ideological presuppositions. These presuppositions however were not put to the test within the theory but it was perfectly framed and underpinned as a set of unexamined postulates. Thus in the section of press or media advertising has become a ground on which opposing traditions of audience research may be fought out.

Finally its links with process of consumption means that advertising is caught up in wider arguments about the power of audiences and consumers to resist and meaning and pleasure produced by the powerful person which is an assertion of a semi autonomous cultural economy and which operates in parallel to the political economy and even in which the consumers rather that producers are empowered involves a view of shopping as considered or to be taken as an oppositional act, who's guerillas are mainly termed and seen in women, or they are the women, always cause advertising to fail accept their appearances, so there is much advertising but so much advertising only because it can never finally succeed in its tasks, those of containing social diversity within the needs of capitalism and of reducing the relative autonomy of the cultural economy from the financial. Advertising is crucial to both economic functioning of capitalism and a form of 'social communication' offering as a new ways of understanding overselves. At the point advertising is categories as 'consumers' rather than the users offering in response to real human needs the problems of death, loneliness, frustrations the need of identity and respect the illusory satisfaction provided by the consumption of material goods. In advertising 'magic systems' these goods identified with human values and desires in orders to obscure the 'real sources' of satisfaction whose discovery would involve radical change in our way of life. So the media has to make a choice in between capitalism and the socialism a man as an audience a listener with perfect consideration he is a man as a user of all advertised goods.

First the allocation of advertising finance between media influences the overall shape of any country's media industry which make ad-documentary and media films so on changing trends in advertising allocation within media sectors influenced the character of each medium causing for an example the political imbalance of the press and the overwhelming orientation of women's magazines towards the young middle class reader. And finally a need to respond to advertising pressures produces highly conservative television and commercial radio schedules and a popular press which dipoliticised.

In the media or the press outside the determinations exerted by the advertising industry is very less coherent and more contradictory and advertisement itself were are polisomic, than is often supposed. Finally she argues that readers responses can be read off neither from the economic interests of the advertisers nor from the advertising text itself. Meanings, may be radically alerted and realigned in accorded with usage. What is needed is analysis which recognises as well as the complex forces of production and the varieties of advertisement from which they produce.

The reason why it's argued that the need for relationship and human meaning appropriated by advertising is one that if only it was not diverted could radically change the society in which we live. The main analysis in media that how advertisement work which draws on samioties, its psychoanalysis constitutes an engagement in a sort of running battle, with advertising a battle waged in order to make that change possible. The extract reproduced here outlines the argument that as sign systems, advertisements are parasitic, appropriating, existing symbolic systems and there associated—cultural values as their referent system. Thus I see the 'ads' use distinctions existing in social mythologies to create distinctions between products.

The press analysis of the use of hands in advertisements continues the argument that ads not only reflect but also help to construct the ideological structures and frameworks in our society. All the hands in the section of out side press are always gendered in advertisement and through her analysis of specific examples which explored the meanings of 'masculinity' and 'femininity' constructed through these representations.

In connection of press outside the advertisement has become a 'critical tool' just to run a newspaper to hold the radio or the advertisements in television, as such. It is evidenced by young people's decodings and the pleasures generated by the increasingly sophisticated cultural form of advertising may be used to subvert and fragment existing networks of power knowledge.

On discussing about the consumer culture in and the press and media where the advertisements for the consumers are but to market them the label only press stands as such. There the press is the only conclusion to feed the people for there search of things which in market is being meant for them. But for this there is a double danger and also an illusion of freedom. While the sphere of consumption is indeed that in which many will seek to express their sense of freedom and their personal power as it remains the case that in the sense of personal identity which is created by others and marked aggressively and also seductively. Secondly the emphasis on consumption as the sphere of individual empowerment ignores the material realities of a society whose unequal distribution of wealth disenfranchises millions from this sphere of freedom.

Thus the media and mass communication both are under

one sect of free press to solve the financial phenomena of the world defined as media world so on.

But one more point to be seen as a mean to handle the situation of that platform where advertising if not succeeded so taking its hundred years development is a much more necessity to carry it on for open and outside press to hold the formation of newspaper and to carry circulation as well as soon.

**Commercial Communication: Advertising**

I see that here the advertisement has developed from the simple announcement of shopkeepers and the persuasive arts of a few marginal dealers into a major part of capitalist and business organisation. This is important enough but the place of advertising in society goes far beyond this commercial context. It is no doubt an increasingly a source of finance for a whole range of general communication to be extent that in 1960 when our press has started highlighting the ads is various manners which was almost a master payee to the press outside including the advertisements of government section also with its policy to hold and communicate to the people as such and All India Radio itself is a big consumer of adds in it with numerous kind of highly ways to go on and our majority television service and almost all over newspaper as I said and periodicals could not even exist without the 'ads' fortune in the last forty years and now at an increasing rates it has passed the frontier of the selling of goods and services and also has become involved in the teaching of social and personal values. It is also rapidly interesting the world politics. In a sense advertising is also the official art of modern capitalist society it is mainly what we put up in our streets and use to fill up the half of our newspapers and magazines and it commands the services of perhaps the largest body of writers and artists with their attendant managers and advisers in the whole of society.

Since I find that it is an actual social stands of advertising, we shall only understand it with any adequacy if we can develop a kind of total analysis in which the economic, social and cultural facts are visibly related. So I may find it that taking advertising as a major form of a modern social communication that can understand our society itself in a new ways.

It is often said now a days that our society is too materialist and that advertising reflects this we are in the phase of relatively rapid distribution of what are called 'consumer goods' and advertising with its emphasis on bringing the good things of life is taken as central for this reason but it seems to me that in the respect our society is quite evidently not materialist enough, and rather this paradoxically is the result of failure in society means and its values and ideals.

The most impossible to look at modern advertising without realising that the material object being sold is never enough this indeed is the crucial cultural quality of its modern forms. If we were not really but sensirely materialist, in that part of our living in which we use things we should find most advertising to be in an insane or some how crazy irrelevance. I can say that beer would he enough for us, without the additional promise that in drinking it we show ourselves to be manly, young in heart or neighbourly. So as washing machine would be useful machine to wash clothes rather than an indication that we are forward looking or an object of envy to our neighbours. But if these association sell beer through press and media and also washing machines, as some of the evidence suggests, it is clear that we have a cultural pattern in which the objects are not enough but must be validated, if only in fantasy by association with the social and personal meaning, which in different cultural pattern might be more directly available. The short description of the pattern we have 'magis' a highly organised and professional system of magical inducements satisfactions, functionally very similar to magical system in those similar societies but rather strangely co-existent with a highly developed scientific technology.

So I find this kind of contradiction is of the greatest importance in any analysis of modern capitalist society. The coming of large scale of industrial production necessarily raised critical problems of social organisation which in many fields we are still only struggling to solve. In the production of goods for the personal use, the critical problem posed by the factory of advanced machines was that of organisation of the market. The modern factory requires not only smooth and steady distributive channels but also definite indications demands without which the expensive processes of capitalisation and equipment would be too great to risk. The historical choice posted by the development of industrial production is between the different form of advertisements and planning which fill the press section and the electronic media with full of illustrative ads, in the society and in the central places so on. In our own century the choice has been and remains between some form of socialism and a new form of capitalism. Though the press our modern advertisement taking on its distinctive features is in just this economic phase is one of the most important of these devices and it is perfectly true to say that modern capitalism could not function without it.

Even though the essence of capitalism could not function is that the basic means of production are not socially but privately owned and the decisions about productions are therefore in the hands of a groups occupying a minority position in the society and in no direct way responsible to it. So obviously since the capitalist wishes to be successful he is influenced in his decision by what other members of the society needs. But here people are influenced by consideration of industrial convenience and likely profit and his decisions tend to be balanced of these varying factors. The challenge of socialism still very powerful elsewhere but in India it is deeply confused by political errors is essentialy that decisions about production should be in hands of the society as a whole in the sense that control of the means of the production is made part of the general system of decisions which the society as a whole creates. The conflict between the capitalism and socialism is now commonly seen in terms of competition in productive efficiency and I have no doubt to say that much our future history of 'press' even on the world scale will determined by the results of our competition. Yet the conflict is really much deeper than this and also a conflict between different approaches to and forms of socialism. The fundamental choice that emerges in the problem set to us by modern industrial production, in the problems set to used modern industrial production in between man as consumer as user. The system of organised magic which is modern advertising is primarily important as functioned obscuring of this choice.

In the section of press and electronic media one more point

to come up as a force of young people indulged in 'art trade' doing for outside press, as models graphics designers and they take it as a remote to sense their carrier in this section of press. As I see that art in the section of press is such for which young girls and boys are forced to do at school, then the pressure of art galleries, theatres and concert halls which are covered by the press.

An interesting T.V. commercial made by some of an agency shown on channel in it every Sundays with advertising services to potential marketing design makers. The advert opens with a shot of most modern young man in stylish flat watching television. At the commercial break he get up and goes to make a cup of tea or to do anything and for the moment the camera focuses on the empty chair and the complete abandoned T.V. set. Then it cuts to the kitchen but you see still hear the noise of the ads coming from the unwatched television. The young man returns to his chair with his cup of tea just as the commercial break ends. And here over the final frame a voice-over informs us that there more than 400 commercials on T.V. everyday. What's so special about the person concern he can simply select it. But it enquires about the potentials of the ad as there should man or women or who to do more with these.

As the same we see the press release from the state, the film confronts the views with the question of whether or not people pay attention to commercial breaks. As the same time it conveys the another message. It represents young people as discriminating and hard to reach and suggests that they are likely to ignore all but the most challenging and entertaining commercials. The view of young people is one which is increasingly prevalent among advertisers and their clients frequently expressed to us in interview. Articles in trade magazines which is research conducted by advertising agencies, about the advertisement themselves and a spate of recent conferences organised for marketeers about the difficulties of targeting and persuading contemporary youth are further evidences of this kind of growing preoccupation.

# Eleven

# Growth of Advertisement

**As Development So Commercial Advertisement**

I see all over in press magazine, radio television the world of advertising to day a concerned is regularly expressed about how to reach and suggests that they are all likely to ignore all but the most challenging and entertaining commercials. This view a young people is one which is increasingly prevalent among advertisers and their clients and ways very frequently expressed to us in interview. As I see within the world of interview today concerned is regularly expressed about how to reach young people and how to persuade and gratify them given what is referred to in trade as their high level of television literacy so that the clues may be picked up and covert messages quicker.

But in commercial columns of the press I see the vision of traditionality to enforce the business through press ads. Politics is dealt in international sides of the news imparts conducted by the press soon and the human stories picked by the reporters from all side of press and published in newspapers are another attraction on to people whom concern. But it is all the concerning matter of outside press with the third sense and three dimension stories of those pressing points where it clinches owner both.

The way our advertising and consumership is both overlapped open the press, it is difficult to say, which is the key reason to hold the economy of the press so on for more than we realise. Here in the matter a large scale of efforts are being made so often with impressive success just to channel our habits of purchasing and the decisions, made and the thought process which is taught by the press itself. I feel to say that one of the most influential thinkers of left in this sphere advertising in an inherent aspect of consumer capitalism and its pursuits of profits is capable not only of convincing us to buy, but of creating false need of indoctrinating us into social conformity and thus ultimately of suppressing political opposition. More recently the commentators of both Left and Right who have been preoccupied by what they consider be a decline in moral standards as well as more academic analysts of advertising have been concerned to establish the effects of a constant diet of television programmes and the commercials, particularly on young viewers who are considered to be the most risk of being a corrupted and duped by entreaties to buy.

Here the talk of the subject for these soap opera used in television and the radios could be said is totally constituted as a sort of ideal person may be father, mother or any kind of relation, who normally shown to be possess a greater knowledge and wisdom than all her children, whose sympathy is large enough to encompass the conflicting claims of her family as she identifies with them all and who has no demand or claims on her own, as she identifies with no one character exclusively. Here in media the connection of melodrama and mother is an old one. This kind of concept is all over the world as such. Even in literature if any book bring the female readers to see the world as one extended family, the world would be vastly improved.

So I feel that it is important to recognize that soap-operas serve to affirm the privacy of the family not by presenting an ideal family but by portraying a family in the constant turmoil and appealing to be understanding and tolerant of the many evils which go on within that family as we in Swabhiman, or in Sansar-but Sansar portrays the faith upon God. But in other sense there the spectator mother, identifying with each character intern, is made to see the large picture and extend her sympathy to both the sinner and the victim. She is thus in a position to forgive all. As a rule only those issues which canbe tolerated and ultimately pardoned are introduced on soap opera. This list includes carrier of woman, premarital and extamarital sex, alcoholism divorce, mental and even physical cruelty. Soap operas contrary to many people's conception of them are not conservative but liberal and the mother is the liberal par excellence. Constantly presenting her with the many sidedness of any question which, by never reaching to any conclusion, nowadays soap-opera undermine them her capacity to form unambiguous judgements.

These remarks must be qualified. If the soap-operas keep us caring about everyone if they refuse to allow us to condemn any of the character and actions until all evidences is in and of course there is never one of that character whom we are allowed to hate unreservedly: the villains, the negative image of the spectators idea self. Although much of the suffering on soap opera is presented as unavoidable the surplus suffering is often the fault of the villaines who tries to make thing happen and control events better than the subject spectator can. The vilianess might very possibly be a mother trying to manipulate her children's lives or ruin their marriages or perhaps she is a woman avenging herself oil her husbands family because it has never fully accepted her.

This character can not be dismissed as easily as many critics seem to think the extreme delight viewers apparently take in despising the vilainess testifies to the enormous amount of energy involved in spectators repression and to her resentment at being constituted as an egoless receptable for the suffering of other. The vilians embodies the spill off fury which in the word like 'truly' a famine, women's particular, as we have seen, the spectator has the satisfaction or seeing men suffer the same anxieties and guilt that women usually experience and seeing them receive similar kind of punishment for their transgressions. But that anger is naturalised at every moment in that it is the special object of the spectators heart-throat hatred. The spectator encouraged to sympathise with almost everyone, can went her frustration on the one character who refuses to accept her own powerlessness, who is unashamedly self-seeking. Women's anger is directed at women's anger and an eternal cycle is created.

And yet if the villains never succeed, then she obviously never permanently fail either. When as occasionally happens a villains reforms, a new one immediately supplant her. Generally, however, a popular villains will remain true to her character for most or all of the soap operas thrive they present a continual reminder that women's anger is alive, if not exactly so well.

The soap opera stimulates women's desire for connectedness is through the constant, claustrophobic use of closeup shots, often only the audience in television is privileged to witness the character's expression, which are complex in and intricately, coded, signifying triumph, bitterness, 'despair' confusion and thus the entire register, in fact soap operas contrast sharply with other popular forms aimed at masculine visual pleasure, which is often centered on the fragmentation and fetishization of the female body. In the most popular feminine visual art, it is easy to forget that characters even so insistently are close-ups of faces employed. Here one of the media critic remarks— "A face in close-up is what before the age of film only a lover or a mother ever saw." Soap operas in media appear to be the one visual art which activates the gaze of the mother, but in order to provoke anxiety about the welfare of others, close- ups provide the spectator with training in reading other people in being sensitive to their feelings at any given moment.

So the central television experiences are so profoundly decentering experience as this opera as an art of being centre off. As soap opera even provide the training in the art of being off centre that must be said that to note in passing that it is probably no exident that the nightmare of soap opera its spin-offs and imitators are flourishing in a period of economic crisis and rising unemployment. Where the housewife of course is in one sense she is perpetually employed her work like a soap opera, is never done. Moreover as I have said her duties are split among a variety of domestic and familial tasks and her television programmes keep her from desiring a focused existence by involving her in the pleasure of fragmented life. Although daytime commercials and soap operas are both set overwhelmingly within the home, the views of the home seem antithetical for the chief concerns of commercials precisely the ones soap operas censor out. The saggy diapers yellow wax build up, and carpet smells making up the world of day time television ads are rejected by soap opera in favour of 'Another world' as the very tittle of one soap opera announces a world in which characters deal only with the large problems of human existence as crime love, death and dying. But this antithesis embodies a deep truth about the way women function in culture, as both moral and spiritual guides and household drudges, so now one and the other are moving back and coming forth between the extremes and but obviously finding them difficult to reconcile.

In media these soap opera as a formal properties at daytime television thus accord closely with rhythms of women's work in the home. Individual soap operas as well as the flow of various programmes and commercial tend to make repetition, interruption and distraction pleasurable. But we can go even further and note that for our women viewers itself often takes place in a state of distraction. But now as we are television we can see that it goes beyond film in this respect or at least the day time programme in some ways recapitulates the work situation anywhere, the viewer is physically passive, immobilized and all his allention is focused on the object before him. Even the most allegedly 'mindless' programme requires a fairly strong degree of concentration if its to make sense. But in television since I see the housewife's 'leisure' time is not so strongly demarcated, her entertainment must often be consumed on the job. This account the part of realistic 'feel', for soap opera.

Whenever you see a soap opera in television which I have considered the both section of media as an important thing is that there is always for a person to consider a remarks ramifications, time for people to speak and listen lavishly. Actions and climaxes are only a secondly importance. This may seen willfully are only of secondary importance. This may seen willfully to misrepresent the soap-operas. Certainly they appear to contain ludicrous a number of climaxes and actions, people are always getting blackmailed, having major operations, dying having or conducting extra marital affairs which inevitably results in pregnancy, being kidnaped, going mad and loosing their memories. But just as in real life it takes a wedding or a funeral to reunite scattered family so soap opera catastrophes provide all convenient of occasions for people to come together, confront one another and explore intense emotions. One advantage of placing the family people in hospitals for example is that because they immobilized. They are forced to take the time to talk to others and listen to what others have to say to them. And friends and family members imprisoned in waiting room can discuss, their feelings about the latest tragedy and from their sense the waiting often seems interminable so on to analyze the predicaments of their mutual friends as well as the state of their own relationship. Thus indirect contrast to the typical main narrative films in which the climax functions to resolve difficulties and to complicate rather than to simplify the characters lives.

Further more as with much women's narrative dialogue in soap operas is an enormously tricky business. Again I see the language here of a kind that takes itself for granted and assumes it is always possible to mean no more and no less than what one intends. More accurately in soap operas the gap between what is intended and what is actually spoken is often very wide. Secrets better left buried may be blurted out in memories moments of intensity or they are withhold just when a character most desires to tell all. This is very different from a night-time television programmes and classic. The full revelation of a secret on these shows usually begins or proclaims the restoration of order. The necessity of the confession, the means through which we gladly submit to power is wholeheartedly endorsed. In soap operas of the other hand the effects of confessions are often ambiguous, providing a relief for some of characters and dreadful complications for other. Moreover it is remarkable how seldom in operas a character can talk another into changing his/her ways ordinarily it takes major disaster to bring about self-awareness just to give a stop feeling sorry for you self speech and the character undergoes a drastic personality change. Perhaps more than men, women in our society are aware of the pleasures of language though less signatures about its potential use as a perfect instrument of power.

Not only do soap-operas suggests an alternative kind of narrative pleasure experienced by women, but they also, tell us a great deal about what called 'women collective fantasies'. To the dismay of many feminists critics, the most powerful fantasy embodied in soap operas appears to be the fantasy of a full self-sufficient family. So here I see that the day lime television promises that the family can be every-thing, only one is willing to stay inside it. For that women confined to her house, the day television fill out the empty spaces of the long day with its programme the 'Ghar Angan', 'Khana Khajana' and so all others as of the long day when she is home alone, channels her fantasies towards love and family dramas and it all promises her that the life she is it can fulfil her needs. But it does not call to her attention her aloneness and isolation and it does not suggest to her that it is precisely in her solitude that she has a possibility for going a self.

It all concerns with family channel to feed up the public, but further the way press outside deals with the universal declaration of the same Human Rights where these kinds of people who are suffering due to families and society. For them where to go and whom to discuss things happened, the press and media in one-way tells about the right and about human rights to say something for getting justice. Here press inside the government media and outside both are equally helpful and siding bias about women children both.

As in India everybody has the right freedom of opinion and expression, this rights include freedom to hold opinions without interference and to see, receive an impart information and ideas through any media.

Given the percievence in this debates it is not surprising that certain ideas now have become part of received wisdom a common sense way of viewing the world. Thus we have the context in which the question of television advertising the youth is likely to conjure images of under-educated, undiscriminating and undiscipline young people who are addicted to T.V. and who mindlessly imbibe the advertisers messages along with the materialist's values of the consumer society, which all is followed by the press with its separate advertising section. But the characteristic of this view is the notion that there exists a very simple cause and effect relationship between advertising and the purchasing of the commodities. It is not only assumed that advertisements work but than the young are more likely than any other sector of population to be taken in by psychologically informed scheming of the marketeers. Youth are considered to be more vulnerable, more gullible and more inclined to be persuaded to buy totally useless things.

Significantly and interestingly this is a far more demeaning view of youth than that held by the advertisers themselves. As has already being indicated that the advertising industry is highly respectful of the critical skills and visual literacy of young people. Indeed as emerges clearly from my work of research to think over it no other age group is considered as discriminating, cynical and resistant to the 'hard sell'. Further, more no other group is as astute as at decoding the complex messages, cross references and visual joke of current advertising. These critical skills are untutored and seem to arise out of an unprecedented intimacy with the cultural form of television commercial. No other generation has been so imbued with the meanings produced by quick edits, long shots, zooms, by particular lighting codes and combination of sound. The young have a unique mastery. So I have to communicate this on to those who are concern with that the section of press has made all such person insiding making a view of an advertising media, through that not only the press is benefitted but these model people are also highly paid for and sometime above board. The finance through press and media ads sometimes are a totality to run the newspapers so on and the same in radio and television ads and sponsorship of any programme. It do give the popularity to programme and a heavy finance to run the programme as an most essentiality and those ads have been given by the government of India it has its money value but sometime the categorisations of the angle of the newspaper or the ads to private commercial channels do differ in policy thought have been stopped but all under current so on.

In same series I am taking one long shot of soap opera as I have already talked about the operas and films of yester-years an still popular today.

**Programming As an Entertainment**

However I feel that I get divided in terms of today and tomorrow among the common people. As I have already talked about All India Radio and Doordarshan, let me take here the Star T.V. in Asia as it takes an open road and silver screen both in its programmes introduced in India and elsewhere. This television channel provides an automobile and its programmes and pictures which are invented at about the same-time, just in time for the century that both would dominate, the movies and the motion in channels, base on films and soap opera to that of sect which turns the point.

So in terms of policy of press it does favor the press. But when you sit in dark it turns a light to you not being felt so alone with its programme. Here Asia Sat in India was launched in 1990, provided the first privately owned satellite communication, network covering all over Asian, based in Hong Kong and licensed by the same government in 1990 December the STAR TV. launched its free-to-air service in October 1991. The northern and southern footprints of Asia Sat covers 38 nations from Egypt to Japan and from Indonesia to Siberia, capturing a potential of 2.7 billions half of the world's population. Star TV. initially aimed to attract the top of the five per cent of this enormous audience, but all are well educated, wealthy the professional and the English speaking.

Stars offers a total of five channels, all including thematic channels music videos (M.T.V.) sports, news (B.B.C. World Service Television) and family entertainment as well as a channel of broadcasts in Mandrain Chinese on running on 24 hours basis. With the exception of Chines channel, which broadcasts programme produced in Hong-Kong, Japan, Taiwan, China and so elsewhere, the other four channels carry mainly western programmes obtained, through contractual suppliers or the international market. The English B.B.C. News channel is the only one that mainly provides partial translations into Mandain. The aforementioned five channels are full Star T.V. services. Its southern beam carries an additional affiliated channel, The Zee T.V. a Hindi general entertainment service set up by an Indian partnership of Star T.V. from Star T.V.'s debut in late 1991 until November 1993 the number of households that can receive its signal has increased to more than 40 millions with the majority concentrated in the people's Republic in China, India and in Taiwan.

An examination as a whole leads people to categorise Star T.V. in Asia into four main types first for virtual suppression, regulated openness and also illegal openness and suppressive openness. The democratic criteria are the nature of national policy on satellite television and the state of policy implementation, where an analysis of each type follows.

Broadcasting regulation is the most decisive factor affecting accessively with ability to satellite television some are more open than others resulting in the four types of control identified above. Bill it is accurate to say that most Asian Government 'cite' cultural invation and social ability are reasons for the control of foreign satellite television. They are afraid that alien values and outside information may erode traditional and indigenous culture and disrupts racial religious and political harmony in their societies. In addition they often have a vested .interest in maintaining the status quo of the television industry, which is generally heavily regulated with ownership and control monopolized by the state. For some of the governments broadcast television is an important source of revenue, as well as an agent of an socio-political control. Even in the few Asian Nations where terrestrial broadcasters are commercially owned. These broadcasters tend to pressure their governments to shield them from competition from the sky. The logical measure of these governments is to manage information by restricting its inflow through satellite television.

I find that the outer section of the press a main thought is of language barrier. The diversity of a language barrier poses to spread of a regional satellite television link Star TV. particularly in Asia where a wide range of languages exists. Including Star T.V.'s associate Hindi channel and all other four English language channel one of which is the B.B.C. World Service Television carries a partial chines translation. Sports Music channels broadcast in English do not require advanced linguistic skills on the part of the audience. However language comprehension is essential to channels offering dramas, movies and information. English is emerging as the language of the rich and the educated in Asia and throughout the world and this is clearly the most important factor in Star T.V.'s choice of English as its major broadcasting language. However to wide and deepen its penetration Star T.V. and schedule all effect is a competitive position in the range of media choice in a nation. Although the Star T.V. tends to fill its channels with low cost programme required through the international market this products are quite competitive for the reason mentioned earlier. If Star T.V. wants to complete with the strong and terrestrial programming in places like Japan and Hong Kong television. Star T.V. tries not to violate the national regulations, creed and beliefs of various countries or to any ideological and political bias.

Undoubtedly, this tension creates constraints over its. programming policy. A case in point is the decision of Star T.V. and M.T.V. Channel not screen Madonna's video 'Erotica' as its America counterpart did in late hours. But the chief of a Star T.V.'s M.T.V. explained that 'Erotica' is obviously designed to shock and outrage and we are here to entertain, when you are dealing with wider range of religion, cultures and beliefs, it is hard to say or see not offending someone and we are very conscious of this.

In the short run Star T.V. has to take a cultural gaps among nations into our consideration when making programming policies. In the long run cultural differences may will be less of a problem as a cultural homogenization especially among Asian middle .class, intensifies. How this cultural homogenization may occur is discussed further in the conclusion.

Leaving it at the place where it crosses the road I tend to handle the soap opera's of tomorrow which almost depends entirely on the sense of an ending as the soap operas are important to their viewers in part because they never end as it encourages our identification with one character, soap operas invite identification with numerous personalities. And where as it is structured around two basic-enigmas, in soap operas, the enigmas poliferate like to find out somebody's wife's sister's baby is really an artificial insemination? And with the lady submit to her sister's blackmail attempt or will she disclose the truth to her husband and also it the truth is discovered than what will happen to enemies? It is to be tuned up for tomorrow not in order to find out the answers but to see what further complication will differ the resolution and introduce new questions. Thus the narrative by placing ever more complex obstacles between desire and fulfillment. So make anticipation on end and end in itself. Soap opera invest exqisite pleasure in central condition of a women's life, waiting whether for her phone to ring for the baby to take its nap or for the family to be reunited shortly after the days final soap opera has left its family still struggling against dissolution.

So I see that according to hermeneutic code with propounds the enignas functioning by making expectation, the basic conditions of truth and that truth these narrative soap opera's tell us, and a make us inquisitives just to find what is 'at the end' of expectation. This mainly designs implies a return to order for expectation is a disorder, but of course a soap operas do not end. Consequently truth for women is seen to lie not at the end of expectation, but in expectation, not in the 'return to order' but in disorder.

For most of the women a family is naturally a family is the

only support and these soap operas offer the assurance of its immorality. The television or radio both by the dramas broadcasted by the radio as they present it to viewers with a picture of a family which though it is always in process of breaking down, stays together no matter how it is intolerable its situation may get. Or perhaps more accurately the family remains close precisely because it is perpectually in a chaotic state. The unhappiness generated by the family can only be solved in the family remains close precisely because of its perpetually in a chaotic state. The unhappiness generated by the family can only be solved in the family. Misery becomes not as in many nineteenth century moves, base on women's character. So the consequence and the sign of the family breakdown, but the very mean's of its function and perpetuation. As long as the children are unhappy, as long as things don't come to a satisfying conclusion, the mother will be needed as confidante and advisor and her function will never end.

But some of the novels are the frequent shifting of perspective identifies the reader with a variety of characters in order to ally her with the mother/father and with God who, in their wisdom, and understanding, an make all hearts of the world go away, thus ensuring the 'right' essentially of the world order.

And most revolutionary part of writing is that this soap opera, however denies the 'mother' this extremely fluttering illusion of her power. On the one hand it plays upon the expectator's expectations of the melodramatic form, most continually stimulating the desire for just a conclusion to the story, and on the other hand. On the other hand, it constantly presents the desire as unrealisable by showing that conclusion only lend to further tensions and much more sufferings, thus soap operas convince women that their highest goal is to see family happy and united. While consoling them for their inability to realize this ideal and bring about a familial harmony.

I see it has always reinforced by the character of the good mother on soap operas. In the contrast to the manipulating mother who tries to interfere with her childrens lives, disintegrates her advice, which she gives only when asked, is temporarily soothing but usually ineffectual. So I see her primary function is to be sympathetic the tolerate the foibles an all kind of errors of others.

Again I come to the counts of the very main subject the Press as such doing under government regulation with the above television subjects and the same in radio broadcasts. At all these places people dare to handle such themes open in the soap opera and find it to vision open in terms of old saga, with the new ad world of popular marketing to know about all.

I feel that ironically the critic of television untiringly accused as the script writers anticipating the housewife is distracted state are careful to repeat important elements of the story several times. Here the viewer of television are indulging in escapism. In other words both of high art critics and politically oriented critics may be they motivated by different concerns, unite at one platform and divide in another while condemning dynamic television for distracting the housewife from her real situation. My point have been that a distracted, or distractible frame of mind is crucial to housewife's efficient functioning in her real situation and at this level television and its so called distraction along with the particular forms they take are intimately bound up with women's work.

So I find that there are strange words indeed coming from one who purports to be analyzing the ideology of narrative form. They are the perfect illustration of how a high art in media or in the press outside is bias, an eagerness just to demonstrate worthlessness of low art can lead us to make claims for high art as a narrative section of media which would ordinarily be worry of professing. Terms like 'progression' 'irreversible' change a true knowledge and consequences are certainly tied to an ideology, they are linked to have a classical metaphysics.

In the open Press Media, the citizen of all the efforts to be given as a mental feed those who concern have need on analysis as done above with little lower of human psyco condians comes in to everyone's life soon. So here to criticize the classical narrative because for example, it is based on a suspect notion of progress than to criticize soap opera because it is never get us anywhere and I feel that certainly not out of ignorance into true knowledge. But it is a different approach.

So in press outside as its was expansion it is describing women's rediscovery of herself. It is a sort of universe in expansion for which no limits could be fixed and which for all that would not be incoherence. So the similarities between this descriptions and soap opera as a farm are so striking. They suggests the possibility that soap operas may not be an entirely negative influence on the listener or viewer. They may also have the force of negation of the typical (a masculine) modes of pleasure in our society. This challenge is more over every like the one being mounted in current and films theory. Theorists have recently being pointing out the pleasures of the kind of text which breaks the illusion of unity and totality provided the reader or spectator by the classic text. Hence the emphasis since the structuralists have been on descentering the subjects but as we have seen women are in their lives, their work and in certain forms of their pleasure already decentered-off centre. It is important that feeling of being the centre of creation is typical of the ego structure bourgeouis male. This fact seems to be crucial importance to anyone interested in formulating a feminist asthetic. Indeed I would like to argue that soap operas are not all together at odds with an already developing though still embryonic feminists attaches.

**Development and Progress of Communication**

The analyses or newspapers recently which does provide a thought of international communication policy especially with which India is concerned about the North American Free Trade Agreement and the general agreement out Trade and Tariffs. Our purpose is to consider the implications of recent regional and international policies for attempts to promote global communications equality through UNESCO and the International Telecommunications Union. We argue that by shielding information communication policy from public participation and by shifting international communication policy out of UNESCO and the ITU, NAFTA and GATT institutionalized transnational politics of a sort of limited democracy.

So an alternative conception democracy should be a promoted through press to stand on this base where country is going to have a new policies of politics. But the normative principles of the new democracy might be applicable to the new analysis of international communication with the consistence of the theory of universal communication. So we address this question by working out the theory of Pragmatic Democracy and after a more substantive theory even to mark the simple communicative democracy as constructed upon theory of public sphere and the ideal speech situation. All these theories are conducted by the press in the shape of limited technical pragmatic and communicative democracy as such. And so there are compared across several measures and used as the basis for a critic of Telecommunication and Information Services.

Press outside has always stated communication as a policy stated all over as an organized industrial policy where I feel that revolution has already been thought of in communication terms. As I find at the point that revolutionary process are political process and mainly projected by the parties in polity of the country which tries to make the newspapers. It is an outstanding understood term base even sometime with the orientation of the partipolics but normally in interest of perks in purse of that papers wing. But sometime any party needs a thought backing by as for example only few decades with the flourish of publishing in newspapers that not only some ways celebrates but also rethinks the French Revolution of 1789 will take a new media forms and most communicative networks been set at the centres of its analysis of today newspaper with the oriented though under current which we can see in the present literature caught at vague which mainly publish those who are pro to the thought.

Here I would like to say that no press or Media under government regulation bags the orientation like till the ruling government follows the opt of that only think under the government pressures as such. So if we have a look upon 7 Bahadurshah Zafar Marg. The newspapers published there are the sect and sectioned thought of press outside but in pressure of Inside Government Press so on. The Group of Birla as well oriented to Congress wings, Goenka with press cuddled Shourie with Hindutva visiting thoughts. In Uttar Pradesh from small to big newspaper underpaid by Samajwadi Party' and the paper like Dainik Jagran under current a B.J.P. oriented and paid inside are the Pride Present of today Press working outside is an actuality so on.

The newspaper like neo-rich rich society are termed to soften the policy of that government, which is ruling under popularity.

As Rashtiya Sahara, a commercial brand of the neo-rich society I turned up to secularist Bartiyata with peeking help of people. But 'under-current with heavy flow of money defending towards the equality in socialistic pattern of the society helping to those in need of social and moral security. At the other Hindustan as complete non Hindu paper float the Marxism with Lenin thought may be the need of Art, Literature and Culture, as it has been so divided, here literate literacy teach is the language and predicts that the language and literature are different but away from Sur, SurTulsi Kabir Parampara. But in thought Kabir is always a sensation is these literature, the way Kabir has emulgated all kind of thought of cast, creed and norms of the society and he breaks the pinpoint of any kind of religion. This newspaper does have an elaborated kind of fulfilments in the news with accuracy and is dominantly sticked up to one point programme submitting new as a sound table talks.

In the contemporary world that media and press are the part of our political problems and part of the solutions, essential elements of representative political structures as well as vehicles for their over through, at issue is how certain form of media can function to support popular mobilization particularly within representative contexts.

But the media and press is also divided here as small media, big media, little media, community media, radical media, group media, all has been crucial is a notation of these media as participatory public phenomena, controlled neither by the big states nor big corporations. Thus the distinction between big and small can not depend on particular kinds of technologies or even on their putative audiences but rather on the manner of use of all technologies.

I see even broadcast media could have a different shape as suggested by Brecht over sixty years ago.

Even I feel that radio should be converted from a distribution system to a communication system. Radio could be the most wonderful public communication system imaginable mainly if I see for television in the same media from where the gigantic system of channels, could be, that is, if it were capable not only transmitting but of receiving or making the listener not only hear but also speak not of isolating him but of connecting him. This means that radio would have to give up being a purveyor and organise the listener as purveyor.

I can say for an outside press that this is an activist model for the 'empancipatory use' of the press and media which focuses on the popular involvement rather than on professional production on horizontal rather than the passive absorption of the very kind of Indian mass-mediated culture and values whether in Western countries democracies locally based and organized, non-profit, most participatory forms are many and various. They include local free newspapers, community radio and television channels, citizen's video community computers and so on.

So I feel that such media projects are all developed by the pressure groups about what I have little talked above just to see and think of this kind of development in media and all sort of these pressure groups are politically organised or under counter culture a ficionades and local communities, and even under minority groups.

So it may known that these alternative, participatory media and press not only satisfy demands of different contents, catering to tastes, interests and orientations not catered to by mass media output and sometimes challenging that output but are also vehicles for direct participation in the mediated .communication process and for the extension of voices of groups and ideas otherwise not heard. The very existence of this mass-media environment is a measure of the vibrancy of a democratic society. Downing stresses the importance of self-managed dissonant media which have posed a genuine alternative to the media patterns of both West and East.

The kind of thought I want to describe in the book press inside outside might be a covering of public communication, so this shift the focus to an autonomous sphere of activity independent of the state and country with popular production of messages, a public coming and into being and also the voicing of one's own opinion to state and language orchestrated voices, to the use of channels and technologies that are readily accessible and available, and to messages that are in the main produced and distributed freely as opposed to private, corporate production for the profit or control by so many of the country organisations.

That the point where we call such media the people's voice 'Janvani' 'Yagvani' and so I even see that the peoples voices might be more apt and pro.

So in the end I find the essence of repressive societies is that political activity is somewhere restricted and as part of that restriction comes a control over public communication. And it is argued for any social and moral transformation to get under way their appears to be one prerequities that underlines all. In big countries a big media environments, the possibilities for the more familiar elements of democratic participatory political organization such as political groups - and parties, unions and interest groups with their regular and open meetings and an independent political press or electronic media were utterly circumscribed.

Press outside also holds a cultural 'synchronization' cultural systems where vaning due to that. That is why about the press some horror tales are told as to prop-up the tails of tales in human figure and political upsets and one conclusion is still seems unanimously shared claims a prominent media researcher. The impressive variety of the world's cultural system is waning.

One more point at this place as a most notable I want to omit that the impact of media on the creation of demigods is also an important factor. There one can not ignore the fact that providing extensive coverage to the stars of any field in print and on air does play a significant role in placing them on pedestal.

But with a noted point the pressure the press sometimes is very much pressed upon such a problems like Punjab, Kashmir, Tamil fronts as the press of Punjab elaborated the simple and straight problem of Hindi and Punjabi speaking into the dividive part of rationalism of Hindu Sikh race clash which further turned in to diffusion of terrorism in Punjab.

Most of the riots and so other communal violence take place just because it does contains the anxiety sensationalism spreaded by the press outside all around.

Now I come to that very point where the press outside and the press inside both are equally responsible to educate and inform to the society or to people in common.

But to see both nucleative points are missing here in the press as such. Press and media as I have already defined several times. But one clinching thought still remains that whether today the press is an industry, management any constructive Institution, a House or a medium where newspapers only projects this kind of any subject : But I find it is no way a truth but it is a public oriented subject to be defined with the communication of people and telecommunication as I have already located on the front where tele—and our subscribing telephone are also considered a main current or press on its clutch.

So I would like to say that both section of press in their duties somehow other are specially oriented to the ruling government or to those section of society which basically needs a voice. Press outside is mostly concerned with anti-establishment form working against the government and bias to society.

But with society you mainly carry on only human stories, which is being given a very little weightage to the press almost at one side of the column. So I still say that most of the newspapers are filled with all kind of political news with illustration of those political persons and figures who are to state, the statements goes beyond its means and protocol and press holds it on at frontage of the newspaper without any if any but, some with the policies of the government when they are announced turns their head to people telling them about. All such subjects are focused to media-hype just for telling that they are for and to you and you only and people have to see it in their frontface, and page.

Again this is a serious argument. But there is perhaps only a thin line between defence of authencity and an antiquarianism which often turns out to be vicarious. After policies and events where the parties and the polity political I see that the people are so assumed to press covering in this field where the relationship between local and imported culture which can only be a competition of the press at both section. The press information Bureau produces a kind of entertainment to people by their registered artists to link up them with art and culture and the right ups of Department of Cultural Affairs float an established assumptions about cultural purity and authenticity probably came to the surface here.

But through press and media we see a real world, but simply then a search of post marxist media studies has been substantially shorn or those intellectual features which gave the field of press outside a degree of unity. Which has been returned to multiple knowledge problematic draws extensively on the problems of established disciplines and then adds to them issues of combination and adoption.

**Social Impact of Television**

But our press is facing a new but risky future situated rather uncertainly on the fringes of social sciences and also film studies, it can also be considered a most important part of active communicative press which can not situate itself primarily as an arts project without a potentially fatal degree of contraction but it might proke several more objection. Among these it might be argued that the shaping influence of feminism and post modernism upon the post Marxist character of the field needs more attention and the part of the active press outside.

So the mode press deals with ideology is also worth a measure of separate consideration on its pivotal importance to the field as initially constituted is most critical stock taking. Here no shift of opinion or attitude concerns as I told with dictions expressions or conventions with keep a tight enough hold on the factors which need to be addressed in their interarticulation. Open argument about these issues, particularly as they appear in a range of current press research contexts is now one of the most pressing requirements.

Press also needs to cross a new road to arrive within the institutionalized order of academic inquiry. Its a house-style of boldness and disrespect its electicism and its conceptualizing zeal have brought dividends in the context of the older often evaluatively conservative disciplines. But as many of the discipline thinks about the press the same quality could easily work against its possibilities for steady and self-assessment and for theoretical and also methodological reconstruction as precisely a multi-disciplinary field of social research in the section press as such.

The mode of expression offered to press is overtly textual is underlined by the fact that there can be no general set of explanations for the carrier of whole categories of exported national production. So here the press could be seen behind the global vision but to think about what does the globalisation mean in actuality. The so called proposed sense of globalisation mean in terms of press that international subsidiaries in order to maximize material, human and financial resources. So here while agreeing with he premise that there are increasing international interdependences is in world commerce and politics and other social human relationships.

Three per cent reservation for seats in Parliament and the State Legislature for women. It is just located in newspapers now as news of passing out this bill just as the passage of 73rd Amendment in 1992. As everybody finds that the current Bill is being find O.K. and virtually even identical to the one which was drafted by United Front. And in today position the Bill is being sent back to the Law Ministry even then I feel that it will come back with some reply.

Here I would like say that the Press is made free to bias towards 'women'. So I would like to quote here the statement about the Bill by that head of C.P.M. Indrajeet Gupta who is not conceptionally alloyed with B.J.P. but through him the C.P.M. and C.P.I. both agrees that this Bill should be presented and passed just as it is at present with no stain. And it is agreed by them that granting any separate reservation to Muslims will be almost impossible unless the secular nature of the constitution is changed. And I feel both the B.J.P. and congress are opposed to it and so the Indrajit Gupta said that Bill should be passed in its own form and as it is.

This is the story of women-united and women divided, but stated by the press as Samajwadi Party is much more committed to the minorities tried to oppose the Bill and later on apologised for that itself. But continued this demand in public. Here the role of the press is only at that stake to flash the story in favour of women who want to share power, with all other major political parties.

But from the time of Gandhi only press itself stating that women's are the bias to press, as they are suppressed so much and they are half power in a complete personality equally to men. So now why not any press is taking or talking any kind of action talk that there is no need of any reserved right for that with no difference. According all other human right all men and women have equal right in all senses, why so differentiate them as a separate body which seeks way of thin line to come forward and see things in there own - stride so on. But upon the issue Press can only flash and project this issue but if I consider the statement given by Clinton that the explosions in both countries will suffers both of them in disturbing the piece. So both countries should talk mutually it is and, was all right but to think why our other section of minorities feel depressed and not in self confidence to hold the government rules if not imposed but to sustain the feeling, so on, that they are meant to ask separate and firm reservation for them as Scheduled Castes and Tribes both are to think of living their reserved right even protesting against the stated word *Harijan*. The main cause is that after the partition unlike Hindus in Pakistan. So the voice of Mulayam Singh supported to them as a matter everybody is free in our democracy to form a popular government their own favours to hold the politics in country so on. So we can't blame him also as if B. J.P. took the side through media with Ram and then to Raj—Mulayam Singh snatched the press in the side to peep others against Muslims or minorities.

Both are sailing on the same boat finding the rivers end in Indian Politics unlike Nehru at a time bringing 4 per cent left Muslims to support at their party giving them important posts and positions so, but all it was injected in people's mind through the press and media, even by feeding them and holding press as their own property to switch the political mission as launching rational Herald, Kaumi Awaj and after that Nava Jeevan. But all of us know that any proper if oriented specific section and even not free and frame the opinions in its own editorial it simply flopped to any end.

But the paid press when they are pressed pressure group of politics some how try to purchase their contributors and writers who can motivate the flow of mind by setting addiction to the people mind politics.

As is a power share I see the Press outside is all above that where the policies of politics are made to be the projection of press create agendas sometime with stamping effect on people and some time it is damaging to the society. Now after politics the press outside has a strong stamping effect on finance and economy of the country. Here the press under the ruling party government does not have any concern accept the showdown welfare of the people in common itself.

So many magazines and papers are published in concern and all private kind of channels are on this bias of the show on condition as and additional wing to support the popularity of products. And on free press it all 'has been fully examined by the Indian Economist to keep the country fit at the economic border that the former CEO, Percy Barnevik concerned with Swiss multinational A.B.B. Ltd. who at that of his visit just marked in his observation over ministers to deliver their speeches in which were trying to point the glories picture of our country's future but were slumped to answer the question about the plans for the immediate future. He was not to believe that who can not of today and tomorrow how can he link of future.

So here the power of press in economic section make our ministers in politics to feel the facts of earthy matters conducted by Indian Economists, consulting about to small industries growth to biggest Industry in India—side by side siding the problems of common man fighting for his livelihood. By all the press inside the government media is never and never able to tough, the facts owned in truth as such as if goes even against the country's good. They are silent here. Our open press is much concern in these matter to hold the future of the country's economic conditions.

At the moment. as we are passing through the old and new set of pressed holds in the press and media both as informally press outside has been considered or under consideration to be declared as industry. But it never such problem, when a neo-rich finance societies took over the charge of press and tried to turned in exploiting mafia tugged with old and ever questioned term yellow journalism. These papers stared a kind piracy in print media and the statement of politician, and the writers too were one of the main contributing part to it with their money and comfort bias attitude getting though press provocation so on. But it was only possible thing in local norm, not in polities and among the politics of Brand concion figures already catered by Big Banners of Industries and these Big Banners were always in search to purchase talents to float and market them at their responsive festivity of the Newspapers so on. And the other side Government Press which till now was an informative wing and educative form to see the society turned into middle person in its authoritative form to see the press outside working into their terms and condition as such.

There is a small hunt left in my subject whether, both the section, of press are dependent upon each other or they are at a draw of two different lines as such. Here I want to go back to my menories of 1975 to 1980. At the time of Emergency imposed upon people by the ruling government (here I would not say Mrs. Gnadhi) as a concern to stop roars and' voices against the government, the Press Information Bureau and Law a placed form of government to keep eye upon whom it concerned to as Research Analysis Wing and more than 100 departments of Government of India were used as an untold secret services for the ruling government with no such kind of popularity hold as it was already a loss of public opinion. I see that more over before the Maruti licensing terms, till now the first term Late Gandhi was accused of attempting to suppress the freedom of the press as everybody knows about that and nothing to say about. I have to say that at the time Ministry of Information and Broadcasting was used by the government to defuse the ownership with a large circulation by drafting a specific scheme to hold it and in public no body was to utter against this. So the ninety per cent of shares in each such newspaper were proposed to be allocated to the staff and hardly 5 per cent would remain with existing share holders and no share holder would have more than half a vote per share in the management and policy decisions. And the other half shares of the fifty per cent of total would be invested in a person-appointed by the Government. But naturally this scheme was naturally created a considerable amount of criticism. But the brain behind was in action was of Sanjay Gandhi, but here Mrs. Gandhi ruled as mother not a Prime Minister of India, like Nehru as she had all inhibitions of her father but better than that to handle the situations. But the thought of newspaper owner was to be questioned if carried through, it would mean that government would have all intents and purposes to control of the chief newspapers. Here Mrs. Gandhi wanted to become a dictator as an editors as the terms are still continued by those press which comes under such kind of pressures and pressure group. Where the hard eye of press in holding the welfare of the country is almost missing at stake.

But the other side the name of the Prime Minister was used in kinds of rumours in the air about the influence of Late Sanjay Gandhi on his mother and a story mysterious supposed to have over her to bend her to his will, and so on the press by pressing the Ministry of Information and Broadcasting turned the rumour in politics which was a beneficial part of stand up of Janta Party then and in the days condition Bhartiya Janta Party which could not, sustain longer when it came into power it only had one and only job to criticise Late Gandhi and nothing more and also at that time they all best master plan but no way to experience the handing of that. Till now Late Gandhi could sense the point of mistake especially an aroused horror of Bhopal Gas Tragedy which turned the face of world politics to India. She quietly assumed her broken tools and further won the battle of come back Congress and even facing the J. P. roar at a time. But during that period the Sanjay was the real ruler of India nor Mrs. Gandhi. This also gave a sympathetic stinct to the public which allowed her to be back in politics, this all battle was fought on the papers published by opinions and statements (readers, where a section of people were happy in emergency in terms law and order so on but this is not my point of thought and discussion.

But today's talk in out side press from others sections of that opens press which basically distinct in any kind ruling party would definitely see the views of the leaders of opposition's S.P. B.S. P both tried to oppose the bill in parliament but one soft corner is still to be thought in behind the sense of women if I see in my personal viewpoint, that Muslim women are double sufferer than the any of the minorities or Hindus, just that firstly they are women and secondly they are dalits. But It is there kind of religious abbvs to defuse them not to be conducted by any political party as a matter of gain of the party interest feel some how more sensible and sensitive about them to see them suffered in India and in all other Islamic countries. But for that they have build their own house to form the position in politics and in society so on otherwise the all political parties would exploit them at stake, were, women may be of any cost and religions. So the press should follow kind of thought in their openings with common in the press out side definitely not projecting her a show-piece material.

As I have told earlier that in such conditions of pressures on papers so on. News is the chief victim of the corporate squeeze because it is time consuming and you can't guarantee a usable story. But now I see and find in press only a kind of trickiness and world weariness.

**Practical Difficulty of Language**

Mostly a confrontial view of each other in politics as popular personalities are man to be fit for showbiz—and the popular leader—are only to be confronted by the press to make their story current politics. So media and makes a man of images. So why should they not be considerable for press to hold their personality in ever constant limelight.

One more thing is that inside the Government Press languages are also a problem mainly to information section. Lange does not mean 'Bhasha' but the tone of expression in the Press is the only and basics of the pressing point of the press itself so on. It should be noted that Mandrain Chinese is spoken by more people than any other language in the world. About half of the population served by Star T.V. is Chinese, mainly concentrated on the land and scattered in to other Asian countries. The Chines constitute the largest potential audience. Recognising the Star T.V. dedicated one of its channels to Mandrin language programming. Once the language barrier is overcome limitations of accessibility in China can be attributed, mainly to the state restrictive policies. Satellite television programing directed as a specific language groups greatly enhances competitiveness with terrestrial television as evidenced by the success of Star T.V. Mandrin Channel in Tiwan.

The prohibitive affect of the linguistic barrier is evidenced by cases like Indonesia, Thailand and South Korea. In these countries satellite reception methods are generally allowed. However the penetration of Star T.V. is insignificant in each country's population understands English, the languages now used by Star T.V.

The cultural gaps in programming in Star T.V. of satellite television in relation to programme types, quality, variety and language advising opinion there should be a bias in the Press outside but this should be towards the 'man' as man in common with their all goods and bads holding in life the Press outside should take it as warning that 'No freedom has been given to press to destroy anybodys' freedom as this question roared at a time of Princess Diana's death f caused by a chase of mediahood. And the political reporting should be placed only at distance from rulers and rulings which could aligned to all powers of politcs and society both.

At last both section of Press inside and outside are connected and powerfully committed to the 'Masses' as such and try to give oxygen to people not the gossip of rumour and malicious thought by peeping in other interiors. Press is the problem but white lies are little difficult to digest when others are difficult to swallow even. So keeping away sort of Bofors better both the press should align with power and support to the masses.

# INDEX